THE DIST... SURNAMES OF NORTH STAFFORDSHIRE

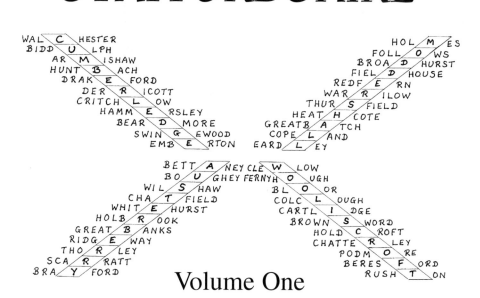

Volume One

Surnames derived from local placenames and landscape features

by

EDGAR TOOTH

CHURNET VALLEY BOOKS
1 King Street, Leek, Staffordshire. 01538 399033
email: picture.book@virgin.net web: freespace.virgin.net/c.hinton/

© Edgar Tooth and Churnet Valley Books 2000
ISBN 1 897949 54 5

Printed in Malta by Interprint Limited

Acknowledgements

I would like to thank the following people for their invaluable assistance during the preparation of this book:

The staffs at the William Salt Library, Stafford, Stafford Record Office, Hanley Reference Library (Arts and Archives), Meir Public Library, the Family History Societies at Audley, Betley and Bentilee, and the Keele History Department.

I am grateful to my colleague Michael Paffard at Radio Stoke for his illuminating observations on so many local surnames. I gladly acknowledge David Horovitz, Jim Sutton and David Hey (Sheffield University) for their superior knowledge on placenames and John Levitt for his unrivalled erudition on local dialect.

My special thanks to John for his help with illustrations and Mrs Florence Daniels for some of the photographs.

CONTENTS

Sources most frequently used in the text and their dates:

1272-1308	Inquests on the Staffordshire Estates of the Audleys.
1327, 1332	Lay Subsidy Rolls of Staffordshire, granted by Edward III to meet the expenses of the war with Scotland.
1532	A list of families in the Archdeaconry of Stafford.
1539, 1640	Staffordshire Muster Rolls.
1666	Staffordshire Hearth Tax Returns.
1841	Scriven's report on children in the Staffordshire Potteries.
1851	White's Directory.
1875/76	Keates's Gazetteer and Directory.
1887	Postal Directory for the Potteries and Newcastle under Lyme.
1907, 1912	Directory for the Potteries and Newcastle under Lyme.

Plus miscellaneous lawsuits, assize rolls, manor court rolls, churchwardens' accounts and parish registers.

PREFACE

One of the key dates in the history of surnames is the year 1066, when William, Duke of Normandy, defeated Harold, King of England, at the Battle of Hastings. Before the Norman Conquest the overwhelming majority of the English population had Celtic, Anglo-Saxon or Scandinavian names, and, generally speaking, it was only one name each. As long as this situation prevailed, where everyone bore a first name that differed from those of his family and friends, surnames were simply not on the agenda.

With the arrival of the Normans the process of name-giving underwent a dramatic transformation. The three and a half centuries between the battles of Hastings and Agincourt (1066-1415) are known as the 'Surname Period', since this is when the bulk of our surnames became fixed and hereditary. Several crucial factors contributed to this phenomenon - the stabilisation of society, the expansion of trade and the gradual increase in population. During this period it soon became customary for each individual to possess a fixed surname in order to define his or her position in the community. The surname could be taken from a homestead, village, hamlet or town where the individual was born - Tunstall, Fenton - or from some particular geographical feature in the neighbourhood - Heath, Brook, Ford. It could have been taken from the trade or occupation followed - Cooper, Turner - or from a title or rank held - Knight, Squire. It could have been a nickname describing some physical, moral or temperamental trait - Little, Brown, Strong, Smart, Bold. The surname may have preserved a personal name - Edwards, Williams - or it may have been taken from the father - Johnson, Adamson - or mother - Dyson, Amison.

Like fossils in ancient rocks, these surnames contain clues to how our ancestors lived and organised their societies. In them lie hidden long abandoned christian names, steeped in mythology, obsolete trade names associated with archaic rural crafts and nicknames whose original meanings are lost in the mists of time. They are memorials of an age when standards of living and morality were light years removed from those of today, but they are part and parcel of our heritage and can only deepen our understanding of local history.

Finally it is perhaps relevant to point out that there are many distinctive surnames that remain concentrated in the area of North Staffordshire to this day. Similarly other distinctive names are concentrated in other counties - just compare with the telephone directories in Cornwall, Suffolk or Cumbria with ours in Staffordshire. Even with the increasing mobility of people over the past two centuries, the population of North Staffordshire has remained remarkably static.

SOME SOURCES

HISTORY, GAZETTEER, AND DIRECTORY, OF **STAFFORDSHIRE,** AND THE CITY AND COUNTY OF THE CITY OF LICHFIELD,

COMPRISING, UNDER A LUCID ARRANGEMENT OF SUBJECTS,

A General Survey of the County of Stafford AND THE DIOCESE OF LICHFIELD & COVENTRY;

WITH SEPARATE

HISTORICAL, STATISTICAL, & TOPOGRAPHIC DESCRIPTIONS OF ALL THE

BOROUGHS, TOWNS, PARISHES, VILLAGES, HAMLETS, MANORS, AND LIBERTIES, IN THE

FIVE HUNDREDS OF THE SHIRE

SHEWING THEIR EXTENT AND POPULATION,

Their Agriculture, Mines, and Manufactures; their Markets, Fairs, Races, Festivals; their Eminent Men; the Lords of the Manors and Owners of Soil and Tithes; the Patrons and Incumbents of the Church Livings; Antiquities, Public Charities, and Institutions; the Civil and Ecclesiastical Jurisdictions; the Names and Addresses of the principal Inhabitants; Mediums of Public Conveyance by Land and Water; the

SEATS OF NOBILITY AND GENTRY;

LISTS OF PUBLIC OFFICERS; And a Variety of other COMMERCIAL, AGRICULTURAL, & BIOGRAPHICAL INFORMATION

In One Volume, with a large Map of the County.

BY WILLIAM WHITE,

AUTHOR OF SIMILAR WORKS FOR NOTTINGHAMSHIRE, AND THE NORTHERN COUNTIES OF ENGLAND.

PRINTED FOR THE AUTHOR, BY ROBT. LEADER, INDEPENDENT OFFICE, SHEFFIELD

MILITIA LISTS and MUSTERS
1757 - 1876

Jeremy Gibson and Mervyn Medlycott

KEATES'S

GAZETTEER & DIRECTORY

OF THE

STAFFORDSHIRE POTTERIES,

NEWCASTLE AND DISTRICT.

1875-6.

HANLEY:
J. KEATES, PRINTER & PUBLISHER, CHEAPSIDE

THE
Natural History
OF
STAFFORD-SHIRE.
BY
ROBERT PLOT. LLD.
Keeper of the
ASHMOLEAN MUS
And
PROFESSOR of CHYMIS
in the
UNIVERSIT
of
OXFORD.

To shall Describe the Land, and bring the Description hither to

OXFORD
Printed at the THEATER, Anno M. DC. LXX

The Printed
MAPS of STAFFORDSHIRE
1577 - 1850

1920.
BUCKNALL-CUM-BA
1762-1812.

Stafford
Parish Register

EDITOR AND HON
PERCY W. L. A
Woore Manor,

DEANERY OF STO

Bucknall-cum
Parish R

PRIVATELY PRINTED FOR THE STAFFOR

All Communications respecting Registers and the cost of the parts sho

☞ Attention is especi on inside o

Staffordshire Pedigrees

BASED ON THE VISITATION

OF THAT COUNTY MADE

BY WILLIAM DUGDALE ESQUIRE

NORROY KING OF ARMS

IN THE YEARS 1663—1664,

FROM THE ORIGINAL MANUSCRIPT

WRITTEN BY GREGORY KING,

(SUCCESSIVELY ROUGE DRAGON AND LANCASTER HERALD)

DURING THE YEARS 1680 TO 1700.

EDITED BY

SIR GEORGE J. ARMYTAGE, BART., F.S.A.,

AND

W. HARRY RYLANDS, F.S.A.,

EDITORIAL SECRETARY OF THE HARLEIAN SOCIETY.

LONDON:
1912.

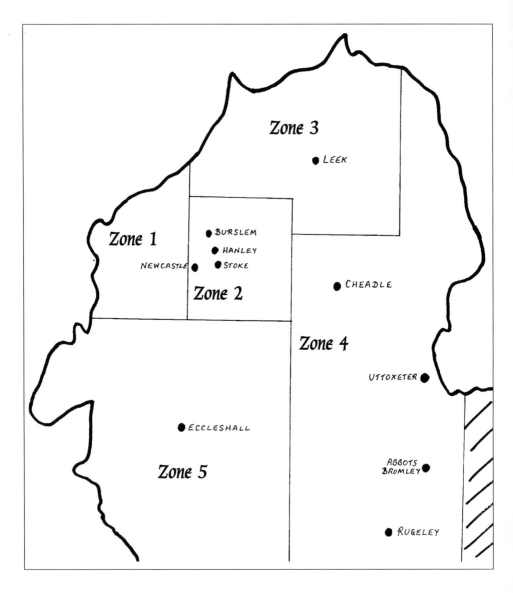

North Staffordshire split into the five zones for this book

INTRODUCTION

In his book entitled *The Homes of Family Names in Great Britain* published in 1890, H.B.Guppy attempted "to ascertain the homes of familiar surnames and to ascertain the characteristic surnames of each county". As his basis he decided to take the names of farmers, "the most stay-at-home class of the country", as he puts it. He culled these names from Kelly's Post Office Directories, rejecting those with a relative frequency of less than 7 per 10,000 of the farmers in any given county. According to his findings, the surnames most typical of Staffordshire are as listed in the accompanying table.

Ash	Clowes	Howson	Sharratt/Sherratt
Clowes	Colclough	Jeavons/Jevons	Shelley
Bagnall	Corbishley	keeling	Shemilt
Bakewell	Cumberledge	Kidd	Shenton
Baskeyfield	Deakin	Lakin	Shirley
Batkin	Durose	Leese	Shoebotham/
Beardmore	Eardley	Leighton	Shoebottom
Bickford	Elsmore	Lindop	Stoddard
Boden	Fallows	Lovatt	Swetnam
Boon	Farrall	Loverock	Tomkinson
Bott	Fern	Lymer/Limer	Torr
Bould	Forrester	Malkin	Tunnicliff
Boulton	Goldstraw	Marson	Turnock
Bowers	Hambleton	Mayer	Warrilow
Brindley	Hammersley	Mottram	Whitehurst
Brunt	Heler	Myatt	Wilshaw
Cantrill/Cantrell	Hodgkins	Orpe	Wint
Chell	Hollingsworth	Parton	Wooddisse
Clewlow/Clulow	Hollins	Pyatt	Woodings

The characteristic surnames of Staffordshire as taken from *The Homes of Family Names in Great Britain* by H.B.Guppy, published in 1890.

On the surface the tabulated material looks very impressive, but as soon as we dig deeper its deficiencies become readily apparent and often quite misleading. Let us analyse each category of surnames in turn in order to clarify the situation:

GUPPYS TABLES

1) Trades, occupations and offices

The five representatives here are: Cantrell, Deakin, Forrester, Lymer and Stoddard. Prior to the Industrial Revolution all these are more typical of north Staffordshire rather than the south of the county, but there are some pitfalls for the unwary.

The surname Cantrell/Cantrill is usually a term for a singer who led the choir in a cathedral or monastery, but there is also a place called Cantrell in Devon which cannot be ruled out of the equation: 1640 Muster Roll:Ralphe Cantrell of Alstonefield; 1666:Laurence Cantrill of lpstones.

Deakin is just another form of Deacon, sometimes referring to the actual office of deacon or an ironic nickname for someone who assumed the bearing of a deacon; 1332 Subsidy Rolls:William le deken of Bagot's Bromley near Blithfield Reservoir. Yet in Staffordshire Deakin is confused not only with Dakin from Daykin - "little David"; Swynnerton parish registers1769/1770, where Robert Deakin of Yarnfield is also entered as Robert Dakin; but also with Dickin - "little Richard", since Deakin's Grave in Cannock is recorded as Dickin's Grave on an 1821 map of the county. The vacillation between Deakin and Dakin (Daykin) simply reflects the North Staffordshire "dee" for "day", which baffles many an outsider.

Forrester is rather more straightforward. Soon after the Norman invasion of England in 1066, William the Conqueror established as royal forest or game preserve large tracts of land that embraced villages and wasteland as well as woods. To police these great royal forests a huge army of officials had to be recruited in order to prevent poaching, to guard against trespass and all other offences contrary to forest law. One of the most important of these officers was the "forester" himself, whose duties corresponded roughly to those of the modern gamekeeper; 1316:Thomas le forester, mayor of Newcastle under Lyme. Forester is often contracted to Forster; 1298:Thomas le forester (forster) of Dimsdale, and then further reduced to Foster, as evidenced by Lawrance Forster of Audley (1689), alternatively cited as Laurence Foster in the same year.

By the close of the seventeenth century the Forester/Forrester/Forrister and Foster spellings far outnumber the Forster forms. In addition, the name Foster may denote a foster parent or nurse, a maker of scissors, a shearer or cutler, or even a maker of saddle bows, from Anglo-French "fuster", especially around Walsall, which has long been associated with the manufacture of saddles and bridles.

The surname Lymer/Limer is widely accepted as a builder or labourer who used lime for whitewashing houses, but more to the point in North Staffordshire is a worker in the building trade who burnt lime in a limekiln for mortar. In the north of the county, limestone has been used for centuries for farming and building purposes, and scattered around the Moorlands are several limekilns - eg. at Consall Forge and Froghall in the Churnet Valley, and south of Cauldon, where the Cauldon Low limestone quarries are situated; 1584:Richard Lymer otherwise Willcoxson of Cheadle.

The horse was such an essential part of the medieval economy, it gave rise to a multitude of surnames with equine associations - the marshall groomed it, the knight rode it, the smith hammered out horseshoes, the lorimer and sadler designed the harness, the skinner and tanner used the hide and the stud horse was cared for by the "stodeherd"; 1395 Assizes:Richard Stodeherd of Bradnop. Hence the surnames Stoddard/Stoddart; at the parish church of St. Edward the Confessor at Cheddleton, on September 19th 1757, Hugh Stoddard of Grindon married Elisabeth Robinson, also of Grindon.

Burslem Church early 1800s

Tunstall Windmill late 1700s

There are some glaring omissions from Guppy's list in this particular class. Typical of north west Staffordshire are names such as Arrowsmith - "arrow maker", Bill - "maker of billhooks", Cadman - "maker of casks or barrels" or "servant of Cade", Cork - "seller of purple dye", Lander/Launder/Lavender - "washerman, washerwoman", Machin - "mason", Proctor - contraction of "procurator", attorney in an ecclesiastical court, Spooner - "maker of roofing shingles" rather than "spoon-maker", Tellwright -"tile maker".

As far as north east Staffordshire is concerned, the following have slipped through Guppy's net: Armitt - "hermit", Dresser - "stoneworker," who "shaped" or "dressed" millstones, (cut an intricate pattern of grooves in them), Flackett, from Middle English "flakette" - a linen or flax cloth covering for a bed, a maker and seller of such material, For(e)man - "swineherd", Copestake - "woodcutter", Leadbeater - "worker in lead", Pakeman - "hawker, pedlar", Wain - "driver of a wain" (wagon), Poyser - "official in charge of the public weighing machine", Stonehewer/Stonier/Stanier - "hewer of stone".

2) Nicknames

Under scrutiny in this section are the nine names Averill, Bott, Bould, Keeling, Kidd, Lovatt, Orpe, Pyatt and Sharratt/Sherratt. Nicknames are as old as speech itself, arising quite spontaneously from that unique human quality, a sense of humour. Thus, William Kyde, taxed at Tunstall (Stoke-on-Trent) in 1332, would have acquired his name as a result of being a lively lad, frisky and full of energy like the kid or young goat he looked after for the lord of the manor - the modern surname Kidd. Similarly with John Lovot, assessed at Keele in 1327; his name comes from an Old French word for a wolf cub, and this alluded to his playful nature - Lovatt/Lovett, which ramifies strongly across North Staffordshire before the advent of the Industrial Revolution.

John Pyot of Leek, who left money for the purchase of bells for Horton church in 1537, had an ancestor with a reputation for being an inveterate chatterbox like the "pyet" (magpie) that nested in the local woods.

Keeling and Sharratt/Sherratt are two quintessential Staffordshire surnames. Adam Kelynge, a tenant on the estates of the Audley family at Talke in 1298, was either a fishmonger who sold "keeling", a type of cod, or possibly a "slippery customer" after the manner of the fish he sold. The high incidence of the name Sharratt/Sherratt in our county is down to the fact that it has two distinct origins. Firstly it is a nickname for a person of outstanding qualities who set a shining example to all those around him, as embodied in Richard Sherard from a 13th century deed in the Staffordshire Chartulary - literally "shining hard", or it can be a reduced form of Sherwood, because Ralph Sherward of Cheddleton (1529), crops up as Ralph Sherott in 1532. If the original surname is Sherwood, then this goes back to Sherwood near Clive in Shropshire or Sherwood in Nottinghamshire - " wood belonging to the shire".

This duality of origin extends to Bold/Bould, which is either a nickname for a brave individual, as exemplified by Thomas Bold, resident at Kingstone near Uttoxeter in 1332,

LOCAL BILLHEADS
WITH NAMES FROM
THIS SECTION

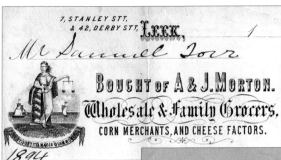

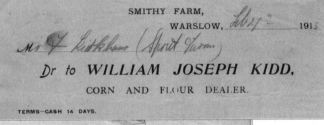

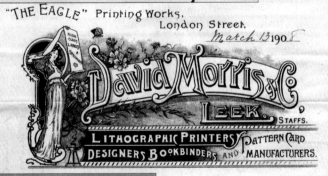

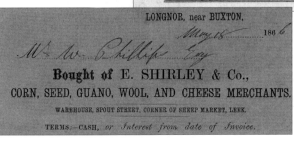

or from The Bold just north of Blithfield Reservoir - "dwelling, building" - home of Richard de la bolde in 1327. The place is now known as Booth.

Orpe is of doubtful meaning, but it is perhaps connected with the Saxon word "eorp" -"dark, swarthy", an obvious allusion to a person's sinister appearance; James Orpe, syngulman is noted as one of the inhabitants at Wootton under Weaver in 1532.

Averill, a name borne by William Averill of Burslem (1730), is from the Old French word for the month of April - "averill", and it was bestowed on a child in order to warn others that his or her moods fluctuated like the inclement April weather. A less attractive option is that the name was given simply because the child in question was born in that particular month.

The monosyllabic Bott looks innocent enough on the outside, but one has to peel away layer after layer to get at the truth. Some sources suggest a nickname from Old French "bot" - "toad", or an old Saxon name "Botta". There may be some link with a medieval word "butte", which occurs in "halibut" - a flat fish or flounder which was only consumed on holy days, and in the surname Bodfish; 1461:Thomas Botfysshe of Froghall. The name would consequently describe a fishmonger who sold flatfish or flounders. Problems accumulate during the sixteenth century, when Bott(e) spellings frequently interchange with Boot(e) and Butt, thus bringing into play other meanings, e.g. an occupational term for a maker or seller of boots, a nickname from Middle English "butt", applied to a person of thickset build, or an archer who resided by some archery butts, or even two other Saxon personal names - "Butt" or "Butta".

In this category several surnames derived from nicknames have escaped Guppy's attention. Indigenous to north west Staffordshire are Flint and Steel(e), both alluding to someone who was hard and unflinching; Grocott, made up of "grew" - "crane (bird)", plus "cock", a highly suitable soubriquet for a person with long, spindly legs; Lightfoot - "a runner or messenger with a light, springy gait"; Proudlove - "proud to be in love"; and Wildblood - "a fiery-tempered individual". Over in the north east, Guppy has missed Frost and Snow, both implying people with a lack of ardour or warmth of feeling; Gold/Gould - "golden-haired" or "rich"; Jolly - "lively, life and soul of the party"; Goodfellow - "good companion"; and Peach - a nickname for someone who had committed some sin, or a grower and seller of peaches.

3) Personal names and petnames

The candidates here are: Batkin, Brunt, Hodgkins, Howson, Jeavons, Lakin, Loverock, Malkin, Myatt, Shemilt and Tomkinson. Of Biblical origin are the quartet Batkin, Malkin, Myatt and Tomkinson, pet names formed from Bartholomew, Mary, Matthew and Thomas respectively. Examples; 1767:George Batkin of Stone, married to Mary Sutton of Swynnerton; 1666:Joseph Malkin, chargeable for tax on one hearth at Bucknall; 1731:Mary Myatt of Biddulph, married to John Dickens; 1847 Endon Tithe Map:Samuel Tomkinson, holder of five acres of land at Brown Edge.

The Germanic contingent is represented by Hodgkins and Howson, derivatives of Roger and Hugh; 1708:Dorothy Hodgkins, married to Joseph Platt at Audley; 1877:W.Howson and Son, wine and spirit merchants, Newcastle Ironmarket .

Lakin is a Staffordshire variant of Lawkin, that is 'Law", a pet form of the Latin "Laurentius" - "Laurence, Lawrence" plus the diminutive suffix "-kin". For example, Richard Lawken of Tamworth (1609) turns up as Richard Lakin in 1611. Up to the Industrial Revolution this surname is virtually confined to the south eastern sector of the county. The Scandinavian contribution extends to Brunt and Shemilt. Brunt is a late modification of the Old Norse name "Brandr", Old Danish "Brand" - "fire-brand, sword", via Bront; 1624:Richard Brant of Norton in the Moors; 1532:James Brontt of Morridge Side (Leek); 1728:Sarah Brunt of Wolstanton. Shemilt is of doubtful origin, although it has been derived from the female Scandinavian name "Svanhildr", as borne by William, son of Swanylde, bailiff at Newcastle under Lyme in 1405. There is no way of confirming whether the latter specimen did eventually develop into the modern Shemilt and so the matter must remain unresolved for the time being. A William Shemelt was living at Stoke in 1668.

Loverock, too, is disappointing. Undoubtedly it is a survival of the Saxon personal name "Leofric", made famous by Earl Leofric of Mercia, husband of the equally celebrated Lady Godiva. The name means "beloved ruler". Instances of Loverock are lacking, but in the parish registers of Rocester we find 1772:Robert Lavrack (sic) and 1791:Thomas Leverock (sic) of Alton. However, these might be from Middle English "laverock" - "lark" - a nickname for someone with a sweet singing voice.

The final name in this section - Jeavons/Jevons - is basically a south Staffordshire surname, traceable chiefly to the Welsh "Ieuan", a form of John; 1655:John Jevons of Audley. It can also be from Old French " jovene" - "young", used to distinguish father from son as in 1277:William le jovene of Colton.

Guppy has failed to pick up on a whole host of surnames here, which are absolutely crucial to any investigation into North Staffordshire nomenclature. They range from the Saxon names "Goodwin, Woolridge, Dodd, Haycock, Harding, Waltho", to the Scandinavian "Orme, Kettle, Haynes, Thurstan, Osbourne"; from the Germanic "Ansell, Emery, Grundy/Grindy, Jervis, Raybould, Till, Timmis, Walklate (a double diminutive of "Walho")", to the Breton "Allen, Bryan, Harvey" and the Welsh "Batho, Craddock, Degg, Maddock(s), Morgan, Brittle, Vaughan, Onions". Not to be ignored are the Biblical "Bateman, Mitchell, Meakin, Mycock, Daniels, Jenkinson, Tams, Tonks", nor the Classical "Alcock, Austin, Bennett, Lockett, Martin, Palin, Nicklin, Pearson, Silvester".

4) Topographical names

Topographical names or "toponymics" involve the most elementary types of surnames of all and specify exactly where a person lived at the time when he or she acquired their surname. It might be any prominent landmark in the immediate neighbourhood - a local meeting spot, such as a tree or a stone, or any physical feature in the landscape readily discernible by or accessible to the local inhabitants of a small medieval village, like a grove, brook, ford or heath. Such basic names, so closely related to the earth from which they sprang, obviously reflect the topography of the individual county in which they are found. For example, the north eastern region of the county bordering on the Peak District abounds with hills, rocky outcrops, valleys and nooks, and it is only reasonable to expect surnames connected with such natural features hereabouts, whereas the north western sector of Staffordshire with its more wooded terrain ought to be characterised by tree and wood names. Indeed, this is very much the case, but only a fraction of these very important names appear on Guppy's list; Ash - dweller by an ash tree; 1912:Arthur Ash (carter), Frier Street, Longton; Fern - dweller among the ferns; 1851:Edward Fern (grocer and tea dealer), Market Street, Longton; Hollins - dweller by the holly or holm oak; 1700:Copwood Hollins of Cheadle; Leese - dweller by the pasture or glades; 1887:George Leese (blacksmith and wheelwright) of Queen Street, Burslem; Wooddisse - dweller at the house in the wood; 1787:John Wooddisse of Uttoxeter - although the most common spelling is Woodhouse; 1851:Thomas Woodhouse, proprietor of a beerhouse in Princes Road, Burslem. Wooding(s) denotes habitation at a place where wood was cut; 1588:Roger Wooddinge of Ellastone.

Fallows refers to someone who set up home near some newly cultivated land, but in Staffordshire it regularly alternates with Follows, as evinced by the Wolstanton parish registers, where William Fallows (1740) appears as William Follows in 1742. Guppy misses this variant altogether.

The three remaining toponymics - Clowes, Torr and Wint - have the upper hand in the Staffordshire Moorlands. Clowes, together with Clews and Clough, all designate residence in or near a ravine or steep-sided valley; 1700:Ellen Clough of Audley, married to William Corn; 1841:Margaret Clewes, aged 13, paper cutter for Elijah Webster at Messrs William Davenport and Co, Longport; 1750:Aaron Clowes, proprietor of the Talbot alehouse at Burslem. The topographical term "torr" - "high rock, peak, hill" - occurs in local landmarks such as Gib Torr near Morridge Top and Drabber Tor north east of Alstonefield, and so the surname Torr alludes to a person who dwelt by a rocky peak; 1666:Thomas Torr, paying tax on one hearth at Ecton near Warslow. Again, Guppy fails to weed out the local variant Tarr; 1851:Daniel Tarr (farmer) of Heaton (Rushton Spencer).

In fact, this is the whole crux of the matter. All authorities on surnames tend to neglect these local corrupted forms. In vain will local and family historians scour the relevant dictionaries and gazetteers; they will never come across what they are looking for, because they are searching in the wrong places. In many instances these local variants will be found lurking in parish registers, because they do not appear until very late in the proceedings. Yet it is this mass of surnames which is more representative of our county than the ones which usually crop up in all the surname dictionaries.

Wint is another classic illustration of this process in action. It describes a dweller by

Knutton Constablewicke.

Clayton.	Hearthes Chargeable.
Mr. Terricke	Eleaven
Richard Baddaley	Foure

Hanford.

Thomas Corbett	Two
Elizabeth Corbett	Three
Thomas Brerehurst	Sixe
John Whitehurst	Three
Humfrey Dixe	One
John Fisher	One
George Slayney	One

Dimsdale.

Edward Brett, Esquire	Nyne
William Bourne	Two
Thomas Wattson	Three
William Tomkinson	Foure
Francis Beech	One
Coulton Latham	Three
George Berkes	One
William Burges, Senior	One
William Burges, Junior	
John Eardley	
Thomas Whittingham	
John Smyth	
Roger Rowley	

Knutton.

William Sutton
Thomas Pattson
John Ball
John Beech
John Lowe
Thomas Hollins
Mrs. Clownam
William Perry
Richard Webster
Thomas Lawton
John Beech
John Baddaley
William Oarme
Robert Mason

1666 Hearth Tax Returns

STAFFORDSHIRE

Staffordshire Record office, Stafford.

Militia Ballot Lists
1812-13. Baswich and Walton [D.3361/10/11].
1824. Tettenhall Regis [D.1018/2].

Militia Muster Rolls
1794. 'Militia men sworn at Cheadle' [D.1554/161].
1803. Trentham Loyal Volunteers [D.593/L/1/26].
1819. Newcastle Volunteer Armed Association [D.1460].

Note. There are no relevant 18th and 19th century militia records at Lichfield Joint Record Office, Walsall Local History Centre and Wolverhampton Archives Department.

Public Record Office, *Kew.*

County Regimental Returns (names listed without location in the county)
Militia: **1st Staffordshire: 1780-1876** [WO.13/1943-70]; **2nd Staffs.: 1798-1805, 1851-76** [1971-82]; **3rd Staffs.: 1798-1800, 1853-76** [1983-89].
Supplementary Militia: **1st Staffs.: 1798-1807, 1808-16** [WO.13/2551-2]; **2nd Staffs.: 1803-15** [2553]; **3rd Staffs.: 1798-99** [2554].
Local Militia: **Central, East, North, South, West: 1808-16** [WO.13/3610-4].

Staffordshire Militia and Muster Lists

a winding path; 1543:Thomas Wynte of Alstonefield. But William Wynt (husbandman) of Wetton (1552) also appears as William Went in the same year, on the analogy of the local pronunciation of "splint" which is always "splent". In other counties the surname Went specifies habitation by the cross-road.

Guppy's list of toponymics is woefully inadequate for north Staffordshire. Hill and valley names of vital importance comprise Banks, Cliff(e), Low(e) and Edge, Bottom(s)/Botham, Dale, Slack and Slade. Woodland names are legion; Shaw - dweller by a copse, and Bradshaw - dweller by a broad copse; Lunt and Lowndes, from the Scandinavian "lundr" - "grove". Tree names too are everywhere; Birks, Scandinavian version of Birch - dweller by a birch tree or some birches; Braddock - dweller by a broad oak tree; Greatolder - dweller by a stout alder; Stubbs - dweller by some tree stumps. Typical of the north west are Snape - dweller by poor pasture, and Vyse - dweller by a boundary, whilst Heath is probably the most characteristic of all North Staffordshire toponymics - dweller by some heath(land).

5) Placenames

This class, which is by far the largest category of all, incorporates all those surnames derived from placenames or "locatives", not only in England, but also in France, especially from Normandy. Several in Guppy's list are undoubtedly to be traced to localities within the county of Staffordshire. Bagnall, for instance, goes back either to the village of Bagnall east of Milton or Bagnall near Alrewas. The pedigree of the family of Bagenhall alias Bagnall in Ward's *History of the Borough of Stoke-upon-Trent,* shows that John Bagnall was mayor of Newcastle under Lyme on no less than five occasions - 1519, 1522, 1526, 1531 and 1533.

The region around Broadmoor Plantation between Croxden and Upper Tean occurs as "Berdmor(e), Berdesmore" etc in the later Middle Ages, and survives as the Staffordshire surname Beardmore/Beardsmore; 1875:Theophilus Beardmore (beerseller) of Stafford Street, Longton. In the Croxden Abbey Chronicle for the year 1528, there is a locality in Combridge recorded as "Lytle Warrelowe", which clearly lives on as the prolific North Staffordshire surname Warrilow in all its divergent forms. A secondary source is a place in Acton Trussell and Bednall cited as "Warelowe" in 1574; 1532:John Warelow of Dilhorne; 1741:Ann Warrilow of Cheddleton.

Whitehurst near Dilhorne gives rise to a very common local surname; 1851:Margaret Whitehurst (shopkeeper) of Bradley Green, Biddulph; as does a locality known as "The Hammersleys" in the 1781 land tax returns for Cheddleton; 1841:Josiah Hammersley, teacher at the Boys' Sunday School, Longton. In the same land tax list a certain James Tomkinson occupied land in "Cummerlidge" owned by Mrs Hollins. This must be the base for the surname Cumberledge/Cumberlidge; 1887:George Cumberlidge (tea merchant), Windmill Street, Tunstall.

Chell is from Great Chell on the extreme northern edge of the Potteries conurbation;

1851:Mary Chell, licensee of the Black's Head, Custard Street, Leek; and the surname Colclough is preserved in Colclough Farm off Colclough Lane, north west of Great Chell; 1851:John Colclough (earthenware manufacturer) of Shooter's Hill in Normacot parish. This is another surname par excellence of our county.

Over in the north west we come to Eardley (End) north of Audley, source of Eardley; 1851:Frederick Eardley of the Dog and Partridge, Hot Lane, Burslem. Heighley near Betley, once the stronghold of the Audley barons during the Middle Ages, is corrupted to the modern surname Heler, probably on the analogy of a name like Pedley, which often switches with Pedler (Pedlar); 1912:J. Heler (farmer) of Adderley Green, Audley.

The village of Maer near Chapel Chorlton is pronounced locally as "Mare", which in turn becomes the surname Mayer, as proved by William Mare of Norton in the Moors (1807), who signs his name in the parish register as William Mayer. In other English counties the surname Mayer is an occupational term for a mayor, or at least, some kind of official name for someone who held the position of mayor. Again, Guppy would not be aware of the actual Staffordshire derivation owing to his ignorance of local dialect and pronunciation.

About two miles from Maer, to the south east, is the hamlet of Bowers, principal origin of the widespread surname Bowers; 1851:William Bowers (farmer) of Hilderstone.

Two localities in the south of the county which have bequeathed North Staffordshire surnames are Bickford west of Penkridge, home of Robert de Bykeford, taxed at Coldmeece in 1327, and Perton near Wolverhampton, recorded as "Parton" on Kip's map of 1607/1610. It is this form that proliferates in all areas of the county; 1907:Alfred Parton (potter's miller) of Cauldon Road, Shelton.

A handful of names listed by Guppy are frequently attributed to external sources, e.g. Boden, Brindley, Farrall, Leighton, Marson, Shirley and Wilshaw. Nevertheless, more acceptable solutions for all these are under our very noses. To be sure, Marson (or Marston), Leighton, Shirley and Boden can all quite rightly be traced to any one of numerous locatives in many English counties (as any glance at a National Gazetteer will verify). Yet all have better local alternatives. Marson (Marston) is derived either from Marston north west of Hopton in the Trent valley, or Marston near Wheaton Aston. At Church Leigh, south of Lower Tean, William Marston, baptised in 1721, is called William Marson on his tombstone (1787). In the main the Staffordshire Leightons have their roots in a lost locality found as "Layton in Pyrell Hundred" in the 1539 Muster Roll, probably near Bagot's Bromley; 1907:Moses Leighton (fried-fish dealer) of Waterloo Road, Cobridge.

Without a shadow of a doubt Shirley, near Foxt in the Churnet Valley, is the focal point for many a Staffordshire family called Shirley; in 1881 William Shirley had a cheese factory at his farm at Rewlach south east of Fawfield Head. The surname Boden/Bowden has two principal evolutionary lines, one stemming from Booden Farm in Haughton, south west of Stafford, whilst the second comes from Boothen near Trent Vale, recorded as

Boothen or Bowden Bridge in 1689; James Bowden married Catherine Wauker at Seighford on November 26th 1581.

Two Cheshire localities often adduced in any discussion concerning the surname Brindley are Brindley west of Nantwich and Brindley Green near Sandbach, but the best claimant could well turn out to be our own Brindley between Lapley and Haughton (Kip's map of 1607/1610) and Brindley Heath near Rugeley; 1851:John Brindley (woodman) of Madeley Holme, Croxden. In all probability there are a good number of families in Staffordshire called Farrall/Farrell with Irish ancestry, from "0 Fearghail" - "man of valour", but equally some must take their name from the place Farewell near Lichfield, since it crops up as "Farrall" in the seventeenth century; 1887:Richard Farrall (coal merchant), Railway coal wharf, Tunstall.

Wilshaw is easily the most deceptive surname in this group. To all intents and purposes it is from the county of Wiltshire and an instance such as 1414:Robert Wilteshire of Normacot seems to go along with this theory. However, the name ramifies largely in the north eastern sector of the county, particularly around Alstonefield, Fawfield Head, Leek, Cheddleton, Ellastone and Uttoxeter, and here the origin is Willshaw near Hollinsclough; 1851:George Wilshaw (shopkeeper), Rushton Marsh, Rushton Spencer.

Locatives brought into Staffordshire by immigrants from other counties also feature prominently on Guppy's list. Derbyshire supplies us with Bakewell from the old Peakland town of Bakewell on the River Wye and Lindop from Lindop Wood in Edensor south of Chatsworth House; 1875:William Bakewell (hatter) of Waterloo Road, Burslem; 1851:John Lindop (farmer) of Chatcull, west of Standon. Cheshire furnishes a very interesting selection; Clewlow from Cleulow Cross about three miles north of Rushton Spencer; 1770:Mary Clewlow of Kingsley married John Locket of Cheddleton. Corbishley and Curbishley go back to Corbishley near Alderley Edge; 1875:Edmund Corbishley (beerseller) of James Street, Stoke; whilst Goldstraw is a local corruption of Goostrey near Holmes Chapel; 1855:William Goostrey of Cheddleton, also quoted as William Goldstraw. Mottram is either from Mottram in Longdendale or from Mottram St. Andrew near Alderley Edge; 1851:Henry Mottram (tailor) of Scaldersitch, Sheen. Hollingsworth is to be traced to Hollingworth township in Mottram in Longdendale, Hollingsworth (Smithy) in Prestbury parish or possibly Hollingworth near Rochdale, Lancashire; 1907:James Hollingsworth (drayman) of Portland Street, Hanley. Swetnam is a shrunken form of Swettenham, east of Holmes Chapel; 1851:Lewis Swetnam (victualler) of The Green Man, Croxden and Turnock is derived from Turnock Farm in Siddington; 1875:John Turnock (grocer) of Talke Pits.

Lancashire contributes a trio of locatives; Durose, Tunnicliff and Shoebotham. Durose has been taken as a toponymic for a dweller in the rows of houses in a street, but this is nonsensical. It is a local perversion of the Lancashire placename Dewhurst near Great Harwood in Blackburn parish. For example; 1646:Thomas Dewerst of Rocester is identifiable with Thomas Duerst in 1649 and Thomas Durose in 1645. The transition works as follows: Dewhurst is first of all contracted to Dewers as in Robert Dewers of Lapley (1612), who gains an extra "r", turning into Robert Deweres in 1615 - compare the local pronunciation of "drawing", which comes out as "drawring" with the added "r" in the middle. The final change from "Deweres" to "Dewres" and eventually to "Durose" is then child's play; 1776:Henry Dewhurst of ye George in Leek; 1907:Thomas Durose (waggoner) of Adelaide Street, Fenton. Without these late spellings in the local parish registers, the link between Dewhurst and Durose would hardly be given a second thought.

Tunnicliff(e) comes from Tonacliffe north of Rochdale; 1806:Mary Tunnacliff of Stoke-on-Trent, married to Thomas Beetlestone (bricklayer). Shoebotham and Shoebottom are local shortenings of Shufflebotham, which is derived from Shipper Bottom Farm near Shuttleworth in Bury parish; 1690:Parnell Shoebottom of Burslem; 1851:James Shufflebotham of Ravenshall, Betley.

From Shropshire we get Elsmore, which is traceable to Ellesmere a few miles north east of Oswestry; 1851:John Elsmore (linen and woollen draper) of Liverpool Road, Stoke.

The remaining locatives - Shenton, Shelley, Boulton and Hambleton - are open to several interpretations. Shenton is generally traced back to Shenton near Market Bosworth, Leicestershire, but in our county the two outstanding contenders are Shavington near Crewe and Shavington not far from Market Drayton, both of which appear as "Shenton" in the seventeenth century; 1851:Elizabeth Shenton (blacksmith) of Trent Vale.

Involved in the surname Shelley are Shelley Farm in Solihull, Shelley south east of Huddersfield, Shelley several miles south west of Ipswich and Shelley near Chipping Ongar, Essex; 1851:Ralph Shelley (hatter) of Market Street, Longton. Places called Bolton are scattered across the north of England, encompassing the counties of Cumberland, Westmorland, Northumberland, the three Yorkshire Ridings and Lancashire. In addition, there is Boulton near Derby and any one of these localities could have ended up as the surname Bolton/Boulton; 1887:Arthur Boulton (greengrocer), St. John's Market, Burslem. Hambleton/Hambilton and Hamilton are also derived from countless villages and hamlets up and down the country, plus Hamilton in Lanarkshire. However, the two main bases for North Staffordshire families bearing these names are Hammerton Knowl Farm, east of Cleulow Cross, cited as "Hamulton" in the seventeenth century, and Hammerton Hill in Litton near Tideswell, Derbyshire, found as "Homelton" etc in the Middle Ages; 1851:Thomas Hambleton (farmer) of Mixon Haye, Onecote.

The two final locatives, Boon and Baskeyfield, were introduced by the Normans from two villages in Normandy - Bohon in La Manche and Boscherville-le-Perrey in the province of Eure. Baskeyfield boasts the variant Baskerville besides, which is nearer to the original Norman spelling; 1851:Fanny Boon (milliner) of Market Street, Stoke; 1851:George Baskerville, licensee of the Red Lion, Talke on the Hill; 1907:Henry Baskeyfield (carter) of Botteslow Street, Hanley.

It is in this concluding section where Guppy really comes to grief, for in one fell swoop he manages to consign the nucleus of our county's distinctive locative surnames to the wilderness. Not only is Guppy completely in the dark as to the surnames derived from lost villages, such as Drakeford and Chatfield, but he has no inkling of insignificant locations like Fernyhough just off Sandy Lane, Brown Edge, source of the prolific Fernyhough, and Wooliscroft Farm between Cotwalton and Hilderstone, origin of Wooliscroft/Williscroft. At the same time, he is blissfully unaware that Brownsword is a late corruption of Brownsett near Roche Grange, that Betteney is simply a local version of Betley, that Huntbach and Humpage are to be traced to the same locality - Humpage Green near Eccleshall, and that Swing(e)wood is a modified form of Swinchurch Farm near Chapel Chorlton. These are the real heart and soul of the county's locative surnames, which have always been overlooked or misunderstood in the past by writers and scholars, respected or otherwise.

It is all well and good presenting neat tables of a county's surnames, based on research from trade directories in the nineteenth century, but this method merely scratches the surface. No account is taken of the distribution of the surnames during earlier periods, when they were in the process of becoming hereditary, nor is any allowance made for the distortion which they undergo throughout the succeeding generations. This is where local dialect, pronunciation and spelling are of the utmost importance, yet it is in these very departments where Guppy's knowledge and treatment of the characteristic surnames of Staffordshire leave a lot to be desired.

All these factors are essential to any proper appraisal of the history and evolution of Staffordshire's unique nomenclature. It is my intention, therefore, in this series of studies, to demonstrate where Guppy and other writers on English surnames are at fault in their conclusions regarding the surnames of our county. The task is certainly a formidable one, but if my approach encourages genealogists and family historians to look at their own surnames in a different light, then this is reward enough.

MILTON,

Stoke=on=Trent.

Memo. Jackson

Bagnall Grange

Bagnall

24 Apl 82.

Bought of *Charles Sherratt,*

BONE AND ARTIFICIAL MANURE MANUFACTURER.

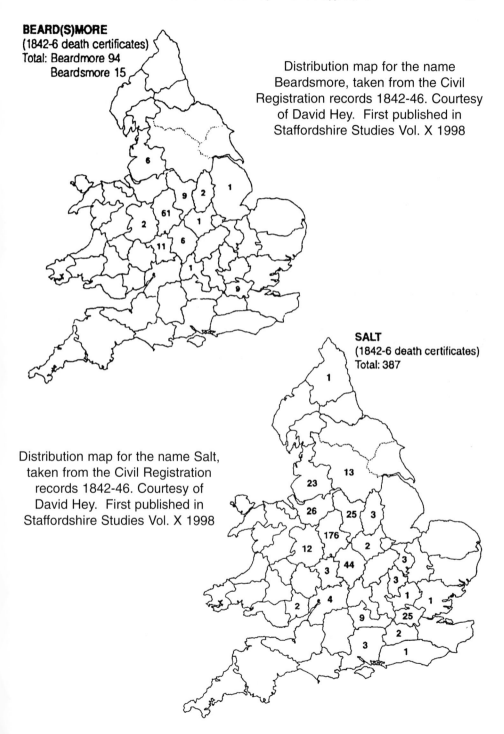

BEARD(S)MORE
(1842-6 death certificates)
Total: Beardmore 94
      Beardsmore 15

Distribution map for the name Beardsmore, taken from the Civil Registration records 1842-46. Courtesy of David Hey. First published in Staffordshire Studies Vol. X 1998

SALT
(1842-6 death certificates)
Total: 387

Distribution map for the name Salt, taken from the Civil Registration records 1842-46. Courtesy of David Hey. First published in Staffordshire Studies Vol. X 1998

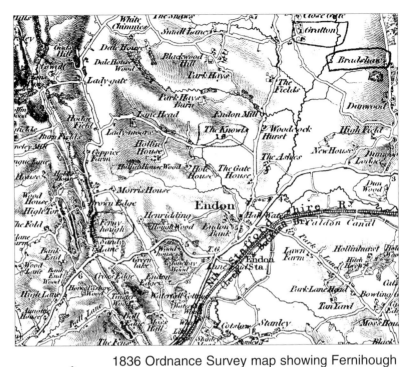

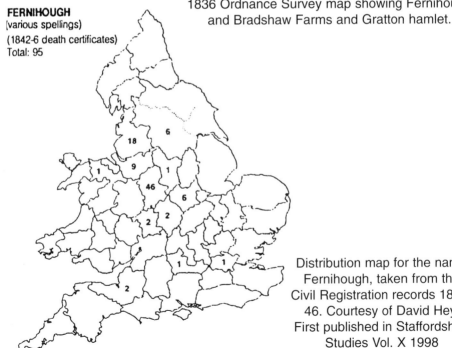

FERNIHOUGH
(various spellings)
(1842-6 death certificates)
Total: 95

1836 Ordnance Survey map showing Fernihough
and Bradshaw Farms and Gratton hamlet.

Distribution map for the name
Fernihough, taken from the
Civil Registration records 1842-
46. Courtesy of David Hey.
First published in Staffordshire
Studies Vol. X 1998

CORPORATION MINUTES, 1520–22

that John Bagnald and Richard Robinson shall have libertie to make a malt mylne on their own coste and charge payinge yerelie theirfore to this Boroughe foure marks at two feasts usuall.

Burgesses elected : Ralph Keelinge and Robert Mylnes, resident and each to pay x^s etc.

Newcastle-under-Lyme
Corporation Minutes

1521 [1521–2]   *Fol.* 57.

Mayor : Ronulfus Eggerton.
Bailiff for the xxiv : John Smyth.
  Pledges : Richard Hall, John Cleyton.
Bailiff for the community : George Smyth.
  Pledges : Thomas Thekenes, Ralph Leighton.
Sergeant for the community : Ralph Telrecke.
  Pledges : William Mathowe, Robert Dason.
Sergeant for the Mayor : Thomas Bradshawe.
Constables : Richard Robynson, John Lymforde.
Receivers : John Cleyton, Richard Brett.
Churchwardens : John Patson, Ralph Leighton.
Custodes Panis : William Wright, Ralph Bagnald.

Memorandum that Robert Launder, John Patson, John Blore and William Greyves have made full payment of certen money the which they weare bounden to pay by obligation vnto John Bagnald then Maior to the towne's vse.

Memorandum that the xxxth day of September A^o regni regis Henrici octavi xiiij^{to} John Bagnald Alderman and Thomas Homersley his suretie acknowledged and bounde themselves to pay to Mr Maior then beinge or to the Reves of our Blessed Lady beyonde the water xxxij^s iiij^d at Easter fayer next cominge to the use of our Blessed Ladye.

Also John Smyth then Bailife and Willm Willott his suretie the day and yeare aforesaid acknowledge themselves to pay some of xxxij^s iiij^d to the use above mencioned at the said day beinge Easter fayer day.

Also George Smyth then Bailife and Rauffe Keelinge his suretie the daye and yeare above written and did acknowledge them selves to paye the lyke some of xxxij^s iiij^d to the use above mencĩoed the day and tyme as afore.

Also Mr Maior and his Bretheren with the great inquest and the smalle are agreed that the Smythes shall have their old costome keepinge up the light as it haeth bin in tymes past. And yf their be any disagreement with any of the occupacõn, they to be ordered by the maior and his Bretheren, Also they be contented to cover the Church porch on this side Christmas daye next cominge.

Yates Map of 1775
showing Newcastle.

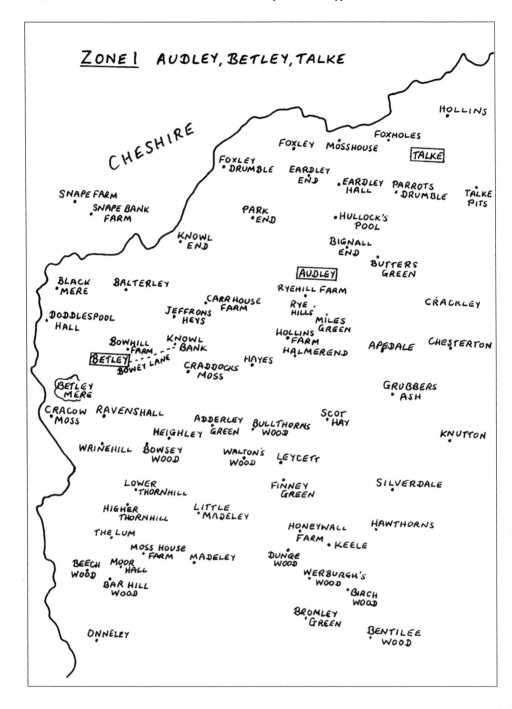

Zone One:
Audley, Betley, Talke

Titterton 27
Audley 27
Lee/Leigh/Ley/Lay/Lye 29
Lear/Leah 29
Lees(e) 29
Betley/Betteney 31
Bentley 31
Bent 31
Broadbent 31
Bromley/Bramley 31
Madeley 33
Heighley 33
Healey/Hayley/Hiley/Hawley/Heler 33
Adderley 33
Green(e) 33
Foxley 34
Year(d)sley/Yardley/Yeardley/Eardley 34
Yenn 34
Heald/Yeld/Eld 34
Hearn(e)/Herne 35
Irons/Hirons 35
End/Ind/Nind 35
Townsend 35
Overend 35
Bowton/Boughton 35
Bufton 35
Town/Toon(e)/Tune 36
Boughey/Buffey/Boffey 36
Hay(es)/Heys 36
Wood(s) 36

Attwood 36
Woodall/Wooding 38
Birch 38
Birks 38
Barks 38
Scarratt/Skerritt/Skerratt 38
Keele/Thornhill 39
Ryalls/Ryles/Royalls 39
Knowles/Knoll 39
Nowell/Newall/Neville/Nall/Knall 40
Hale(s) 40
Littlehales 40
Hallowes 40
Haugh 40
Hales/Hailes 40
Ravenshall/Ramshaw/Renshaw/Ramsill 40
Armishaw/Armshaw/Ormesher 41
Ormesher/Homeshaw/Hampshire 41
Foxall 41
Dumbell/Dumbrell 41
Moss 41
Poole(s) 42
Powell 42
Pooler 42
Pooley 42
Blakemore 42
Snape 42
Lumb/Limb 42
Plummer/Plimmer 43
Lycett 43

AUDLEY, OLD HALL.

Zone One

Every single county in England possesses its own basic stock of surnames which have evolved in that county over the centuries and which remain a distinguishing feature there, to the present day, despite all the periodic shifts of population throughout the ages. Generally speaking, a good percentage of these surnames consists of placenames traceable to a single locality within the county in question. For instance, Yorkshire is characterised by such names as Murgatroyd, Dent, Shackleton, Illingworth, Sutcliffe, Wilberforce and Hemingway, all of which can be traced back with a high degree of certainty to a small village or hamlet in one of the Yorkshire Ridings.

But the question immediately arises - are all the families called Murgatroyd, for example, descended from a common ancestor, who lived in the village of Murgatroyd during the Middle Ages? Of course, without any genealogical evidence, this is almost impossible to prove, unless the original inhabitant called Murgatroyd happened to be a noted landowner in the area. The difficulty of tracing any surname derived from a placename to a single source is highlighted in an article which appeared in the February 1990 issue of the Local Historian magazine. Here John Titterton attempted to pinpoint the origin of his own name using such sources as the Mormon International Genealogical Index, telephone directories, early wills, parish registers, hearth tax returns and others too numerous to mention. He gives a list of Titterton births registered throughout the country covering the years 1837-1890, and out of a total of 855 children baptised as Titterton, 240 occur in Staffordshire and 207 in Derbyshire. Thus, over 50 per cent of Titterton births during this period take place in these two adjacent counties.

But from where did the original Tittertons come? In the Lichfield Episcopal Registers, one entry for the year 1372 records a priest called John de Tydrynton at Sandbach. Now this is certainly striking, because the advowson of Sandbach church was held by Dieulacres Abbey near Leek, and it is in the north eastern region of Staffordshire where the surname Titterton evolves - eg. 1397 Staffordshire Assizes:William de Tyderyngton of Alstonefield. The name persists in the Alstonefield area right through the sixteenth and seventeenth centuries in forms such as "Tydrynton, Tytrynton, Tytryngton, Titerton, Tytterton" and so on, until we finally come across William and Henry Titterton in a lawsuit of 1624. The obvious base is Tytherington between Prestbury and Macclesfield, approximately twenty miles from Alstonefield. There are three other places called Tytherington in England, one near Chipping Sodbury in Gloucestershire, one near Frome in Somerset and one in Wiltshire, on the edge of Salisbury Plain, but whether any of these is implicated in the Staffordshire or Derbyshire Tittertons or Titheringtons is not known. In White's Trade Directory for 1851, John Titterton was running the Jervis Arms at Onecote, and George and Benjamin Titterton were farming land at Bradnop.

So where does this leave Staffordshire's own distinctive brand of surnames derived from unique locations within our county? - names like Audley, Burslem, Chatterley,

Wedgwood, Chell, etc. Are we to believe that every family in north Staffordshire bearing the surname Audley is related to all the other Audleys hereabouts? This is plainly nonsense, for, in addition to the once powerful barons of Audley there were humble peasant families who were born and brought up in the Audley area, some of whom also bore the name Audley. They had no links whatsoever with the landowning Audleys, but they too passed on their family name Audley to succeeding generations; 1907:Charles B. Audley (grocer) of Waterloo Street, Hanley.

During the Middle Ages the power and prestige enjoyed by the Audleys were unrivalled, for they dominated huge areas of North Staffordshire as feudal lords in possession of extensive tracts of land. In 1253 a charter of free warren was granted by Henry III to James (Lord of Audley) in all his estates in the north of the county, comprising Audley, Betley, Chesterton, Bradwell, Bignall End, Chatterley, Tunstall, Burslem, Chell, Thursfield, Whitfield, Bemersley, Endon, Horton, Gratton, Longsdon, Alstonefield and Norton in the Moors. James inherited all these possessions from his father Henry, who was the acknowledged founder of the Audley dynasty. He was the instigator behind the construction of Heleigh Castle and the foundation of the Cistercian abbey at Abbey Hulton. In 1223 he bestowed on the abbot and monks of Hulton the vills of Hulton and Rushton Grange (near Cobridge), the wood of Sneyd, the hay or small park at Carmountside, lands in Bucknall and Normacot, and the vills and estates of Mixon, Bradnop, Middlecliff, Apesford, Morridge and Onecote.

Since the Audleys controlled so much territory in north Staffordshire, stretching from the border with Cheshire and Shropshire, in the west, to the border with Derbyshire, in the east, it is no wonder that their influence permeated every stratum of medieval society in the region. Nowhere is this more apparent than in the Inquests on the Audley estates, covering the period 1272-1308. For here we see that by the beginning of the fourteenth century the feudal system as a business organisation is on the wane and indeed, arbitrary forced labour on the demesne lands of the lord of the manor has largely been replaced by varying forms of payment in lieu of "dayworks" or "Autumn works", that is, working for the lord of the manor on special days or at critical seasons of the agricultural year, such as helping out with the ploughing in autumn.

The status of the villein tenants on the Audley estates had changed so radically that by 1299 many were known as "customary tenants" paying the lord of the manor for certain privileges such as excusing themselves for non-appearance at the local manor court, for rights of pasturage called "herbage", and for "pannage" or right to pasture pigs in the lord's waste or woodland. Many of these customary tenants were hiring out their labour to work on the lord's demesne lands under the supervision of the local bailiff or reeve.

At this particular time "copyhold tenure" for manorial land was still in its infancy and up to the individual whims of the lord of the manor. This legislation regarding land ownership had been introduced by Edward I in order to enable the eldest son in even the most humble family to inherit the land which his father had worked all his life - it was no longer the exclusive preserve of the rich barons and landowners with their vast estates. This land could be claimed and awarded only at the local manor court, and it was held "by copy of the Court Roll". This system, which is the basis of English inheritance, is known as "primogeniture".

It is not known how widespread this particular practice was on the Audley estates, but even if it were merely in its embryonic stage it would be a major factor in the stability of any close-knit medieval community, because it would encourage each individual "copyhold" tenant to stay put in the same vill where he was born so that his surname was handed on to his son, and his son, ad infinitum. This, probably more than anything else, has contributed to the remarkable continuity of the surnames in North Staffordshire from the end of the Middle Ages up to at least the advent of the Industrial Revolution.

Surnames connected with woodland

The element "-ley" of Audley is a relic of the Saxon word "leah", which referred to a wood, glade or clearing, and only later open land or pasture. Consequently the prolific local surname Lea, together with variants such as Lee/Leigh/Ley/Lay/Lye could contain any one of these meanings, denoting residence by such a feature, or go back to places like Church Leigh, Upper Leigh and Lower Leigh between Tean and Uttoxeter, or Lea Heath near Hixon, and so on. In the 1841 Scriven report on children in the Staffordshire Potteries, Elizabeth Lee, aged 25, had been a cutter and transferrer since the age of 15 at Messrs. Minton and Boyle's China Factory along Trentham Road, Stoke. For piecework she earned 8 shillings per week. Other examples of the surnames; 1851:Thomas Lea (basket and sieve maker) of Merrial Street, Newcastle under Lyme; 1907:Joseph Leigh in charge of the public weighhouse in Parliament Square, Hanley. The most notorious of the local Leigh clan is of course Molly Leigh, the Burslem witch who lived in the Hamil between the years 1685-1748. She shunned the company of other people, preferring to live on her own with her black raven for a pet. Her grave in St. John's churchyard, Burslem, lies in a transverse position (north-south), in order to pacify the ghost of the deceased.

Some surname writers conjecture that Leah/Lear is a variant of Leigh, but this is unconvincing, although there is a 1684 reference in Brocton by Baswich to the Leas alias Leahs house, which does indeed point to this conclusion. Sarah Leah married William Pot (husbandman) at Swynnerton in 1756, and Daniel Lear was owner of a beerhouse in High Street, Longton in 1851. The Biblical name Leah, borne by the sister of Rachel and the first wife of Jacob, was not used as a christian name in England until its adoption by the Puritans in the seventeenth century, and so this line of enquiry can he dismissed forthwith. The most promising line seems to be the fieldnames known as The Lear, Near and Over Lear in Huntington near Cannock, which preserves Old Norse "leirr" - muddy place. Hence it could be a toponymic for a dweller by a swampy stretch of land.

The plural form Lees, preserved in Brown Lees near Knypersley, Leys near Froghall, Tean Leys and Leese Hill near Loxley and countless other places so called across the

county, survives as Lees and Leese, both of which are even more prolific in north Staffordshire than the singular variety; 1640 Muster Roll:Robert Lees, member of the impressed band at Cheadle, enlisted to do service against the rebellious Covenanters in Scotland; 1887:Joseph Leese (grocer) of Greengates, Tunstall. An alternative source for Lees(e) is the Saxon "laes" - "pasture", denoting residence there.

The original site of the settlement at Audley is accredited to Aldgyth, its female Saxon founder, who must have been a woman of considerable importance in the local Saxon hierarchy. Curiously, two other places in this same zone contain female Anglo Saxon personal names - Balterley - "glade of Baldthryth" and Betley - "glade of Bette". The former apparently does not survive as a surname, but Betley certainly does; 1851:John Betteley (auctioneer) of Stafford Row, Hanley; 1907:Frederick Betteley (butcher), stall 37, Meat Market, Burslem. In North Staffordshire it also develops into Bettany/Bettaney, as in the parish registers for Seighford, where Joseph Betteley (1762) is buried as Joseph Bettany in 1806. In 1907 Thomas Bettany was a noted carter in Normacot Road, Longton. Occasionally there is confusion with Bentley; Johnathon Bettoney, resident at Bucknall in 1810, is also known as Johnathon Benteley in 1808. Yet Bentley is principally from Bentilee Wood south of Keele, Bentilee near Abbey Hulton, recorded as "Bentteley" on the Yates map of 1775, or Bentley, two miles west of Walsall, all designating a clearing overgrown with bent grass; 1851:James Bentley (cabinet maker) of Liverpool Road, Stoke; 1851:Edward Bentley (baker and flour dealer) of Bow Street, Newcastle under Lyme. The first part of this name - Old English "beonet" - "bent grass" - gives the modern surname Bent - dweller by a grassy plain or heath, as in Henry del bent, taxed at Leigh near Checkley in 1327, whose name lives on in The Bents near Withington. Joseph W. Bent (miner) was living at Bold Street, Northwood (Hanley) in 1907. The compound Broadbent refers to a dweller by some broad grassy expanse of land; 1851:John Broadbent (plumber and glazier), Piccadilly, Hanley. The Yorkshire and Lancashire Broadbents probably originate mainly in Broadbent, north of Oldham, midway between Higginshaw and Watersheddings.

South of Keele, just off the Whitmore road, lies Bromley Green, which could well turn out to be the focal point of the surname Bromley in north west Staffordshire. Yet there are other contenders to the Bromley throne with excellent credentials, comprising Gerrard's Bromley near Podmore and three places in the vicinity of Needwood Forest - Abbot's Bromley, famous for its ancient Horn Dance, Bagot's Bromley and Bromley Hurst. All commemorate a settlement built in a clearing where broom once grew. At an assembly in Newcastle under Lyme Guildhall on 11th April 1654, Edward Bromley was one of four "lewners" appointed for a three month assessment. A lewner was a tax inspector who collected "lewns", church taxes levied by the parish. The variant Bramley (with the same meaning as Bromley) is much rarer; 1851:William Bramley (schoolmaster) of Stowe by Chartley.

Madeley west of Keele and Madeley south of Croxden have both contributed to the

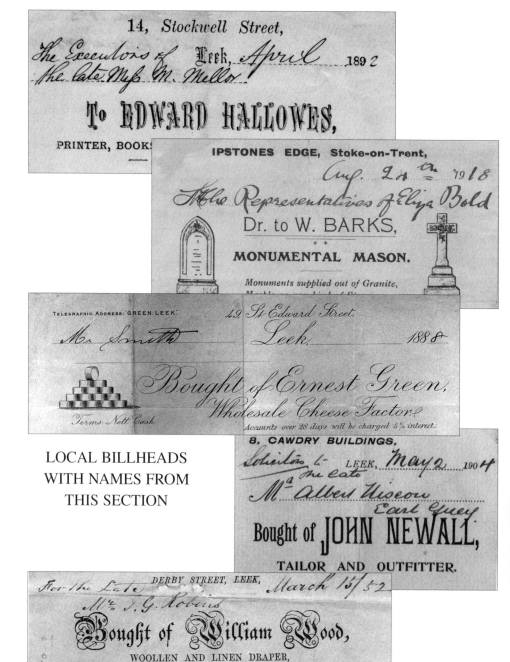

LOCAL BILLHEADS
WITH NAMES FROM
THIS SECTION

spread of the surname Madeley, although the name may also have been brought into the county by immigrants from Madeley near Telford. These three places probably refer to a forest that once belonged to a Saxon called Mada. Madely near Gloucester - "glade where mowing was carried out" and Madley near Hereford - "good place" - are definitely out in the cold here as regards possible sources; 1887:Mrs M.A. Madeley (bookbinder) of Albion Street, Hanley; 1907:David Madeley (brick and tile maker) of Gibson Street, Burslem.

Just north of Madeley, on a pronounced hill, is Heighley with its scanty castle remains, the nerve centre of the Audley empire during the Middle Ages. The place itself means "high glade (clearing)" and is without question the progenitor of a large number of local families called Healey, Healy, Hayley, Hailey and Hiley. Besides, there are several other localities called Healey in other counties which cannot be ruled out as possible sources - Lancashire offers Healey in Spotland and Healey in Chorley; Northumberland's interest is shown by Healey near Hexham, Healey near Morpeth and Healey near Rothbury; whilst Yorkshire submits Healey not far from the Theakston Brewery Visitor Centre and Healey near Dewsbury. All are identical in meaning with our local Heighley. The constant fluctuation in forms of this particular surname is demonstrated admirably by Thomas Hayley of Seighford (1793), who occurs as Thomas Healy in the same year, and Francis Heley alias Bageley in the register of St. Mary's, Stafford (1570), noted down as Francis Bageley alias Hyley in 1571. Heler is most likely a modern variant of Heley, modelled on the local pronunciation of "borrow",which often alternates between "borrer" and "borrey"; 1912:T. Heler (farmer) of Eardley End, Audley. Hayley often interchanges with Hawley: Rugeley parish registers; 1677:John Hauley (Hayley), which in turn switches with Halley; 1581:Edward Halley (Hawlye) of Eccleshall. In 1851 James Hawley was in charge of his own hairdressing salon in Lower Street, Newcastle under Lyme. Staffordshire families called (O')Healy, Hely with Irish ancestry, could be for "0 hEilidhe" - "descendant of the claimant" or "0 hEalaighthe" - "descendant of Ealathach".

Adderley Green, north east of Heighley, together with its namesake Adderley Green (Longton) are probably to be ignored as origins of the surname Adderley, because they were most likely named from previous landowners of that name, and so our possibilities are narrowed down to Adderley near Dilhorne and Adderley north of Market Drayton, both referring to the glade of Aldred. In the churchwarden's accounts for Stoke (1589), Raffe Adderley was paid eight pence *"...for washinge of the serplice",* and in 1851, Rupert Adderley was proprietor of the Duke of York in High Street, Longton.

The component "Green", contained also in other places such as Finney Green (Leycett) and Miles Green (Audley), probably alludes to a common, a village green or simply a grassy spot. Hence the widespread surname Green(e), as in William del grene of Madeley (1327 subsidy rolls) implies residence by such a local landmark, but on occasion it may stand for a nickname for someone who was "green", in the sense of "young" or "immature". In the 1841 Scriven report Thomas Green, aged 10, had already been a jigger turner for three years at the earthenware factory owned by Messrs. Meller, Venables and

Pinder, Burslem. He worked first for Thomas Sergeant, then for Thomas Summers and eventually for William Taylor.

Catherine Foxley, buried at Audley in July 1672, must surely have claimed ancestors from Foxley, a mile and a half away to the north, or, failing that, from Foxley near Chatcull. Both locations betray the presence of foxes in the glades and woods when the hamlets were established; 1907:William Foxley (placer), Smith Child Street, Tunstall.

Right next door to Foxley is Eardley End on the Alsager Road, with Eardley Hall a stone's throw away to the south east. In his 1733 survey of Audley parish and Talke hamlet, Richard Parrott mentions a certain absentee landowner by the name of Esquire Ocker of Okeover, who employed a coachman John Whittell. Previously he had been under contract to Mrs Eardley of Eardley Hall until her death. The Eardleys of Eardley were of yeoman stock, as exemplified by Hugh de Erdeley yoman of Audley, summoned to the local assizes in 1413. Most families in North Staffordshire by the name of Eardley have a family tree going back to this place, but its actual meaning is unknown. At any rate, it is alternatively described as "Yeardley Ende" in 1512 and as "Yardley End" in 1621, thus presenting us with the other modern variations - e.g. 1669:Ralph Eardly (Yardley, Yeardley) of Standon. In 1655 William Yardley, a Quaker of Dairy House, Horton near Rudyard, was imprisoned for speaking out in Leek parish church, and in 1887 Thomas Eardley had set himself up as a boot repairer in his shop at Newport Lane, Middleport.

Yeardsley (Hall) near Whaley Bridge, Derbyshire exhibits forms such as Erdley, Yeardley in the 1600s and 1700s, and must be regarded as a secondary source, especially for Yearsley spellings, e.g. 1907:Cornelius Yearsley (school teacher) of Derby Street, Cobridge. Yearsley, a few miles south of Rievaulx Abbey in the North Riding of Yorkshire, could also play a part in the proceedings at some stage. If the name Yardley came into Staffordshire from other counties, then we are also looking at Yardley in Birmingham, Yardley in Thaxted (Essex) and two locations in Northamptonshire - Yardley Gobion and Yardley Hastings.

The couplet Eardley-Yeardley parallels the dialectal "(h)ead-yed". The same modification is evident in Endley-Yendley; 1562:John Yenley of Ellastone (1563:John Endley). These could be for Hanley (Handley) via Henley (Hendley), since Roger Hendeley is resident at Kingsley in 1532 and Thomas Yenley (Yendley) is amongst the inhabitants at Alton in 1606. In 1907 Enoch Hendley (joiner) was living in Ronald Street, Longton. Endon and Endon Bank occur with a similar development; Leek parish registers: 1661:Thomas Sutton of Yen; 1671:Anne Bentley of Yen Bank, hence the rare surname Yenn, 1589:Margerye Yen of Ellastone.

The modern surname Held/Heald/Hield(s) signifies a dweller near a slope or rising ground, as in 1327 Subsidy rolls:Thomas de la helde of Tunstall, whose name is preserved in Yeld House near Chatterley (1836 Ordnance Survey map). The dialect variant "yell" is found in Yell Bank in Gnosall. The vacillation in the forms is confirmed by Ann Heald of Ellastone, wife of John Heald (1631), registered as Ann Yeald in 1628. Occasionally the name loses the initial aspirate; 1851:Sarah and Jane Eld (boot and shoe makers) of Gaol Street, Stafford; 1907:Thomas Eld (oddman) of Edge Street, Burslem.

Hern(e)/Hearn(e)/Hearns is a toponymic for a dweller in a nook or corner of land, from an old Saxon word "hyrne"; 1360 Assizes:Rosa in the hurne of Ronton; 1907:Thomas Herne (warehouseman) of Penkville Street, Stoke. The sense implicit in the fieldname Yearn in Dunston near Penkridge is "spot of land in a river bend". This survives as the surname Yearn, but unfortunately local examples are not forthcoming. Other variants include 1739:Joseph Hiorns of Abbot's Bromley and 1907:Thomas Irons (boot, shoe and clog manufacturer) of Leek Road, Smallthorne. Whether the unattested Ion(s) belongs here is debatable.

The suffix "-end" as displayed in such localities as Eardley End, Bignall End, Halmerend, Knowl End, etc, indicates that they were situated at the extreme of the parish and away from the parish church which was at the centre. William attende, taxed at Penkhull in 1327, dwelt at the end of the village, and his name lives on as Ind and Nind; 1875:James Nind (butcher) of Knutton; 1907:J.A. Ind of Park Terrace, Leek. This is virtually synonymous with the much more widespread Townsend/Downend; 1327:William atte touneshende of Ipstones; 1851:Dorothy Townsend, licensee of the Nag's Head, Market Place, Uttoxeter; 1907:John A. Downend of Leycett. In 1716 Mostylee water mill in the Moddershall valley was bought by Stephen Townsend, a Stafford dyer, most likely because it was being used at that particular time for the fulling of cloth.

Overend and Overhand (no examples) refer to residence at the upper end of a village - compare the fieldname "Overende (1339)" in Rugeley; whilst Bowton/Boughton/Bufton denote a dweller above the village; 1851:Richard Boughton (linen and woollen draper) of Market Place, Burslem; 1907:Frederick Bufton (waggoner) of Hind Street, Tunstall. Town(e), Toon(e) and Tune simply allude to residence in the village itself, from the Saxon "tun", which is such a common element in placenames; 1887:Joseph Toon (coachman) of Rectory Road, Hanley; 1907:Sarah Tune of Albert Street, Longton.

The last family to hold the lordship of the manor of Audley was the Bougheys, whose most illustrious member was probably Thomas Boughey of Aqualate Hall in Shropshire. He could justly claim his title of lord of the manor in the nineteenth century as a result of his vast wealth accumulated in land and industrial undertakings in coal and iron. Bowey Lane (1833 Ordnance Survey map), the modern Bowhill Lane, which runs from Betley to Knowl Bank, is a reminder of the original locality from where the Bougheys obtained their name. This is recorded as "Boghay, Bochay" etc in the Middle Ages, a compound of Old English "(ge)haeg" - "enclosure, an enclosed piece of land" and an obscure first element, although there might be some allusion to its bow shape, or possibly an enclosure where wood was obtained for making bows. The latter is certainly a tantalizing theory, because, prior to the establishment of a village at Audley, the surrounding countryside was extremely fertile and heavily forested with woodlands of mainly ash, oak, beech, birch and yew. Traditionally the stave of the English longbow has always been made from yew, hazel, ash or elm and any one of these trees would surely have been in good supply in a place called "Boghay". During the Middle Ages the Audley area was renowned for the quality and prowess of its bowmen and archers, many of whom served the King's cause in the wars against France, achieving glorious victories at the battles of Crecy, Poitiers and Agincourt. Boughey has two other modern variants - Boffey and Buffey, and all three are well represented locally; 1608:Edward Boughey (churchwarden) at Swynnerton; 1907:William Buffey (ironworker) of Victor Street, Hanley; 1912:John Boffey (labourer) of Clayhills, Tunstall. Boffey and Buffey are alternatively derived now and then from Beaufour in Calvados, Normandy, as typified by John de Beaufey at the 1333 Staffordshire assizes.

In places like Scot Hay near Leycett and Jeffrons Heys east of Balterley Hall, the "hay" referred to an enclosure where deer were herded and kept throughout the winter for food, and so an instance such as Henry de la haye of Betley, tenant on the Audley estates in 1298, could stand for a number of things - the person who actually lived by the enclosed piece of land and thus was responsible for the deer herds, or it might be for residence by a forest fenced off for hunting. Any of these meanings is pertinent in the case of the surname Hay(s)/Hayes; 1768:John Heys, overseer of the poor at Betley. The singular form Hay also goes back to a nickname for a high (tall) man, or a Saxon personal name, usually a contraction of one commencing with the element "Heah-" - "high, tall", e.g. Hugh Hai from a Staffordshire deed of the twelfth century.

Only fragments remain of the great woodland scattered across the region - Walton's Wood and Bullthorne Wood at Leycett, Bowsey Wood at Heighley, Dunge Wood, Birch Wood and Werburgh's Wood at Keele, Bar Hill Wood and Beech Wood at Madeley, and so on. The prevalence of the surname Wood(s) hereabouts is a sure sign of the omnipresence of woods in the Middle Ages; 1298:William atte wode of Betley; 1887:Eliza Wood (smallware dealer) of Waterloo Road, Burslem; 1887:James Wood (brick and tile maker), Fenton Tileries; 1912:Frank Wood (engine driver), Wilson Street, Stoke. A very rare source is "wood", the adjective,used in the sense of "wild, frenzied", as in Shakespeare's "wood within this wood" in Midsummer Night's Dream. Attwood retains the original preposition of the toponymic; 1907:Charles Attwood (pointsman), Cliffe Vale Place, Hanley; 1907:William Attwood of Woodlea, Sydney Street, Wolstanton.

By contrast, John Wodhend, resident at Milwich in 1532, was descended from someone who resided at the end of a wood. The more normal modern form is Woodend; 1332:Robert atte wodehall of Dunston near Penkridge, clearly dwelt at the hall in the wood, giving us the surname Woodhall, Woodall, but this would easily absorb a name such as 1327:Peter de Wodhul of Newcastle under Lyme - "dweller at the wood by the hill". 1850:Samuel Woodhall (draper and grocer) of Wrinehill. Woodall is also a weakened variant of Woodwall Green near Croxton perhaps "stream flowing through a wood"; 1580:John Woodwall alias Whyte of Castlechurch; (1589:John Whyte alias Woodall); 1907:Arthur Woodall (potter), Russell Street, Burslem.

MADELEY PARISH REGISTERS

BAPTISMS

Dec. 11 Humphrey s. of Humphrey Bullock,
cordwainer

Jan. 10 Robert s. of John & Margaret Morrice,
husbandman

Jan. 30 William s. of George & Ann Snead, gent

Jan. 30 Thomas s. of John & Elizabeth Leighton,
yeoman

1585

1585 July 1 Thomas s. of Thomas Broomall, labourer

Aug. 23 Ann d. of William Bloore, taylor

Aug. 30 Mary d. of William & Ellen Burton, gent

Sept. 7 Joan d. of Richard Weston, husbandman

Sept. 8 William s. of William & Ann Picken,
husbandman

Oct. 10 Elizabeth d. of Thomas & Margaret
Whittmore, yeoman

Jan. 10 Ann d. of William & Joan Platt

Feb. 6 Alice d. of John & Joan Weston of Moorhall

1586

1586 July 20 Margaret d. of Richard Harding, husbandman

Aug. 22 William s. of Thomas Hawkins

Sept. 19 Elizabeth d. of Ralph & Ellen Leighton,
webster

Feb. 13 John s. of Peter & Ann Ridgway, miller

Mar. 15 Hugh s. of Phillip & Alice Walker,
husbandman

Mar. 22 Ann d. of Lawrence Harrowes, yeoman

1587

1587 Apr. 20 Thomas s. of Thomas Liversage, brickmaker

Apr. 21 Ellen d. of John & Alice Smith, gent

Apr. 28 John s. of Thomas & Margery Heath, bloomer

Nov. 12 Margaret d. of Robert & Mary Snead

Feb. 14 John s. of Peter & Ann Ridgway, miller

Madeley Parish Register 1585

Wooding(s) is either a toponymic for habitation by a place where wood had been cut or a derivative of the Saxon *woding - "the mad one"; 1300 Inquisition:Reginald de wodinges of King's Bromley; 1912:J. Wooding of Alfred Street, Fenton; 1912:Albert Woodings (furnaceman), West Parade, Fenton.

On the other side of the coin, this zone is strangely bereft of surnames derived from the names of trees, apart from Birks, which is a Scandinavian form of Birch - "dweller by a birch tree or a group of birch trees". For example, in the 1666 hearth tax returns at Audley, Richard Berkes junior is chargeable for one hearth whilst Anne Berkes and Jane Berkes are classed as exempt from payment. In the same returns Thomas Berkes is paying for two hearths at Halmerend, John Berkes for one hearth at Keele and John Birkes for one hearth at Madeley; 1912:Jesse Isiah Berks (builder), Brook Street, Fenton; 1912:David Birks (ovenman), Upper Normacot Road, Longton. Barks is possibly a late perversion by analogy with Berkeley-Barkley; 1851:Thomas Barks (farmer) at Brookside, Waterfall.

Birkin is a Danelaw counterpart of "birchen", preserved in Birkin north east of Pontefract; 1851:Thomas Birkin (tailor), Brownhills, Burslem; 1875:Bryan Birkin (shopkeeper) Mill Street, Hanley. In addition, Birch/Byrch/Burch is a topographical name for residence by some newly cultivated land, from the Saxon "bryce" with the common shift of the letter "r"; 1912:William Birch (postman), Ronald Street, Longton; 1912:Harry Birch (forge labourer), Smith Street, Fenton.

The complex Scarratt/Scarrott/Skerratt/Skerrett/Skerritt may or may not belong here - it all depends on two recordings from the Audley estates surveys, that is, Henry Skaryok, who was working 3 acres of land at Horton near Rudyard in 1298. He resurfaces as Henry Scarioc in 1307. If these two spellings are reliable, then they could refer to residence by some scarred oak tree, but there again, if the final "k" or "c" stands for "t", as so often in medieval documents, then this is evidently for "Scariot", perhaps a reduced form of "Iscariot", a nickname for someone who took the part of Judas Iscariot in the medieval Miracle plays. At any rate, the parish registers for Audley and Betley are crammed with the name - eg. 1540:Thomas Skarrett of Audley; 1557:Isabell Skerrat of Betley; 1559:Robert Scarriat of Betley; 1583:Frances Skerriot of Bowsie Wood, and so forth. 'Up north' the surname Skerritt is traced to Skirwith east of Penrith, Cumbria, which was formerly pronounced "Skerritt", whilst elsewhere an occupational term is on the cards for anyone who grew or sold parsnips, from "skirwit" - "parsnip". But the Audley and Betley specimens demolish these theories; 1851:Thomas Scarratt (ironmonger), Gold Street, Longton; 1875:Henry Scarratt, licensee of The Swan Inn, High Street, Tunstall; 1907:William Skerratt (compositor), Campbell Road, Stoke; 1907:Thomas Skerratt (saggar maker), Clanway Street, Tunstall.

Hills and valleys

Keele conceals an earlier "Kiel" - "cow hill" - and survives as Keel(e)/Keal; 1798:Ann and Samuel Keele of Wolstanton; 1907:S. Keele (potter), Havelock Street, Fenton. There may be some confusion with Kell(s), which is from an Old Norse personal name "Kel", borne by Henry Kel, resident at Grindley near Drointon in 1279; 1907:Robert James Kells (waggoner), Foley Street, Fenton.

Lower and Higher Thornhill, west of Madeley, is a likely base for our local Thornhills; 1887:Joseph Thornhill (farmer) of Jamage, Talke; 1912:John Thornhill (placer), Peace Street, Hanley. The place occurs as "Thorn(h)all" in 1644 - "nook of land at the thornbush". Less amenable sources are Thornhill east of Mam Tor, Derbyshire and Thornhill south of Dewsbury - "hill overgrown with thorn bushes."

Hillsides where rye was once cultivated for animal fodder and making bread or ale, are plentiful in many English counties, as evidenced by Ryal north of Corbridge, Northumberland, Ryehill near Hull and Ryhill south east of Wakefield. These end up as the modern surnames Ryal(l)/Ryalls/Ryle(s), but in Staffordshire the more relevant origins are Ryehill Farm and Rye Hills in Audley, Ryehill Farm in Church Eaton and "le ruyhul" (1349) in Essington; 1559:Thomas Ryle of Audley, buried on October 10th; 1841:George Ryles, Inspector of police for the parish of Burslem. Moreover, The Royals in Hatherton, Cannock is recorded as "Ryalls, the Rials" in the 1841 Tithe Awards - "nook of land where rye was grown" - and hence we have the couplet Ryles-Royall/Royle, which is an echo of the dialectal "bile" for "boil"; 1907:Arthur Royalls (flint miller) of Victoria Road, Fenton; 1907:William Henry Ryles (potter) of Oldfield Street, Fenton.

In the Audley estates surveys, covering the years 1298-1307, appear the following tenants; 1298:Richard atte knolle of Betley; 1307:William de knolle of Endon; 1307:Robert de knolles of Alstonefield, and 1307:Peter del knol of Audley. The names of these medieval farmers survive in Knowl Bank near Betley, Knowl End west of Audley, Knowles Farm near Endon and possibly Knowle Farm west of Rewlach or Brown Knoll north west of Alstonefield. All these have contributed towards the spread of the surname Knoll/Knowles/Nowles down the years, not forgetting Knowles near Upper Hulme and Knowl near Hixon. They all preserve the Saxon "cnoll" - "knoll, hill, hilltop" and denote habitation by such a prominent feature. In 1851, Joshua Knowles (carrier), based at the Butcher's Arms, Leek, was transporting goods regularly via Longnor, to Bakewell and Sheffield. So far, so good, but the surnames Knoll and Knowles overlap with several other names, and the actual forms are very tricky to decode. In the Swynnerton parish registers, the locality known as Knowl Wall near Beech, is written down as 'Nowall" in 1739, and as "New Wall, New Hall" in 1812, thus becoming embroiled with three other totally different surnames. Nowall clashes with Nowell/Nowill/Noel - Old French "noel" - "Christmas", a baptismal name for a child born during the festive season. The Augustinian Priory at Ranton was founded circa 1150 by Robert son of Noel (Lord of Ellenhall) and the two variants Nowel and Knoles occur in this general area - eg. 1318:Philip Nowel, and 1632:William Knoles, both of Seighford.

The spellings New Wall and New Hall come into conflict with Newhall, Newall/Newell - "dweller at the new hall", presumably a servant employed there in some capacity or other. Richard Nowell of Sugnall Magna (1532) is cited as Richard Newell in 1539. At Stowe by Chartley there is even confusion with Nevall/Nevell; 1574:Richard Newall, as opposed to 1609:John Nevell and 1633:William Nevall. Nevell/Nevall and Neville are French imports from any one of umpteen places on French soil called Neville - "new town", which corresponds to the equally ubiquitous home grown Newton. Also at Stowe by Chartley a form such as Elizabeth Nawell (sic) for 1585, suggests an intermediate spelling between Nowell and the modern Nawl/Nall/Knall. In the 1539 muster roll at Marchington, for example, Richard Nalle is a correction for Richard Knowall. In 1838, George Nall, bookseller, stationer and printer in Sheepmarket, Leek, was also postmaster for the town; 1907:Thomas Nall (miner), Hot Lane, Burslem; 1907:John Nawl (labourer), Peace Street, Northwood, Hanley.

The Saxon "halh" - "nook, recess, remote valley" - developed a special meaning in the north of England, that is, a piece of flat alluvial land by the side of a river. Thus, instances such as 1332:Geoffrey in le halgh of Seighford and 1300:Alice atte hale of King's Bromley, could contain any one of these connotations, giving the modern Haugh/Hauff/Hale and Hallowes. Richard Hallowes (died 1589), evidently kept a school at Alstonefield, combining his teaching duties with his office of parish clerk. In May 1640, William Hales was elected bellman at Newcastle under Lyme and his pay was 18 pounds per annum. Besides being town crier, proclaiming throughout the town the council orders and instructions to all the inhabitants, he was obliged to collect toll on all corn to be sold in Newcastle. This plural form Hales/Hailes is from Hales near Almington or Sheriffhales just across the Staffordshire-Shropshire border, north west of Weston under Lizard, or Halesowen in Worcestershire, all for "the nooks". Littlehales near Lilleshall Abbey - probably "small nooks" - also survives as a surname; 1907:Jabez Littlehales (miner), Gordon Street, Burslem.

Ravenshall near Betley - "Hraefn's nook" - was the home of Stephen de Raveneshalow, taxed there in the 1327 subsidy rolls. In Staffordshire the ending "-shall" is often converted into "-shaw", as in Mottershall-Mottershaw later on; Betley parish registers 1730:Samuel Ravenshaw. Yet the surname Ravenshaw is usually for habitation by a raven wood or from Ravenshaw Wood near Lichfield. It is further compressed to Ramshaw/Ranshaw/Renshaw/Renshall - e.g. Thomas Ravenshaw, buried at Seighford in 1682 is probably identical with Thomas Renshaw (1635); 1907:William Renshaw (confectioner), Goldenhill Road, Fenton. Moreover, Ravenshall itself occurs in the Betley parish registers as "Ramisall" in 1590 and as "Ransell, Rensall" in 1690, possible forerunners of Ramsell/Ramsall; 1907:Benjamin Ramsell (farmer) of Whiston Bridge, Kingsley, and of Renshaw/Ramshaw via a form such as John Renshall, resident at Betley in 1765. Also to be adduced as origins for the latter names are Ramshaw near Upper Hulme and Renshaw Wood west of Chillington.

Another correspondence of the Ravenshall-Ravenshaw type is Armishall-Armishaw, which is perhaps from Armishall Bank in Acton Trussell, south of Stafford (1850 Tithe

Award) - and meaning "Eorm's nook of land"; 1851:George Armishaw of The Star public house, Hollington. Also in the frame is a locality recorded as "Ametesawe (sic)" (1275) in the Trentham Chartulary, probably a misprint for "Armetesawe" - "grove of the hermit". The place is in Wall Grange, Leek. In the Ellastone parish registers Ralph Armishaw (1679) is written down as Ralph Ormishaw in 1686, hence the modern Ormesher. Of significance here is Homeshaw Lane in Haslington near Crewe, which was originally "Ormeshalgh" in 1299 -"Orm's nook", and this may well be implicated in Cheshire families of this name, along with Armyshire Hill in Lostock Gralam. In south Staffordshire, John Armyshire (1810) of Brierley Hill, crops up as John Hampshire in 1807, proving that the latter is not exclusively derived from the county of Hampshire. In a roundabout way, all this evidence complements nicely the research done by Redmonds on the surnames of the West Riding of Yorkshire, where Armshaw, Ormesher and Hampshire are traceable to Hallamshire, a district in the West Riding.

Foxall is basically indigenous to the southern half of the county, but examples like 1907:Harry Foxall (ironworker) of Edward Street, Fenton and 1907:George Foxhall (forgeman) of Oldham Street, Hanley, might go back to Foxhall Cottage in Gnosall - "nook of land where foxes hunted" or Foxholes in Talke - "fox burrows (earths)".

Two intriguing fieldnames in this zone are Parrot's Drumble near Talke Pits and Foxley Drumble about two miles north west of Audley. Drumble is a variant of the dialectal "dimble, dumble" and refers to a hollow, a ravine through which a watercourse runs, a deep shady dell, a wooded valley, hence an ideal spot to set up home in the Middle Ages. The dialect word survives as the surname Dumbell: 1907:Henry Dumbell (hairdresser) of Hanover Street, Hanley, whilst Drumble becomes Dumbrell with the switch of the letter "r".

Marshes, bogs, pools, lakes

During the Second World War, in response to the "Dig for Victory" slogans, great swathes of land in this zone were brought under cultivation for the first time, and it was not uncommon for local farmers to plough up whole tree trunks buried long ago in the ancient peat bogs and mosses dotted all over the place in this area - e.g. Craddocks Moss near Knowl Bank, Cracow Moss near Betley Mere, Moss House near Eardley End and Moss House Farm in Madeley. The surname Moss continues the same tradition, denoting a dweller by some primeval bog, swamp or morass; 1327:Stephen atte mos of Balterley; 1912:Thomas Moss (pavior), May Place, Fenton. In 1841, according to the Scriven report, William Moss, aged 8, had been working for five months as a mould runner for William Leir at Messrs John Meir and Son's Earthenware Factory at Tunstall. His wage was one shilling and sixpence per week, with one and a half pence extra for working overtime.

The land around Betley Mere was once covered by extensive shallow lakes and Doddlespool Hall and Farm may hark back to this particular era, although Hullock's Pool north of Bignall End could be more recent. At any rate, the surname Pool(e) is common enough around Audley from the 1500s onwards; 1540:William Poole; 1592:John Poole; 1697:Ellin Pool, etc. It simply denotes residence by some pool, deep place in a river or tidal stream. In 1887 John Poole was proprietor of a draper's shop in Newcastle Ironmarket. Inevitably the name becomes intertwined with Powell; Mucklestone parish registers 1597:Henry up Poell, that is "son of Powell" noted as Henrie up Pooll in 1602. Powell stands for Welsh "ap Howell" - "son of Howel", where the latter means "conspicuous, eminent"; 1887:James Powell (grocer), Bond Street, Tunstall. The extended form Pooler also refers to habitation by some pool; 1644:Judith Pooler of Seighford, married to Richard Purcel on August 4th. Pooley would then be a probable variant on the analogy of Heler-Heley, but instances are lacking.

This same theme is emphasised by Black Mere in Balterley - "dark pool or lake", synonymous with Blakemore (House) in Oulton, Norbury, despite the latter's modern spelling. Also on the agenda here is Blakemere Pool north east of Norbury by the Shropshire Union Canal and possibly "Blakemore" (1487) in Forton, west of Aqualate Mere, Blake Moor in Church Eaton and Blake Mere east of Upper Hulme on Morridge, famed for its legendary mermaid waiting to lure unsuspecting travellers to certain death beneath the murky waters. Any of these localities could have given rise to the surname Blackmore/Blakemore; 1590:George Blackmore, son of Hugh Blackmore, baptised at Audley on May 3lst; 1907:James Blakemore (miner), Adelaide Street, Fenton.

Barely two miles north west of Balterley, across the Staffordshire border in the neighbouring county of Cheshire, we come to Snape Farm and Snape Bank Farm west of Englesea Brook. These preserve the Saxon word "snaep', which could mean anything from "land of a boggy texture", "inferior winter pasture" to "poor grazing land" or "scanty grass for sheep". Consequently the surname Snape could go back to this region of Cheshire or indicate residence by a spot, notorious for its poor, damp pasturage. Auxiliary sources include a locality known as "le snape iuxta Levedale" (1364) near Penkridge, Snape north west of Ripon in the North Riding of Yorkshire, Snape near the Maltings in Suffolk and Snape Green south east of Southport, Lancashire. From the Reformation onwards the surname proliferates across the whole of North Staffordshire. Amongst the able-bodied contingent in the 1539 muster for Madeley was Robert Snape who was equipped with "a jack and a peyr of splentes", that is, an ornamental jerkin or jacket with pieces of iron sewn on for protection, and strips of overlapping armour for shielding arms and elbows; 1851:William Snape (nailor), Garshall Green, Milwich; 1875:Samuel Snape (police officer), Hartshill, Stoke.

The Lum, near to Bower End, Madeley, means "the pool" and must be propounded as a major source of the local surname Lum(b), backed up by Lum Edge two miles north west of Warslow, with external pressure from Lumb in Rossendale, Lancashire and Lumb south west of Halifax; 1887:Samuel Lumb (family grocer, retailer and outdoor beer seller) of Wilson Street, Stoke. It is fundamentally a West Yorkshire surname. The rare local Limb could be a variant, mimicking a doublet such as Plummer-Plimmer - "worker in lead"; 1887:Gershon Limb, headmaster of Chell Board School, home address, Church Street, Tunstall. The Plummer-Plimmer interchange is confirmed by the Rocester parish registers, where James Plummer (1652) is entered as James Plimmer in 1629.

One surname on its own here is Lycett, from Leycett north east of Madeley, of doubtful meaning. One hypothesis is "an animal fold in a meadow" but this is pure guesswork; 1875:Samuel Lycett (grocer), Broadmeadow, Chesterton; 1887:Charles F. Lycett (manufacturer of window blinds), Fountain Place Buildings, Burslem.

1846, and the former have one in *Red street*, built in 1833. The *National School*, in Butt lane, was built in 1847, at the cost of £480, raised by subscription and grants. It is attended by about 90 children. The *Free School* in the village was built by subscription in 1760, and was endowed in 1761 with seven acres of land, purchased with £100 given by John Bourne and Richard Edensor. This land is let for £15 a year, for which, and the use of the school-house, the mistress teaches 14 free scholars. A new school-room was added about 12 years ago. The *Church Land*, purchased in 1752, with £200 from Queen Anne's Bounty, is subject to a yearly rent-charge of £3. 18s., to be distributed in bread amongst the poor of Talk-on-the-Hill, in consideration of £90 poor's money, used in the purchase of the said land.

A page taken from White's History, Gazetteer and Directory of Staffordshire, 1851 (second edition, first edition 1834).

AUDLEY.

Post-office at Eliz. Dean's. Letters despatched 4½ in the afternoon, *via* Newcastle-under-Lyme.
Bebington John, watchmaker, &c.
Briscoe Josiah, revenue officer
Broad James, blacksmith
Davenport Wm. police officer
Davies Robt. Evens, ironmonger, (and at *Tunstall*)
Francis Rev. Wm. chaplain of Newcastle Union
Hall George, Free schoolmaster
Harrison Daniel, gentleman
Hilditch Thos. butcher, and Mr Jno.
Maddox Mr Rd. || Proctor John
Morris Benj., Wesleyan schoolmr
Proctor Joseph, blacksmith
Rigby Robert, colliery agent
Smith Jane, National School
Sproson Thos. plumber, painter, &c.
Steel Wm. sen. nail maker
Vernon Richard, surgeon
Warburton Ths. John, and Salt Wm. surgeons
Weaver Geo. ironmonger & nail mfr
Wilbraham Rev Chas. Pp., B.A. vicar
Williams John, higler

INNS AND TAVERNS.

Boughey's Arms, (commercial,) Jno. Harding, (and maltster)
Bull's Head, Eliz. Procter
Butchers' Arms, Samuel Hilditch, (and parish clerk and regr)
King's Head, John Warham, (and plumber, glazier, and painter)
Red Lion, Edward Lawton

BOOT & SHOE MKS. | FARMERS.
Darlington Abel | Bailey Thos.
Hilditch Chas. | Booth Daniel
Hilditch John | Burgess John
Hilditch Thos. | Darlington Wm.

Fox James
Harding John
Johnson Samuel
Jones John
Lewis Samuel
Richardson Saml.
Rigby Robert
Rubotham Wm.
Weaver Geo.
White Martha, (& beerhouse)
White Joseph
GROCERS & DPRS.
Dean Eliz.
Hilditch Chas.
JOINERS, &c.
(* *are wheelgts.*)
Brassington Chs·

Hayes Chas.
*Malpass Ralph
*Procter Chas.
Ravenscroft Ths. (& cabt. mkr.)
SHOPKEEPERS.
Henshall Chas.
Procter Chas.
Ravenscroft Ths.
TAILORS.
Emberton Jph. (and draper)
Hayes George
Procter John
Prophett Joseph
Williams Saml.

BIGNALL-END.

*Marked * are at Boond Hill, and + at Bignall Hill.*

Boughey Sir T. F. Bart, coal master; h *Aqualate Hall*
+Hares Thomas, engineer
*Hulse Wm. tailor
+Procter Ralph, whitesmith
+Riley Wm. shoemkr. and toll colr
Wood Nichls. Price, Esq. coal owner, *Bignall Hill House*

FARMERS.
Betteley John
+Dean James
*Emberton John
*Jackson Farmr.
+Massey John
*Pool Peter
Tomkinson Arthr
Warburton Rph.
NAIL MAKERS.
*Brindley Chas.

*Brindley Saml.
Brindley Wm.
*Johnson Danl.
*Riley Isaac
*Steel Wm. jun.
SHOPKEEPERS.
+Dean James
*Emberton John

ZONE 2 STOKE-ON-TRENT AND NEWCASTLE UNDER LYME

GREENWAY BANK

TRUBSHAW
WHITEHILL
THURSFIELD LODGE
BRINDLEY FORD

WEDGWOOD
RIDGEWAY
OXFORD

COLCLOUGH FARM
WHITFIELD
HEAKLEY HALL FARM
STOCKTON BROOK
STANLEY

SANDYFORD

ASHWOOD
HOLLY WALL
GREAT CHELL
NORTON-IN-THE-MOORS
YELD HILL HOUSE
BADDELEY GREEN

CHATTERLEY
TUNSTALL
STANFIELD
BRADELEY

HIGH CARR
RAVENSDALE
SMALLTHORNE
BAGNALL

MILTON
LIGHT OAKS

BRADWELL
BURSLEM
SNEYD GREEN

BEASLEY
CHESTERTON
COBRIDGE
ABBEY HULTON
WETLEY MOOR

NORTHWOOD
LITTLE EAVES
GREAT EAVES

WHITLEY
BUCKNALL
WASHERWALL

BASFORD
HANLEY
TOWNSEND
ASH BANK

KNUTTON

SHELTON
BENTILEE
HULME

NEWCASTLE UNDER LYME

STOKE-ON-TRENT
FENTON
ADDERLEY GREEN

GRINDLEY HILL
PENKHULL
BOLTON GATE

CLAYTON
BOOTHEN
SANDFORD HILL
WESTON COYNEY

SEABRIDGE
ROWLEY WOOD
TRENT VALE
SIDEWAY
LONGTON

BUTTERTON
MEIR

BLURTON

NORTHWOOD
HANFORD

LIGHTWOOD
GRINDLEY

TRENTHAM

Zone Two: Stoke on Trent and Newcastle under Lyme

Colclough 47
Wedgwood 47
Burslem 48
Wedgut 48
Bridgewood/Bridgett 48
Northwood/Norwood 49
Lightwood/Ledward/
Ledwood/Leathwood 49
Field/Fielding/Fielden 49
Fieldsend/Fieldhouse 49
Thursfield 49
Whitfield 51
Stanfield 51
Chatfield 51
Drakeford 51
Oxford 55
Sandford 55
Hanford 55
Han(d)ford/Handforth 55
Ford 55
Well(s) 55
Wall 55
Attwell 55
Waller/Weller 56
Wallbanks 56
Bradwell 56
Hartwell/Hartle/
Hartill/Hartell 56
Halliwell 56
Cresswell/Carswell/
Cas(e)well 57
Follwell/Fullwell 57
Brook(s) 57
Brookhouse/Brockhouse/
Brockhurst 58
Brooksbank 58
Bourne/Burn 58
Burns/Byrne 58
Bourner 58
Hulme/Holmes 58
Hollins 59
Holly/Hollis/Hollier/Ollier 59

Homer 60
Carr/Kerr 60
Ridgeway 60
Holloway/Holdway/
Halloway 60
Greenway/Greenaway 61
Stanway/Stanaway 61
Blakeway 61
Redway/Radway/Rodway 61
Way 62
Bytheway 62
Highway 62
Street/Streeten/Streeter 62
Stanistreet 62
Lane/Lone 62
Stoke(s)/Stoker 63
Stocker 63
Stubbs/Stubbings/Stebbings 63
Trentham/Tantrum 63
Sneyd/Snead/Snee 64
Tunstall 64
Croft(s)/Cruft 65
Holdcroft/Howcroft/Alcroft 65
Bancroft 65
Toft/Taft/Tuft 66
Heath 66
Whittle/Whittell/Whitehall 67
Hill/Hull 67
Hillman 67
Underhill/Undrell 67
Eaves 67
Seabridge 67
Cliff(e)/Clive/Clift 67
Vale 68
Bagnall 68
Holt 68
Bucknall/Buckland/
Buckner 68
Coppenhall/Copeland/
Copnall/Copner 69
Shaw 70
Trubshaw 70

Shore 70
Shay/Shave/Shafe/Shea 70
O'Shea 70
Oaks/Noakes/Oakes/Nokes 71
Rock/Rook 71
Rocker 71
Knock/Knox 71
Braddock 73
Holyoak 73
Ash/Nash 73
Frain 73
Thorne(s) 73
Hawthorn(e)/Hordern/
Horderne/Hardern 76
Bradeley/Bradney 76
Chatterley 76
Baddeley 77
Hanley/Handley 77
Buckley 79
Grindley/Grimley 79
Blakeley 79
Chell 79
Brindley 80
Rowley 80
Hackerley/Ackerley 80
Beesley 80
Norton 81
Sutton 81
Weston/Wesson 81
Aston/Asson 81
Easton/Eason 82
Hilton/Hulton 82
Shelton/Shilton 82
Blurton 82
Longton/Langton/Landon/
Longdon/Longden 83
Clayton 83
Fenton 84
Rushton/Ruston/Russon 84
Milton 84
Chesterton 85
Butterton 85

Zone Two

This particular zone harbours more indigenous locative surnames than anywhere else in the county. Many of these have ramified greatly over the whole of North Staffordshire since the Middle Ages, and are to be traced to some small inhabited locality, a detached farm or hamlet, often no longer to be found on modern maps, or simply commemorated by the name of a local thoroughfare. Such is the case with Colclough, which is preserved in Colclough Farm, off Colclough Lane by Goldenhill Municipal Golf Course. In the medieval manor court rolls for Tunstall it is spelt in a multitude of different ways, but the most regular form is "Colleclogh", which points to a ravine or steep sided valley where charcoal was obtained or where coal was extracted. The pedigree of the Colclough family of Oldcott, Tunstall, shows that Hugh Colclough granted Blurton and Cocknage to his son Richard during the reign of Henry V. At the dissolution of the monasteries in the 1530s, Sir Anthony Colclough took over the lands of Tintern Abbey, County Wexford, whilst his son Thomas was handed the lordship of Hanley under the honour of the Duchy of Lancaster. By contrast, according to the churchwarden's accounts for Stoke upon Trent in 1688, John Colclough was paid seven shillings *"......for sawing and worke at the Bridge"*. This refers to Fowlea Bridge over Fowlea Brook. In 1841 Samuel Coleclough was employed as a saucer maker at the firm of Batkin, Walker and Broadhurst in Longton. It is curious to note that Cowclough in Rochdale parish, Lancashire, is also found as "Colleclogh" in the Middle Ages, and the odds are that this locality too spawned some families called Colclough, some of whom may have ended up in our county to mingle with our own native Colcloughs.

One mile north east of Colclough on the 1836 Ordnance Survey map, lies the tiny village of Wedgwood, adjacent to the old Biddulph Valley Railway line. This is the birthplace of the ancestors of Staffordshire's most illustrious son, Josiah Wedgwood, one of the great pioneers of the Industrial Revolution. It is recorded as "Wegewode, Weggewod(e)" etc in the Tunstall manor court rolls, spellings that hint at a wood shaped like a wedge, that is, tapering at one end; 1875:Josiphiah Wedgwood (carver and gilder), New Street, Burslem; 1875:John Wedgwood (licensed victualler) of the Golden Ball in Bridge Street, Newcastle under Lyme. The only trace left of the original locality is Wedgwood Farm north of Fegg Hayes, now the site of a modern housing estate.

Josiah himself was born at Burslem on the 12th July 1730, the youngest of a family of thirteen children. Burslem, the Mother town of the Potteries, started out as "Burwardeslym" - "that part of Lyme belonging to an Anglo Saxon known as Burgweard (fortress guardian)". The "Lyme" suffix refers to the old forest of Lyme, which once stretched from Shropshire, across Staffordshire and Cheshire and into Lancashire, swallowing up Macclesfield Forest on its way. It is a Celtic word and indicates an original elm wood. It survives also as the final component of Newcastle-under-Lyme. In 1857

Thomas Platt was serving his apprenticeship as a blacksmith under George Burslem of Madeley and in 1907, Ernest Burslem (platelayer) lived in Smith Street, Fenton. One fascinating fact to emerge here from the pedigree of the Burslems of Burslem is that the issue of Thomas Burslem, who married Mary Ford of the Moss in 1590, included two daughters, Catherine and Margaret. Catherine married William Colclough, who was constable of the manor of Tunstall in 1620, whilst her sister Margaret married Gilbert Wedgwood. Their son, Burslem Wedgwood, was churchwarden at Burslem in 1639. Thus, these three surnames, so prolific in this zone since the Middle Ages, were at last intertwined by marriage, forming a kind of interlocking elite, distinct from the rest of the community. Yet a similar precedent was being set by local men and women at the opposite end of the social scale, as illustrated by the following marriages from the Audley parish registers:

1542: Robert Sneyde and Sibilla Yeardley.
1548: James Yeardley and Agnes Rowley.
1555: Richard Baddeley and Margery Podmore.
1566: William Handley and Elizabeth Colton.
1609: Randolph Whytoughe and Margaret Ashley.
1615: Richard Buckley and Anna Sneyde alias Ball.

The parish registers for Norton in the Moors evince an identical trend:

1579: Roger Bagnolde and Margerie Drakeforde.
1580: Thomas Badiley and Elizabeth Benteley.
1595: John Drakefforde and Jocosa Cartledge.
1594: Walter Rowley and Alice Bradshawe.
1616: William Thursfield and Joane Drakesford.

These distinctive locative surnames, derived almost exclusively from small hamlets and villages in north Staffordshire, were thus passed on from one generation to the next, and this situation must have been going on since at least the time when surnames were becoming hereditary, that is, about the beginning of the fourteenth century. If that is the case, then it is hardly surprising that they reign triumphant in our local nomenclature.

In his *History of the Borough of Stoke-upon-Trent*, John Ward inserts a Burslem Dialogue between John Telwright and Ralph Leigh, who met in Burslem market place in 1810. Ralph Leigh refers to *"...Mester Siah Wedgut's wheit ware..."*, - namely Josiah Wedgwood's white ware. Clearly Wedgut is a local corruption of that time for Wedgwood, with loss of "w" as in the dialectal "backerts" for "backwards" and "okkerd" for "awkward". This missing out of the letter "w" is also evident in the pairing Bridg(e)wood-Bridgett, as in the Stoke-on-Trent parish registers, where Joseph Bridgwood (1723), occurs as Joseph Bridgett a decade after. The point of origin of this name is apparently an unidentified locality somewhere between Packmoor and Knypersley, from whence came

Stephen de Bruggewode, taxed at Biddulph in 1327. There again, the surname could denote residence by a bridge in or near a wood. Any connections with the Celtic Saint Brighid are without foundation, although she was once regarded with much veneration both here and in Ireland. On the contrary, the surname Bridget in Ulster is an abbreviated form of Uprichard - "son of Richard"; Compare John ap Richard who enrolled in the local militia at Weston on Trent in 1539. This gives us the local surname Prichard. In 1851 William Bridgett of Trentham Road, Longton, was classed as a stonemason, and in 1887 Michael Bridgwood kept the Vulcan Inn, along Market Street, Fenton.

Northwood near Birches Head, Northwood, Hanchurch and Northwood not far from Calwich Abbey are prime movers in the spread of the local names Northwood and Norwood, with a toponymic for a dweller by a spot situated north of some wood or other, also feasible. Charles Norwood was Minister of Fulford Constablewick in 1666, and in 1907, John Northwood (potter's presser) lived in Campbell Terrace, Birches Head. As for Lightwood between Longton and Meir Heath and Lightwood near Cheadle, the sense inherent is a wood with trees far apart letting lots of light through rather than light-coloured wood. This dual alliance must be responsible for our local Lightwoods; 1851:Ralph Lightwood (boot and shoe maker) of Friar's Street, Newcastle under Lyme. Leathwood/Ledwood and Ledward(s) may belong here also as later variants via such forms as Thomas Leightwood (church warden at Swynnerton in 1600), and 1774:Stephen Lateward of Newcastle under Lyme. The "Leight, Late-" spellings are local pronunciations of "light". Samuel Ledward was the architect of Burslem covered market, which was opened for public use on Saturday, October 1st 1836.

Almost forming a perfect triangle around Wedgwood Farm are Thursfield to the north west, Whitfield to the south east and Stanfield to the south west. All three compounds contain the element "feld" - "open land, land under cultivation" and thus the surname Field(s) is either for a person who lived by such land or goes back to Field on the River Blithe west of Bramshall; 1327:Roger de Felde of Chesterton; 1907:George Field (miner) of Cromer Street, Wolstanton. Allied names in this context are: Fielden - "dweller in the fields"; 1907:Evelyn Mary Fielden of Blakeley House, Dilhorne; Fieldsend - "dweller at the end of the field"; 1912:Mary Fieldsend, proprietress of dining rooms in Commerce Street, Longton; and Fielding "dweller in open country"; 1907:William Fielding of Fern Villas, Clive Street, Shelton. Fieldhouse and Felthouse signify residence at a house in a field or open country; 1851:Daniel Fieldhouse (coal merchant) of Albion Street, Longton; 1649:Francis Felthouse (alias Bacon) of Rocester. The names are also preserved in Felthouse Wood, Ashcombe Park, Cheddleton, Fieldhouse in Waterfall, etc

Thursfield bears witness to the Scandinavian invasions of the ninth century, since it is recorded as "Turvoldesfeld" in the Staffordshire Domesday folios - "open land of Thorald or Thorvaldr (Thor ruler)". The letter "r" in this surname is prone to much jumping about, now in the middle of the name; 1851:Charles Thursfield (baker and flour dealer) of Stafford Street, Longton; now at the front; 1666:Henry Thrusfeild (sic), exempt

from hearth tax at Adbaston (west of Eccleshall). This shift of "r" mimics the dialectal "brid" for "bird".

William de Whytfeld, who appears at the Tunstall manor court in 1362, clearly came from Whitfield south of Wedgwood, but later families called Whitfield or Whitefield may have had ancestors in Whitefield near Knutton (Whitfield - 1775 Yates map), "Whyteffeld" (1545) in Penkridge or "Whytefeld" (16th century) in Shareshill, south of Cannock. The initial syllable in all these probably refers to chalky or limed soil; 1528:Thomas Wittefeild, elected burgess at Newcastle under Lyme; 1875:John Whitfield (grocer) of Heathcote Road, Longton.

Stanfield, midway between Little Chell and Burslem, was a settlement built on stony terrain. In 1844 George Stanfield occupied a cottage at Kibblestone, owned by the Reverend Francis Kitchen, and in 1887 James Stanfield was working as a dairyman for Trentham Dairy, Well Street, Newcastle under Lyme.

Chatfield/Chadfield, alas, has not yet relinquished its secrets. Just one single scrap of evidence has come to light as to its origin and that is a field name in Castlechurch, Stafford, recorded as "St. Chadesfield" in the reign of Elizabeth I. This is a stretch of open land dedicated to St. Chad, patron saint of Lichfield Cathedral. Instances of the surname are very late on the scene and prove nothing, e.g. 1666:Thomas Chatfeilde of Uttoxeter; 1797:John Chatfield of Keele; 1851:Edwin Chatfield (watch and clock maker), High Street, Longton; 1875:Thomas Chatfield (beerseller) of Stoke Road, Stoke. It may, after all, be a lost place like Drakeford. Despite the fact that it occurs in great profusion in the medieval manor court rolls for Tunstall, Drakeford has not been actually identified. It is clearly one of these local habitations which was abandoned for one reason or another in the Middle Ages, through some disastrous crop failure or more likely because of infestation by plague. One particularly virulent outbreak ravaged Staffordshire during the last few months of 1349. An inquisition post mortem at Mucklestone, dated 2nd October for that year, records the calamity and its aftermath: "*....there are there 5 acres of meadow which used to be worth 5 shillings and now they are not worth more than 2/6d, and this on account of the pestilence. And there used to be there 30 shillings by the year of Rent of Assize at the Terms of the Annunciation of the Blessed Mary and St. Michael, and now there are only 10 shillings at the same terms, by reason of the present pestilence.*"

In 1666 there are several families called Drakeford paying hearth tax at Talke, Knypersley and Stadsmorlow; e.g. William Drakeford of Stadsmorlow, also noted as William Drakesford in 1620. Coming up to date, in 1907, Albert Drakeford (miner) was resident in Sutherland Road, Longton and James Drakeford of Goldenhill Road, Fenton, was a potter's packer. The logical conclusion to draw from all this is that the original point of departure must be in the neighbourhood of Tunstall. The initial element of the placename is the Saxon "draca" - "dragon, sea monster", a very potent symbol in Germanic mythology, preserved in other places such as Drakelow in Derbyshire. The Anglo Saxons believed that buried treasure and the mounds containing it were guarded by a dragon, and

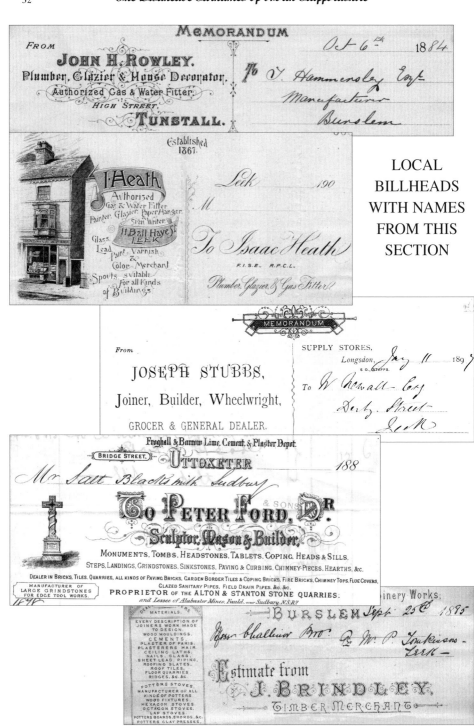

LOCAL
BILLHEADS
WITH NAMES
FROM THIS
SECTION

WOLSTANTON.

SNEYD GREEN.

STANLEY MILL AND POOL.

"GRAPES" INN, TONTINE STREET, HANLEY

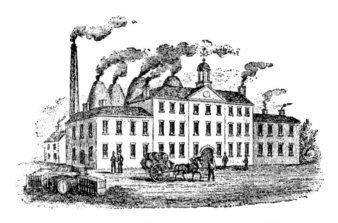

ADAMS POTTERY AT GREENGATES, TUNSTALL, EARLY 1800S

BURSLEM MARKET PLACE, 1824.

so the ford here would have been endowed with some powerful mystical force.

Other "-ford" localities in the area are more down to earth. Right next door to Wedgwood on the Yates map of 1775 is New Oxford, home of Thomas de Oxunford, assessed for tax purposes in 1332 for Fenton Culvert and Bucknall. This is a ford over which oxen were herded; 1907:William Oxford (miner), Mount Street, Northwood (Hanley). In the southern sector of the county the emphasis is on Oxford between Pendeford and Wolverhampton, with minimal intervention from Oxford, the university town. Sandyford, south of Colclough Farm - "sandy ford" - survives as Sandiford (no examples) and possibly Sandford/Sanford/Sampford; 1573:Margaret Sandford, married to James Orehed at the parish church of St. James the Great, Audley; 1907:John Sandford (postman), Trubshaw Street, Burslem. But if Sandford Hill in Longton is an ancient name, then this may be behind some of our local families of this name. Other places that could carry some weight in our deductions are Sandford in Prees and Sandford near Oswestry in Shropshire and Sandford Bridge and Farm in Wrenbury, Cheshire. The fluctuation between Sanford and Sandford is duplicated by Hanford-Handford, derived from Hanford in Trentham parish - "Hana's ford" or "cocks' ford"; 1700:Dorothy Hanford of High Offley, registered as Dorothy Handford in 1702. Handforth, identical in meaning, is most likely from Handforth near Cheadle Hulme, Cheshire; 1907:Edwin Handforth (hat and cap manufacturer), Piccadilly, Hanley. Of course, the number of people who lived in the vicinity of fords during the Middle Ages was legion; 1298:Adam de la forde of Tunstall; 1307:Henry de la forde of Talke; 1372:Richard del foorde of Newcastle under Lyme, and so on, hence the high incidence of the surname Ford/Foord and even Fforde in this zone; 1593:Jocosa Fford of Burslem; 1705:Matthew Forde (blacksmith) of Audley; 1839:Reverend William Ford, Minister at Lane End Church, Longton.

Wells, springs, streams, brooks, wetlands

Old English "well" - "well, spring, stream" - developed quite normally into the modern surnames Well and Wells, denoting a dweller by the well, etc; 1275 Assizes:Richard atte well of Rickerscote, near Stafford; 1433 Assizes:John Atwell of Lichfield (no examples for north Staffordshire); 1887:Charles Wells, licensee of the Blue Bell, Nile Street, Burslem. However, in the West Midlands, and above all in Staffordshire, it is the Mercian word "waella" that prevails, spelt as "wall", as in William atte walle, taxed at Newcastle under Lyme in 1332, and Geoffrey atte wall at Kibblestone in the same tax returns; 1731:Margaret Wall of Kingsley, married to Elias Bagnall of Dilhorne at Cheddleton; 1851:William Wall (cratemaker) of Etruria; 1907:James Wall (plumber), Reid Street, Burslem. Nevertheless, instances such as 1332:Richard del wal of Leek and 1272:Robert del wal of Lichfield are obvious allusions to Wall Grange, Leek and the former Roman fortress of Wall, Lichfield, both of which go back to the Saxon "wall" - "wall". The locative sources are equally valid here.

The same duplicity of meaning extends to the pairing Waller-Weller; 1887:John

Waller (shoeing and general smith), Audley Road, Chesterton; 1666:Richard Weller of Drayton Bassett. There are a number of other scenarios here to grapple with. Besides the obvious dweller by a spring, stream, well or wall, the surname Waller could be an occupational term from the building trade for a builder of walls, whilst in Staffordshire and Cheshire, a person who boiled the brine or attended to the salt pans was dubbed a "Waller". The rare Weller tends to be a toponymic rather than a trade name for a salt boiler.

In local placenames it is invariably the form "-wall" which wins the day - e.g. Washerwall near Werrington - "Waessa's stream" or "stream where sheep were washed", Caverswall -"spring of Cafhere" and Honeywall, Penkhull - "sweet spring." Wallbank(s) describes a person who lived on the bank(s) of a stream. One sad entry from the Ellastone parish registers for 1683, informs us that *"Thomas Wallbank, not having the fear of God before his eyes, hanged himself upon Fryday the 16th of February and was buryed the Friday followinge";* 1851:John Wallbank (linen and woollen draper), Market Street, Stoke; 1875:Walter Wallbanks (cratemaker), Newcastle Street, Burslem; 1875:Frederick Wallbank (potter's fireman), Peel Street, Dresden.

Bradwell crops up as "Bradewalle" in the Middle Ages - "broad stream", but only the former survives as a surname; 1907:H. Bradwell (silk brokers), Britannia Street, Leek. Bradwall spellings persist as late as 1532, when Thomas Bradwall was chaplain at Stoke on Trent. One of his ancestors might have been Adam de Bradewell, resident at Tunstall in 1298. Synonymous with our Bradwell are Bradwall Green, Sandbach and Bradwell south of Castleton, Derbyshire, both of which could have played a part in the dissemination of the surname.

Eva de Hurtwall of Longton, who attended the Staffordshire assizes in 1293, unquestionably had roots in Hartwell near Rough Close - "spring or stream where harts (male of the red deer) came to drink". The final syllable is often clipped, turning it into Hartill/Hartle; 1907:Reverend Edgar Hartill (M.A.), Minister of St. Barnabas Church, Princes Road, Hartshill. If the basic name is Hartell/Hartill/Hartle(s), the sources are Harthill in Cheshire, midway between Broxton and Burwardsley, Harthill in Bakewell parish, Derbyshire, pronounced "Hartle", and Harthill near Sheffield, Yorkshire, all for "hill frequented by stags".

Since time immemorial, wells and springs have fascinated the human mind, mainly because of their reputed healing powers. The Druids, for instance, venerated wells and fountains and placed each natural spring under the care of its own special deity. With the advent of the Christian era, the custom gradually arose of blessing certain wells and springs on Ascension Day, or Holy Thursday. On this day too, took place the familiar welldressing ceremonies at Milton, Uttoxeter, Burton upon Trent and Endon, but Endon is the only village in the county to carry on with this ancient custom. Holly Wall near Sandyford is probably a reminder of one of these local "holy wells", where an extract from the Gospels was read on Holy Thursday. It is more than likely from the locality cited as "Haliwalle, Halywalle" in the Tunstall manor court rolls for 1366 - compare especially

John Brode of Hallewell, Constable of Tunstall Court in 1642. It also survives as the surname Halliwell - a dweller by a holy spring; 1875:John Halliwell (grocer), Rathbone Street, Tunstall; 1907:Mrs Olive Halliwell of Bedford Road, Shelton (Hanley). Also to be considered are Holywell (1841 Tithe Awards) in Blymhill and Brineton (now Holywell Plantation), "Holywell parke" (1462) in Castlechurch and Halliwell near Bolton, Lancashire. Other modern variants of the name are Helliwell/Hellawell and Hellowell, none of which, alas, is attested for our county.

Cresswell,the other side of Blythe Bridge, Creswell near Seighford, and Creswell Green south west of Farewell, all exhibit spellings such as "Carsewalle, Careswalle, Karsewalle, Kersewall", and so on, during the Middle Ages, and designate a stream or spring where watercress grew. This particular triumvirate of locatives is behind a whole barrage of curious surnames. First of all there is the elementary Carswell; 1320:Henry de Carswell of Dilhorne; 1612 Lawsuit:Barnabas Carswell of Eccleshall. But the "r" vanishes into thin air and we have to make do with Cas(s)well; 1907:William Caswell (miner), Sneyd Street, Cobridge, and Casewell; 1851:Joseph Casewell (cow leech), Blackwaters, Woodland Division, Eccleshall. The original Carswell, with the common shift of "r", already seen in Thursfield, turns into Cras(s)well, which then leaves us with the modern Cresswell; on 20th April 1815, Joseph Cresswell, a writing clerk of Hazlehurst near Cumberledge Park, registered a room for Dissenters at Endon; 1851:Thomas Creswell (tailor) of Waterloo Road, Burslem.

The Staffordshire Follwells and Fulwells have several possible branches in their family trees. The most intriguing line goes back to a nickname, recorded by the tax assessors at Alstonefield in 1332, where John Falle in the wall contributes his seven shillings and fourpence towards the nation's coffers. This has nothing to do with falling against walls, for it is our old friend "wall" once more in the sense of "stream, spring, well", hence "fall in the stream". The unfortunate John must have got his weird nickname from slipping and falling headfirst in some local stream whilst out fishing or crossing the ford; 1907:R.S.Folwell (school teacher), High Street, Hanford. Locatives which come to mind here are "Little Fullwalle" (1570) in Cannock and "Foulwell" (1301) in Aldershawe near Lichfield - "muddy spring, stream" - synonymous with external sources such as Fulwell Spinney in Church Lawford near Rugby in Warwickshire and Fulwell near Chipping Norton in Oxfordshire.

One of the most widely diffused of all local toponymics in this zone is Brook(e)/Brookes/Brooks - "dweller by some brook or stream"; 1327:Thomas del broke of Tunstall; 1306:Juliana atte brok of Fulford. All modern variants of the surname are extant; 1912:Henry Brook (accountant) of Birches Head Road, Hanley; 1912:Benjamin Brooks of the Cat Inn, Keeling's Road, Hanley; 1907:Horace Brooke (engraver) of Newfield Street, Tunstall; 1907:John Brookes (marl loader) of Beech's Row, Sandyford.

Richard de Brochuse of Tunstall (1307) evidently dwelt at the house by the brook and his progeny are amongst us now as Brookhouse or Brockhouse; 1598:William

Mylward alias Brockehouse of Hope, near Alstonefield; 1907:Charles Brookhouse (photographer and picture framer), Broad Street, Hanley. Yet these names are easily mixed up with Brockhurst, although the actual evidence is flimsy - compare two entries from the parish registers for Brewood; 1576:Henry Brochouse; 1582:Raphe Sprott alias Brochurste. Brockhurst designates residence near a brook in or by a wood, or close to a wood frequented by badgers. The variant Brickhurst as in John Brickehurst of Eccleshall (1585) suggests that the local name Brick is a rare form of Brook.

The compound Brookbank(s), Brooksbank/Brockbank refers to a person who dwelt by the bank of a brook or stream and is thus virtually synonymous with Wallbank(s), discussed earlier; 1737:Francis Brooksbank, wed to Jane Wardle at Cheddleton; 1912:Edwin Brookesbank (commercial agent) Boulton Street, Wolstanton.

Almost on a par with Brooks for its fertility is the surname Bourn(e)/Burn(e), from the Saxon "burna" - a dweller by a spring, stream or brook; Roger de la bourne, tenant on the Audley estates at Betley in 1307. Applied to streams in the north of England and especially in Scotland, the word is burn", which, in actual fact, is its original pronunciation, hence the vacillation between Bourne and Burn. In the Norton in the Moors parish register for 1817, William Bourne signs his own name as William Burn. One entry from the Wolstanton registers makes sorry reading; 1807:The burial of Thomas Bourne, aged 4 years, son of Charles and Hannah Bourne, who, in consequence of his clothes accidentally taking fire, was burnt. On a lighter note, Mrs Mary Burne was making soda water in Fountain Street, Leek in the late 1880s.

Some writers have associated the surname Bourne with "bourne" - "limit", as used by Shakespeare in Hamlet - *"The undiscovered country, from whose borne no traveller returnes"*, but this assumption can be quashed immediately, since this particular word was not in usage until the sixteenth century, which is far too late for the formation of any surname. Plural forms such as 1907:David Burns (potter), Furnival Street, Cobridge and 1907:Thomas Burns (miner), Brighton Street, Stoke, denote residence by some springs or streams, but Scottish families called Burns, who came to live in Staffordshire, could trace their names back to Burnhouse in Argyllshire, from where the poet Robert Burns got his own name. In Ireland Burns is often equivalent to Byrne(s) - "descendant of Biorn" or "descendant of Bran(raven)"; 1907:Thomas Byrne (grocer and bread dealer), Waterloo Road, Burslem. Bourner, which shares the same meaning as Bourne, is very scarce; 1887:Arthur C. Bourner, Gladstone Street, Basford, Stoke-on-Trent.

Hulme between Weston Coyney and Werrington, Upper Hulme and Middle Hulme south of the Roaches, plus Hulme End near Warslow, make up a group of special importance in north Staffordshire. All these places contain the Old Danish "hulm" -"a small island, a piece of land on a stream, dry ground in a marsh", and are indisputable evidence of a small but scattered Scandinavian community in this region. In an inquisition post mortem made at Stafford before the Lord Reginald de Legh in 1284, it is stated that *"....Henry son of Ranulph de Holm is able to sell to the Lord Abbot and Convent of*

Deulacresse and to assign two messuages and 60 acres of land in Uvere Hulm and Netherhulme to the value of two marks..." (A mark in the Middle Ages was equal to 13/4d). In the same document the two localities are also chronicled as "Ovre Holm" and "Nether Holm". This switching back and forth between Hulm(e) and Holm(e) is duplicated in the surname Hulme(s) and Holme(s), as in the Kingsley parish register, where William Hulme (1608) occurs as William Holme in 1611. On the night of the 19th July 1833, William Hulme, aged 18, with his accomplice Samuel Mellor, broke into the shop of Thomas Mycock in the parish of Waterfall, south of Grindon, and stole a soldering iron, a pair of shears and other articles. They were found guilty at Staffordshire assizes and both were transported for life. The distribution of the various forms is quite clear cut from the fifteenth century onwards - Hulme is the dominant spelling in the Staffordshire Moorlands, whilst Holmes has the upper hand in the rest of the county. Less common are other forms such as Holme, Hume and Hulmes; 1666:Nicholas Hulmes of Uttoxeter; 1676:Thomas Holme of Standon; 1750:Richard Hume of Burslem; 1769:Elizabeth Holmes, witness to the marriage of Henry Brindley and Mary Wilden at Seighford; 1851:James Hulme (professor of music), Waterloo Road, Burslem.

An additional source of the names Holm(s)/Holmes is the Saxon "holegn" - "holm oak, holly", which becomes "holm", hence a person who dwelt by a tree of this type, and "holin", resulting not only in Holmes but also in Holli(e)s/Holl(e)y and Hollins, as in the fieldnames Hollins in Talke and Hollins in Consall. Again, all these different forms ramify strongly throughout the county after the end of the Middle Ages, and, generally speaking, Hollins outnumbers the rest in north Staffordshire, whereas Holly/Holley/Hollis and Hollies are the norm elsewhere; 1618:George Hollis and Francis Norris, married at Stowe by Chartley; 1666 Hearth tax returns:Walter Hollies chargeable on one hearth at Crakemarsh and John Holley likewise at Tean; 1851:Margaret Hollins (milliner and dress maker), Moorland Road, Burslem; 1851:Thomas Hollis, licensee of the Oak public house in Gaolgate, Stafford.

Two contentious surnames here are Holmer/Homer and Hollier/Ollier. Without any doubt Holmer and Homer evolve in the southern half of the county and do not venture northwards until well after the middle of the nineteenth century; 1887:Ann Homer of Birch Street, Hanley; 1887:Charles J. Homer (colliery proprietor), Ivy House, Bucknall New Road. More often than not they are taken as an occupational name for a maker of helmets, from Old French "heumier, heaumier", but no such evidence has been unearthed thus far. On the contrary, they are toponymics, denoting residence by a holm oak, flat land near some water, or by a pool in a hollow, or locatives, traceable to "Holmer Greene" (1621) in Penkridge, Homer Pool in Gnosall, Holmer in Essington (Homer Meadow - 1676), Homer near Much Wenlock, Shropshire, Holmer near Hereford or Holmer Green near High Wycombe, Buckinghamshire. All probably refer to a pool in a hollow.

Hollier is usually construed as a nickname for a lecher, whereas Ollier is a maker or seller of oil. Yet these two surnames occur side by side during the 1500s in the Penkridge parish registers; Thomas Hollyer, buried on June 5th 1573, and Margaret Ollier, baptised on April 5th 1579. The loss or addition of initial "H" is almost universal in local dialects, so there is no problem here on that score, so the likelihood remains that the two names are simply variants of each other and are toponymics for a dweller by a holly bush; 1887:John Ollier (canal assistant agent), Etruria Vale, Hanley; 1912:William Hollier (stonemason), Mellor Street, Burslem.

Another Scandinavian infiltrator - "kjarr" - "marsh, wet moor, boggy copse" - is inherent in High Carr, Chatterley, a lost Carr House, Shraley Brook, Carr Wood and Carr Bank, north of Oakamoor, and the surname Carr, Ker, Kerr - a dweller by a boggy copse; 1833:Paul Carr, aged 18 years, lost his life in a mining accident at Woodhead Coal Pit, Cheadle, on July 20th; 1851:David Carr (sugar boiler), Chapel Street, Cheadle; 1875:George Carr (greengrocer), Mulberry Street, Hanley. The Scottish form of Carr is Kerr, the 35th most common surname in Scotland in 1958, whilst, in Ireland, Carr is used as the anglicised version of several different Irish surnames, including MacElhar, Kerrane and Mulcair. Thus modern bearers in Staffordshire of such names as Carr, Ker and Kerr could well be from the Emerald Isle or north of the Border.

Roads, ways and tracks

In the shadow of Chatterley Whitfield Mining Museum lies Ridgeway, which was once the site through which ran an ancient trackway along a ridge. Sharing the same meaning is the old Chester road between Castle Bromwich and Stonnall, south of Lichfield, once known as The Rudgeway. Both places are of paramount importance in the history of the surname Ridg(e)way, with minor assistance from Ridgeway south east of Crich, Derbyshire, Ridgeway near Sheffield, Yorkshire and Ridgeway south of Redditch, Worcestershire. In 1599 Richard Ridgewaye of Bradwell (mylner, or miller) was bound over for the sum of ten pounds to keep the peace towards John Bagnall (tailor); 1907:William Ridgway (laundryman), Melville Road, Longton. In 1894 there was a smallpox outbreak at Ridgeway and the pupils from this area were advised not to attend the local school, which was St. Anne's Church of England Large School at Brown Edge.

Oddly enough, the headmaster at this particular school from 1845 until 1860 was a certain George Holloway, whose surname is the exact opposite of Ridgeway, a road in a hollow, a sunken road. Thus it is either a toponymic for a dweller by a road in a hollow, or from locations such as "Hollowaye" (1469) in Forton near Aqualate Mere, Holloway in Haughton, Gnosall, Holloway Leasow in Norbury, or Holloway south of Matlock in the Derwent valley, once the home of Florence Nightingale; 1656:Elizabeth Holloway, married to William Jevines at Audley; 1907:Herbert Holloway (saggar maker), Hot Lane, Burslem. There are some other curious variants: Holdway, with an intrusive "d", although this may also go back to an old Saxon personal name -"Ealdwig" - "old war"; 1907:Thomas Holdway (waggoner), Cannon Street, Hanley; and Halloway: 1801:Peter Halloway of Stoke-on-Trent, wed to Ann Brundrick. Here again, Saxon names come into the picture -

"Alfwig" - "elf war" and "Athelwig" - "noble war".

North of Ridgeway we come to Greenway Bank, from whence came Roger de Grenewey, taxpayer at Endon in 1327. This probably refers to a track or road alongside which there grew a lot of green vegetation, shrubs and such like. An alternative source might be the fieldname in Essington south of Cannock, recorded as "le grenewey" in 1335; 1907:Mary Greenway of Colclough Lane, Goldenhill. Later on the surname developed a glide vowel between the "n" and "w", perhaps arising by analogy with the colloquial "Henery" for "Henry" with the final pronunciation influenced to a certain extent by Sideway near Hanford, known locally as "Sidderway" - "track or road by a slope". Unfortunately, examples of Greenaway/Grenaway are not available for north Staffordshire but compare 1731:Samuel Greenaway of Tipton. The modern surname Sidaway could also be traceable to Sidway near Maer (same meaning); 1327:Adam de Sydewey of Knutton and Hanford; 1706:Anna Sidway, widow of Audley.

Completing this unique trio is Stanway/Stanaway "a stone road or paved road", usually situated near some ancient Roman road, as attested by Stanway on Wenlock Edge, Shropshire, which is not far from the Roman road that ran from Wroxeter to Chesterton. This could be the locality which gave its name to Adam de Stanwey, tenant of the Audleys at Chesterton in 1307. It emerges from the Wolstanton parish register that William Stanway, aged 34 years, was buried at Burslem on December 20th 1807, and *"...his death was occasioned by the bursting of the boiler of a steam engine."* In 1851, George Stanway (confectioner and baker) had a shop in High Street, Stoke, and Joseph Stanaway was farming land at Biddulph. Less feasible sources for the Staffordshire Stanways and Stanaways are Stanway near Winchcombe, Gloucestershire, Stanway Green, north east of Stowmarket, Suffolk and two places near Colchester, Essex - Stanway and Stanway Green.

Besides Greenway, colour is also manifest in Blakeway and Redway. Bennett Blakeway, vicar of the church of St. Michael, Horton near Rudyard (1879-1919), carved a chancel screen, which was erected in 1900 as a memorial to William Tellwright of Horton Lodge. His antecedents possibly lived by some dark road, or their roots were in Blakeway Farm south west of Much Wenlock or Blackeway near Child's Ercall (both in Shropshire).

Redway is rather more complicated. It is certainly derived on occasion from a Saxon name "Raedwig" - "counsel warrior", as borne by Redwi, a tenant at Branston in the twelfth century surveys of the Abbey at Burton on Trent. Nevertheless, the surname is more likely to represent residence by a red way, that is a track with sandy soil, or a track with reeds shooting up along its edges, as in the fieldname "le redewey" (1300) in Cheslyn Hay and possibly Redway near Flash (1842 Ordnance Survey map). Radway in Warwickshire, not far from the site of the Battle of Edgehill, fought in 1642 during the Civil War, is either for a red way or roadway, a road fit to ride on, and so could be identical in meaning with Rodway on the Weald Moors, Shropshire, near Crudgington. In all probability, this was where Richard de Roduey came from, cited in a writ centred on Aston in Hales in 1299. Later instances include 1711:John Rodway of Burslem, married to Alice

Ball; 1887:Thomas Rodway (draper) of Lord Street, Etruria. Whether Radway Green near Alsager is involved in this particular group of surnames is impossible to determine on account of the lack of early spellings of the place.

Away from the intricate network of Roman roads criss-crossing the medieval Staffordshire countryside, many people lived by some sort of road, pathway or track leading to the next village or nearest market. Richard above the Way of Farley near Alton in the Churnet valley (1327) and William Bithewey of Longdon near Rugeley (1307) obviously did, and their descendants live on in the names Way(e) and Bytheway; 1789:Joseph Bytheway, buried at Seighford on July 12th; 1887:Mary Ann Bytheway (grocer), Stoke Old Road, Stoke-on-Trent. Some of these lines of communication were "saltways", along which salt was carried by packhorse all across the Midlands, or simply dusty cart-tracks, used for the transportation of hay, such as "le heywey" (twelfth century) in Castlechurch near Stafford, hence Highway/Heighway. Henry Highway was mayor of Walsall in 1851. Occasionally the surname Highway could have been assigned to foundlings who were abandoned on the King's Highway and adopted by another family.

The word "street", contained in Watling Street and Ryknild Street, two very important routes during the Roman occupation of our county, was itself borrowed from Latin "strata" - "paved road, Roman road", giving the surnames Street(e)/Streat and Streeter - dweller by a Roman road or in the street of some medieval village; Ralph de . : strete de Gnoushale (Gnosall), quoted in a thirteenth century deed in the Cartulary of Ronton Abbey; 1875:George Streete (butcher), Heathcote Street, Longton; 1887:Eliza Street (coal dealer), Madeley Street, Tunstall; 1887:Henry Streeter of the Pheasant Inn, Gower Street, Longton. Streeten/Streeton/Streetin(g) denote an inhabitant at the end of the street; 1396:Nicholas atte stretehende of Stafford; whilst the compound Stanistreet/Stoneystreet is from Stanystreet in Worsley, Greater Manchester - "stony road", situated on the former Roman road that ran from Manchester to Wigan; 1875:William Stanistreet (baker), Ellgreave Street, Burslem; 1907:Frederick W.Stanistreet (teacher of music), Wharf Street,Burslem.

Of course,the most familiar rural word for a country path or narrow thoroughfare is "lane"; 1325:Henry in the lane of Caverswall. Longton High School's humble beginnings go back to a schoolhouse built on land adjoining St. John's churchyard in 1760, measuring a mere 25 yards by 13 yards. The land was given by Reverend Obadiah Lane, Lord of the Manor. The medieval variant "lone", as in 1327:William in le lone of Forsbrook, survives as Loan(e) -cf. 1592:John Lone of Hatton and Brewood.

Homesteads and crofts

The present city of Stoke on Trent is the product of the federation in 1910 of six independent towns, namely, the county borough of Hanley, the boroughs of Stoke-Upon-Trent, Burslem and Longton and the urban districts of Tunstall and Fenton. In his novels and short stories Arnold Bennett immortalised them as The Five Towns - Turnhill, Bursley,

Hanbridge, Knype and. Longshaw, standing for Tunstall, Burslem, Hanley, Stoke Upon Trent and Longton. To the eternal frustration of the local 'Potters'', Fenton was omitted. Over nine centuries ago Stoke-on-Trent was put down as "Stoche" by the Norman French scribes in Domesday Book - "dependent settlement on the River Trent" and it did not acquire its familiar suffix until 1686, when Plot called it "Stoke super Trent" in his Natural History of Staffordshire. Yet even before the arrival of the Normans, the Saxon "stoc" was originally applied to a place where cattle stood for milking in outlying pastures. This developed logically into "cattle (dairy) farm", but as such settlements grew with the construction of sheds and huts for the herdsmen, the term came to be used for any outlying farm adjoining some more important place. Thus, localities called Stoke were once most likely insignificant places dependent on some neighbouring village. This would also apply to Little Stoke near Stone, which, together with Stoke-on-Trent constitute the principal sources of the surname in north Staffordshire. But there are scores of other Stokes up and down the country with distinctive suffixes, which might well have filtered through into our county. Stoke(s)/Stoakes/Stoaks/Stooke(s) is well dispersed across Staffordshire at all stages in its evolution; Nicholas Stokes was vicar at Ellastone in 1532, and Henry Stokes was one of the overseers of the poor at Betley in 1755. In 1875, George Stokes (beer retailer) lived in Hope Street, East Vale, Longton.

Contrary to its appearance, Stoker is not an occupational term for a person who tended furnaces on steam trains or steamships, but a toponymic for anyone who lived at a place called Stoke; 1789:Thomas Stoker (mariner) of Newcastle under Lyme. Stocker, on the other hand, designates residence by a tree stump; 1875:A.D. Stocker (commission agent), The Villas, Stoke-on-Trent. The characteristic surname in North Staffordshire for a dweller by a tree stump is Stubbs, although a nickname for a short, stumpy individual cannot be ruled out. From the Corporation Minutes of Newcastle under Lyme for October 25th 1625 it is reported that *"...at the assembly aforesaide Ffrancys Stubbs for his abuse and contemptuos(sic) speeches to Mr. Maior in matters questioned for the good of this Burrowgh which then were related and sufficyently proved, is fyned in ten shillings and censured to sitt a Market daye in the Stocks"*. The allied names Stubbings, Stubbins and possibly Stebbing(s) refer to residence by land cleared of tree stumps; 1667:Margaret Smyth alias Stubbing (widow) of Ellenhall; 1700:John Stebbing of Cheadle.

Trentham - "homestead on the River Trent" - was a royal manor in the eleventh century, belonging to William the Conqueror. An Augustinian priory was founded here circa 1153 by Ranulph de Gernon, Earl of Chester. Soon after the Dissolution of the Monasteries in the 1530s the site was acquired by the Levesons of Wolverhampton, whose spectacular rise to prominence through intermarriage with the Gowers of Stittenham in Yorkshire, culminated in their promotion to Dukes of Sutherland in 1833. One of the Trentham dynasty was Thomas, born in 1575, the second son of Thomas Trentham of Rocester Abbey by Jane, daughter of Sir William Sneyd of Bradwell and Keele. He was elected member of parliament for Newcastle under Lyme in 1601. This alliance of the

Trentham and Sneyd families recalls that of the Colcloughs, Burslems and Wedgwoods, dealt with earlier. The name Tantrum sounds like a nickname for someone with a nasty temper, but it could well be a local variant of Trentham, with shift of "r"; 1907:Joseph Tantrum of Spode Street, Stoke.

Medieval precursors of the Sneyd family of Bradwell and Keele included Henry de Sneyde, who married Margaret, daughter and heiress of Nicholas de Tunstall in 1310. For three or four generations after this marriage the immediate descendants of this union bore either the surname Sneyd or Tunstall; Nicholas Sneyde alias de Tunstall (in the reign of Edward III); Richard de Tunstall alias Sneyde, who fought alongside James, Lord Audley and the Black Prince at the Battle of Poitiers(1356), and Richard Tunstall alias Sneyde, to whom John Tuchett, Lord Audley, and others, granted their lands in Bradwell in 1400. The surname Sneyd only became fixed when another Richard Sneyde took over the manor of Bradwell in 1423. The Sneyds got their name from Sneyd Green, which was bestowed as "boscus de Sneade" by Henry de Audley in 1223 on the abbot and monks of Hulton Abbey. This indicates "the wood of Sneyd" from a Saxon word for a piece of woodland, a clearing, and it is the basis of the majority of local families called Sneyd/Snead/Sneed and Snee with loss of final "d". Other sources at work on a minor scale comprise Essington Sneyd near Bushbury, "Sned" (1487) in Forton near Aqualate and Snead Farm (and Common) in Pensax, north west of Abberley, Worcestershire; 1824:Ralph Sneyd, curate of Caverswall; 1907:Frank Sneyd (bricklayer), Allen Street, Hartshill; 1907:Patrick Snee, Victoria Street, Chell. Sneath as in Anna Sneath of Rocester (1607) is either a Scandinavian variant or from Snaith south of Selby, Yorkshire, the Danelaw equivalent of Sneyd.

From its modest beginnings as a small farm settlement surrounded by outbuildings Tunstall grew into the most northerly of the six towns of the Potteries. Yet in the 1770s it was still insignificant enough to be portrayed as *"a mere street, or rather roadway, with only a few houses, probably not more than a score, scattered about it and the lanes leading to Chatterley and Red Street."* Thomas Tunstall was churchwarden at Newcastle under Lyme in 1575; 1851:James Tunstall (boot and shoe maker), Hunt Street, Tunstall; 1907:Ralph Tunstall (slip maker), Rushton Road, Cobridge. Other contributors to the name Tunstall/Tunstill are Tunstall near Adbaston, Tunstall (or Dunstall Hill) near Wolverhampton, Tunstall (Dunstal) near Abbots Bromley and Dunstall near Barton under Needwood, often found as Tunstall in early documents. Borderline cases are Tunstall south of Kirkby Lonsdale, Lancashire, Tunstall east of Hull, Tunstall near Catterick, Tunstall (Sunderland), Tunstall near Sittingbourne, Kent, Tunstall west of Great Yarmouth and Tunstall south west of The Maltings, Suffolk.

Crofts and tofts

The medieval croft is a far cry from the small farms dotted about today's Scottish Highlands. In the Middle Ages it denoted any piece of enclosed land utilised for tillage or pasture, a small portion of arable land adjacent to the villein's rickety thatched cottage.

This was his own patch of ground, where he grew vegetables such as leeks and cabbages, and herbs and spices like onions, garlic, mustard and parsley to add flavour to his meagre meals. People like 1327:John super le croft of Amerton and Weston near Ingestre and 1332:Robert del croftes of Stafford, cultivated their crops on just such a croft, and their names live on as Croft(s); 1887:Mary Crofts, owner of a warehouse for storing ornaments, bric a brac, Piccadilly, Hanley; 1907:William Francis Croft (drug stores), King Street, Fenton. The variant Craft is occasionally found; 1608:Thomas Crafte of Ellenhall, but this is normally a nickname for a scheming individual. Another mutation is Cruft, as in Charles Cruft, founder of the Cruft's dog show in 1886, but this is absent from the local material.

The present day telephone directory for the Stoke-on-Trent and Newcastle under Lyme area teems with the surname Holdcroft/Hol(e)croft/Houldcroft, yet before the Industrial Revolution its distribution is sporadic, to say the least. In any case, it is not easy to pinpoint the exact origin of this surname. The prime target seems to be a place in Burslem, recorded as "Holecroft (side)" in the Tunstall manor court rolls for 1690. On a Burslem map of 1750 it appears as Holecroft meadow, and it is commemorated by Holecroft Street between Waterloo Road and Nile Street. It describes a croft in a hollow and so is synonymous with a portion of land in Ilam called "Hollecroft" in a suit from the Court of Star Chamber (1542). These two localities are probably the principal sources for the surname in north Staffordshire, bolstered by "le holdecroft" in Shareshill (1342) and "the olde crofte" (1674) in Penkridge - "the old croft". Between 1840 and 1841 David Holdcroft was a travelling preacher around Foxt. He died in 1901 and was buried in the churchyard at Norton in the Moors. Other representatives of the surnames are; 1851:Sarah Holdcroft (keeper of a beerhouse), Ball Green; 1875:Diggory Holdcroft (greengrocer), Union Street, Hanley; 1887:Gregory Howcroft (fruiterer), Hanley Fish Market, plus Allcroft; 1672:Thomas Allcrofte of Stoke-on-Trent quoted as Thomas Oldcroft in 1643. Migrants from Cheshire and Lancashire bearing the surname Holdcroft are probably descended from ancestors with roots in Holcroft in Bradwall near Sandbach, "Holkroft" (circa 1260) in Barrow near Chester, or Holcroft Moss on Glazebrook near Culcheth.

At a session of the Tunstall manor court, held at Burslem on May 8th 1548, it is reported that *"...John Bancroft had died seised, according to the custom of the manor, of and in one cottage and garden in Tunstall, and that Joan Bancroft was his sister and next heir"*. It is almost certain that the Bancrofts mentioned in this extract stemmed from a place known as "Banecroft" in Chell in a thirteenth century deed from the Staffordshire Cartulary. It refers to a croft where beans were cultivated, and is thus identical in meaning with Bancroft near Yoxall and fieldnames called "Bancroft" in Castlechurch, Penkridge and Hilton near Wolverhampton, any one of which could have given rise to later families of this name. The accounts of Thomas Cliffe, one of the churchwardens for Stoke-on-Trent in 1690, disclose that one shilling was *"...giveen unto Humpphery Banckcraft who had a letter of request being impoverished by grate loss of cattell and houses...";* 1907:Hudson Bancroft (miner), Scotia Road, Burslem; 1907:C. Bancroft (basket maker),

Spencer Road, Shelton.

The Scandinavian import "toft" - "homestead" - still retains this sense in the rural dialects of Lincolnshire, where the owner is known as a "tofter" or "toftman". The surname, too, preserves the same connotation, that is, either a worker on such a site or more likely the owner of a toft or homestead, as typified by William del toft, taxed at Bishton and Wolseley near Colwich in 1327. In 1532, Richard Toft was elected as "aletaster" or "warden of assize of bread and beer" at Newcastle under Lyme. These officials are first recorded in 1369, when they took an oath to test faithfully bread and beer in whatever place it might happen to be sold during their term of office and to present whatever default might be found; 1731:Joshua Toft of Hareyate (Leek), buttonman; 1851:Alphonso Toft (engraver), Tinker's Clough, Hanley; 1887:Leonard Toft (family butcher), Swan Passage, Hanley and Crown Street, Shelton. The sequence Craft-Croft-Cruft is reproduced in Taft-Toft-Tuft; Wolstanton parish registers 1764:John Taft (1766:John Toft); 1623:Mathew Tuft of Kinvaston (Penkridge).

Heathland

On the whole the heathland that we know today in Staffordshire has resulted from large scale tree felling since the end of the Middle Ages. Nevertheless, the landscape in our county must have been dominated by large tracts of uncultivated land overgrown by coarse grass and heather prior to this, judging by the omnipresence of the surname Heath in the fourteenth century; 1306:John de le hethe of Fradswell; 1321:Geoffrey del hethe of Hixon; 1369:John de le heth of Newcastle under Lyme, who came into his liberties in that year. Indeed, the surname Heath, which simply denotes a person who dwelt by a heath or uncultivated land, ramifies thereafter in the most astonishing fashion across the whole of North Staffordshire, filling page after page of local parish registers; 1558:Richard Heathe of Swynnerton; 1628:Jane Heathe of Stowe by Chartley; 1632:Thomas Heath (weaver) of Wootton; 1708:William Heath of Butt Lane. Trade Directories of the nineteenth century list 1887:Ann E. Heath (hosier), Waterloo Road, Burslem and 1887:James Heath (tripe dealer) of the Market Hall, Newcastle under Lyme. Two well known bearers of the surname are Robert Heath, mining engineer, born at Burslem in 1816, and George Heath, the Moorland poet of Hall Gate Farm, Gratton near Horton (died 1869 at the age of 25). There is a memorial to him in Horton churchyard, and on his gravestone are the following pensive lines:

> His life is a fragment — a broken clue
> His harp had a musical string or two;
> The tension was great, and they sprang and flew,
> And a few brief strains, a scattered few
> Are all that remain to mortal view
> Of the marvellous song the young man knew.

Hills and valleys

Modern surnames such as Whittle/Whittell/Whittal(l) and Whitehall pose a variety of problems. On the face of it they are toponymics for habitation by a white hill, or from Whitehill near Kidsgrove, but locally the names are also to be traced to Upper and Under Whitle near Longnor - "Whittle" (1840 Ordnance Survey map), or to Whitehough on Ipstones Edge, home of Henry del Whitehalgh in 1358 - "a white nook of land". The fluctuation in the forms is reflected in Anna Whithough (Anne Whitehall) of Bignall End (1625), whilst Randell Whytall of Oldcott, Constable of Tunstall Court in 1615, is paying hearth tax at Oldcott in 1666 as Randle Whitehaugh (Whitehall). If an example like 1609:Lawrence Whithall of Whiston near Kingsley (1610:Lawrence Whitwall) is reliable, then we are also dealing with a reduced form of Whitwell - "dweller by the white spring"; 1887:Joseph Whitehall (stationer), Dimsdale Street, Burslem; 1907:Thomas Whitehall (fireman), Price Street, Burslem.

Three of the most elementary surnames for hill-dwellers are Hill(s), Underhill/Undrell and Hillman; 1776:William Hill, a Blackamoor, aged 22 years, brought from Virginia, baptised at Rocester; 1912:Joseph Hill (sanitary presser), Albert Road, Fenton; 1851:George Underhill (chimney sweeper), Dottell Street, Stafford; 1907:Sydney Underhill (bricklayer), Belgrave Road, Longton; 1887:James Hillman, licensee of The Old Crown, Stafford Street, Hanley; 1907:Mrs Elizabeth Hillman, Hot Lane, Burslem. Many medieval forms of the name Hill exhibit the Staffordshire dialect spelling "hul(l)" as in 1327:John del hul of Penkhull and 1360:Adam del hul of Tunstall, which are thus one origin of the surname Hull. However, Hull is normally a pet form of the Germanic personal name Hugh, since Richard son of Hugh de Flotesbroc (Flashbrook) occurs as Richard son of Hulle in two deeds from the Cartulary of Ronton Abbey (1277 and 1298).

Eaves signified a dweller by the edge of a hill or wood: Clare Eeaves (sic) widow, ineligible for hearth tax at Fenton Vivian and Longton in 1666. The term also survives in Great Eaves, Bucknall. Seabridge, south of Newcastle under Lyme is a deceptive name, since it was originally "Sheperugge" in the Middle Ages, as in William de Sheperugge, taxed at Clayton and Seabridge in 1332. It alludes to a ridge or slope used by sheep; 1875:Sarah Seabridge (hosier), Church Street, Silverdale; 1887:Peter Seabridge (joiner), New Road, Talke. Two strange distorted variants are Sawbridge and Shoebridge, which arose via a form such as Stephen Shawbridge, resident at Swynnerton in 1750.

Cliff and Cliffe are exceedingly commonplace in this zone from the Reformation onwards, and are either from Cliffe Vale south west of Hanley, noted as "Le clif" in 1253, or from a lost Castle Cliff in Newcastle under Lyme, recorded as "the King's wood called Le cliff" in 1263. Henry de Cliffe of Endon (1327) could have come from either locality. Ralph Clyff, wife Agnes and their seven children - two Joans, Catherine, Margaret, Em, William and John, were amongst the inhabitants at Meaford in 1532. At Norton in the Moors in 1579, Johanna Coulcloughe was otherwise known as Johanna Cliffe and in 1608,

Jeffery Cliffe of Newcastle under Lyme was following the trade of ropemaking. If the surname is a toponymic, then the exact sense implicit in the name varies from residence by some steep slope or incline, by some rock, or to habitation near the bank of a river. Other modern variants like Clive/Cleve/Cleave(s) and Clift are much rarer hereabouts; 1851:John Henry Clive (coalmaster), Goldenhill, Tunstall; 1907;Harry Clive (agent for potters' materials), Town Hall, Albert Street, Hanley. Some of these must go back to The Clive in Pattingham, south Staffordshire, found as "The Clyff" in 1532.

The "Vale" part of Cliffe Vale was a late addition and denotes its situation in the valley of the Trent along with its neighbour Trent Vale two miles to the south. However, the surname Vale - "dweller in a valley" - is in very short supply; 1631:Roger Vale farmer of Newcastle under Lyme; 1839:Reverend Benjamin Vale, Rector of the Church of St. James the Less at Longton. In fact the latter was a Londoner by birth, and, during the Chartist riots of 1842 his house was attacked by the rebels and his valuable books, manuscripts and furniture were all burnt or stolen.

The high incidence of the surname Bagnall in our county is due to the fact that it is derived from two distinct localities - Bagnall, a hilltop village near Milton on the edge of the Staffordshire Moorlands and Bagnall near Alrewas, not far from the Fradley Junction on the Trent and Mersey Canal. It is accepted in most quarters that the two places are identical in meaning, but early spellings seem to discredit this view. For instance, Bagnall near Milton boasts medieval forms such as "Bagenal, Badegenhall, Bagynholt" etc - "Badeca's nook" or "Badeca's holt (wood)", whereas Bagnall near Alrewas appears as "Bagganal, Baginhal" and so forth in the thirteenth and fourteenth centuries. This hints at "badger nook". Be that as it may, the two have combined to produce one of the most prolific of all surnames in North Staffordshire. In the 1539 Muster Roll, local volunteers called Bagnall, Bagnold, Bagnald, are registered for Newcastle under Lyme, Fenton and Longton, Fulford and Barlaston. In 1786 the poorhouses at Betley were damaged by fire and Ralf Bagnall was given the job of repairing the roofs with thatch. He was paid 8 shillings and 9 pence for three and a half days work. Trade directories list 1851:Thomas Bagnall (mine surveyor) of Kidsgrove; 1887:William Bagnall (solicitor, town clerk and commissioner for oaths), Glebe Street, Stoke.

If the terminal of Bagnall near Milton turns out to be "holt", then this brings us to the local surname Holt/Hoult - dweller in or near a holt(wood), as in Kingsley Holt in the Churnet valley; 1887:Joseph Holt (boot repairer), High Street, Hanley; 1907:George Holt (potter's placer), Birch Street, Northwood; 1907:Clement Hoult, proprietor of the Eagle and Child Hotel, Etruria Road, Hanley.

In conjunction with Bagnall, Bucknall formed one of the rectories separated and sold from Stoke under the Act of 1807, and of which the advowson was purchased by the Reverend Edward Powys, incumbent in 1843. The place means "Bucca's nook". The surname Bucknall does not become as entrenched across the region as Bagnall; 1875:George Bucknall (pork pie maker), Normacot Road, Longton; 1907:William

Bucknall (painter), Hamil Road, Burslem. Ironically, it is a name borne by John Buknall, one of the monks at Hulton Abbey, whose signature appears on the charter of surrender, dated September 18th 1538, when the Dissolution of the monasteries was in full swing. Bucknall is pronounced locally as "Buckner", hence the modern variant Bucknor; 1804:John Bucknor of Newcastle under Lyme, noted as John Bucknall in 1772. The surname Bucknall/Bucknell could also have been introduced into our county from Bucknall east of Lincoln, Bucknall in Tranmere, Bucknall in Fownhope (Herefordshire), Bucknell south east of Banbury (Oxfordshire), a lost Bucknell Wood in Besford (Worcestershire) or Bucknowl in Dorset. Bucknell south west of Stokesay, Shropshire - "Bucca's hill" must also be in on the act. On Robert Miller's map of Staffordshire (circa 1821), Bucknall is recorded as Buckland. Now this makes very interesting reading, since Buckland End in Castle Bromwich was originally "Bokenholt" in the Middle Ages - "beechen wood" and so we are also confronted by the pairing Bucknall-Buckland. Indeed, in the Castlechurch parish registers, John Bucknoll (1575) is almost certainly identical with John Buckland (1578). If the original name is Buckland as exemplified by 1361:John de Bokeland (knight) of Tutbury, then this is traceable to any one of numerous places called Buckland in many southern counties, all representing land which was formerly held by charter; 1782:Ralph Buckland (miller), married at Stoke-on-Trent on Christmas Eve to Mary Starkey; 1851:Harriet Buckland (milliner and dressmaker), Dale hall, Burslem.

The interplay between Bucknall and Buckland is not unique, for it is matched by the pair Coppenhall-Copeland. Conclusive proof of this apparently impossible relationship is afforded by two entries from the Swynnerton parish registers, where Anne, daughter of John Coppenhall alias Copland and Elizabeth his wife, was baptized on May 7th 1648. This same John is cited as John Coppenhall (Copland) of Blakeley in 1660 (the modern Blakelow not far from Swynnerton Grange). These entries are confirmed by the Burslem registers, since Moses Copnall (1704) is also quoted as Moses Copland in 1707. The transition from Coppenhall to Copeland is as follows; Coppenhall, from the place Coppenhall, south of Stafford - "Coppa's nook", is first reduced to Copnall; 1574:John Copnall (rector of Stoke-on-Trent). Secondly the liquid consonant "l" and the nasal consonant "n" change places, giving Coplan - cf Joseph Coplin of Norton in the Moors (1687), noted later as Joseph Copeland in 1738, and finally the form Coplan gains an extra "d" as in the dialectal "drownd" for "drown"; 1887:Turner Copeland (mineral water manufacturer), Jasper Street, Hanley; 1907:Joshua Copeland (saggar maker), Sant Street, Burslem. Whether Church Coppenhall near Crewe (same meaning) undergoes a similar modification is not known. If the original surname is Copeland, as typified by John de Coupland of Tillington, who appears at the the local assizes in 1307, then the sources are Coupland near Yeavering on the northern rim of Northumberland National Park, and Coupland near Appleby-in-Westmorland, both of which preserve the Scandinavian "kaupland" -"bought land". Migrants from the north of England probably swelled the numbers of families called Copeland/Copland/Coopland/Coupland/Cowpland in the wake of the Industrial Revolution, driven south to Staffordshire and adjoining counties in their search for work as miners in the local pits or as navvies on the canals. Copnell is simply a variant of Copnall; 1907:Jacob Copnell, Heath Street, Chesterton, whilst Copner parallels the local pronunciation of "Tunster" for Tunstall; 1907:John Copner (grocer and beer retailer), Victoria Street, Silverdale.

Copses and trees

Trubshaw close by Thursfield Lodge contains the very common element "shaw" "small wood, thicket, grove", but the initial syllable remains unsolved. James Trubshaw junior of Great Haywood was the architect of Wetley Rocks church, erected in 1833/34 and constructed with local stone from Wetley Rocks quarry; 1851:Charles Trubshaw (wine and spirit merchant), Church Street, Longton. When used alone, the normal sense conveyed by "shaw" is a toponymic for a dweller by a copse, thicket or small wood, as epitomised by individuals such as 1307:Adam atte schawe of Horton near Rudyard and 1379:Richard del schawe of Knutton and Dimsdale, who occupied dwellings in close proximity to one of these topographical features. After the Middle Ages the surname Shaw establishes itself strongly across the whole of north Staffordshire and is intermittent elsewhere. This distribution is corroborated by the 1666 hearth tax returns for the county, where out of a total of 52 recordings, 41 are confined to the northern Hundreds of Pirehill and Totmonslow, compared with only 11 for the three southern Hundreds of Cuttlestone, Offlow and Seisdon. In the will of Thomas Shaw, who died at Alton in 1608, he bequeathed *"To Thomas my sonne all the corne that is in his house....and the hay at the rick at the plum tree....and to my sayd sonne the horse which he sold at Burton faire..."* Later Trade Directories list 1887:George Shaw (cutler), Percy Street, Hanley; 1907:Charles Shaw (shunter), Hill Street, Fenton.

Shaw is sometimes spelt Shore - Audley parish registers:Sarah, daughter of Richard Shore, is baptized as Sarah Shore on June 26th 1697, but is buried as Sarah Shaw on August 19th of the same year. If Shore is the original surname, then this is derived from Shore near Rochdale, which conceals a dialect word for a steep rock; 1887:Thomas Shore (machinist), Pyenest Street, Hanley; 1907:Arthur Shore (engineer), Dundee Road, Hanley. A spelling such as John Shaye of Ingestre (1539 Muster Roll) recalls the Yorkshire dialect variant Shay for Shaw, whilst Shave and Shafe (unrecorded) are strays from Dorset, Devon and Somerset. Shea and Shee can be for Shaw now and again, but they are mainly Irish forms of O'Shea - "descendant of Seaghdha", where the personal name is a nickname for a stately, majestic person; 1912:B. Shea (plasterer), Edward Street, Longton.

Staffordshire was once as densely wooded as any county in England and the forests of Brewood, Kinver, Needwood and on Cannock Chase provided people with shelter, food, medicine and defence from enemies. In fact, trees played such an essential role in their everyday lives that they moulded religious beliefs and outlook. The oak tree was a crucial element in the ancient ceremonies of the Druids, who attached mystic significance to mistletoe, especially when it grew upon oaks - this tradition is still with us at Christmas. The curious horn dance performed annually at Abbot's Bromley has been interpreted as a pagan rite connected with the oak cult of Zeus. But the most famous tree of all is the oak in which Charles II hid at Boscobel (just a mile or so outside the borders of Staffordshire), fleeing from the Roundheads after the Battle of Worcester in 1651. This is the historic Royal Oak commemorated on Royal Oak Day (Oak Apple Day) and familiar on countless public house signs up and down the country.

Many of our medieval ancestors lived by some impressive gnarled oak tree; 1379:John atte oke of Wolstanton, but others preferred the protection of a group of oaks; 1327:Nicholas in le okes of Ronton and Coton, hence the surnames Oak(e)/Oakes, and the locality Light Oaks near Bagnall. At a meeting on 25th February 1799, at the Legs of Man Inn, Burslem, it was agreed that the security of property from fire would be much promoted by having fire engines provided for the use of the neighbourhood. Amongst the subscribers to the scheme was Samuel Oakes, who agreed to pay the sum of two guineas for the purpose of providing three fire engines, one to be stationed in the town of Burslem, one at Tunstall and the third at Longport; 1887:Ralph Oakes (district manager of the United Kingdom Assurance Society), Trinity Street, Hanley; 1912:James Oakes (joiner and coffin maker), Biddulph Road, Tunstall.

In the formation of other surnames of this type, two additional prepositions were resorted to - "atten" and "atter". The former produced such names as 1360:John atte noke of King's Bromley and 1381 Poll Tax Returns:Richard atte nokes of Lapley and Aston. These survive as Noak(e)s, Noaks, Noke(s), Nock and Knock; 1561:Edward Nokes of Audley; 1666:Dorothy Nocke of Eccleshall, paying tax on one hearth; 1755:Ellen Knock spinster of Swynnerton married William Venables husbandman on February 6th; 1912:Arthur Noakes (corn mixer), Pinnox Street, Tunstall. The modern Knock is also a toponymic for a dweller on a hill, from the Saxon "cnocc" - "hill", and this infers that the extended name Knocker could denote habitation either by a hill or an oak tree; 1617:Robert Knocker of Ellastone. The plural forms Knocks and Knox are from Knox in Renfrewshire; 1912:William Knocks (joiner), Freehold Street, Newcastle under Lyme.

The preposition "atter" resulted in a name like 1323:Henry atte rook of Penkridge - Roke/Roake/Rock(e)/Rocks/Rook(e)/Rooks/Ruck; 1607:Francis Rocke of Stafford; 1653:Matthew Rock, elected sergeant to the mayor at Newcastle under Lyme; 1700, April 24th:Augustine Rock of Stoke-on-Trent wed Sara Long; 1851:Thomas Rock (fishmonger) of Piccadilly, Hanley. Variants such as Rock(e) and Rocks are just as likely to designate residence by a rock or group of rocks, whilst forms like Roke, Roake and Rook or Rooks could even be an apposite nickname for a boisterous talker who was as raucous as a rook; 1887:Joseph Rook (bootmaker) of Trent Vale. The fuller form Roker is either a reference to a dweller by an oak tree or is a derivative of "rok, rocke" - "distaff", that is an occupational term from the wool trade for a worker who spun material on such an instrument. At a 1496 session of the manor court at Newcastle under Lyme, John Roker

1734]   *Stoke.*   447

1734, Jan. 3. Sarah Lay, wid. out of the Workhouse.
,, Jan. 11. Edw. Toft, s. of Matth., of Lane Delph.
,, Jan. 12. Mary Rowley, wid., of Handley.
,, Feb. 2. Eliz. Ellis, d. of John, of Handley.
,, Feb. 22. Thos. Rowley, s. of John, of Handley.
,, Feb. 23. John Bloore, s. of John, of Lane Delph.
,, Feb. 25. Cath. Baggiley, w. of Thos., of Moor Side.
,, Mar. 9. Ellen Pye, d. of Rich., of Lane End.
,, Mar. 10. Mary Keeling, of Handley, spinster.
,, Feb. 13. Margt. Barker, w. of Rich., of Lane End.
            ffinis.

MARRIAGES IN THE YEAR OF OUR LORD, 1734.

1734, Apr. 14. Rob. Rowson & Deborah Wood, of Mear Heath.
,, Apr. 15. John Jones & Mary Brown, of Sneyd Green.
,, Apr. 15. Wm. Bennett & Mary Heath, of Burslem.
,, Apr. 16. John Brommall & Anne Alcock, of Mear Heath.
,, Apr. 17. Thos. Lyngott, of Clayton, & Eliz. Brassing-ton, of Trentham.
,, Apr. 18. Thos. Eccles & Hannah ... castle.
,, May 3. Jas. Goodwin & Mary Cler...
,, May 13. Wm. Briscow & Mary Ya...
,, June 2. Jerem. Hall & Prudenc... Newcastle.
,, June 25. Joseph Woolley & Ha... Penkhull.
,, June 30. Thos. Simpson & Reb... Penkhull.
,, July 25. Wm. Ridge & Ellen Benn...
,, July 25. Thos. Mellor, of Yorks., & ... of Bucknall.
,, Aug. 5. Chas. Toft & Sarah Clith...
,, Aug. 11. Wm. Kemp, of Darliston... of Boothen.
,, Aug. 26. Geo. Lovatt, Stone Paris... of ye ffield.

was admitted unto his liberties.

The regularly occurring Braddock camouflages a dweller by a broad oak; 1403:Reginald de brodok of Newcastle under Lyme, or is from Broadoak near Kingsley or Broadoak (Farm) near Bramshall; 1666:James Braddocke of Onneley; 1851:Samuel Braddock (grocer and tea dealer), Sheep Market, Leek.   Holyoak(e)/Hollyoak(e); 1351:John de Haliok of Eccleshall - designates a person who resided by a holy oak (gospel oak), an oak that marked a parish boundary, where a reading was taken from the Gospel during the ceremony of Beating the Bounds on Rogation Days. This annual religious ritual was of great antiquity, and the times appointed were the three days before Ascension Day (Holy Thursday), that is, Rogation Monday, Tuesday and Wednesday, from the Latin word "rogatio" - "an asking", a supplication to the Almighty for his blessing on all the fruits of the earth; 1907:John Holyoake (platelayer), Acton Street, Birches Head; 1907:Ernest Holyoake (blacksmith), Friarswood Road, Newcastle under Lyme.

The ash tree, too, had a unique significance, especially for the Norwegians and Danes who settled permanently in the English Danelaw. In Norse mythology, Asgard, the home of the gods, was a fortress in the centre of which flourished an evergreen ash tree called "Yggdrasil", whose roots reached down into the underworld. Its branches were so lofty that they pierced the heavens. It was the "universal column" which supported the whole world. This pagan belief was probably a decisive factor in determining the site of many of the placenames called Ashby in the Danelaw counties of Norfolk, Suffolk, Lincolnshire, Leicestershire and Northamptonshire. From a more realistic standpoint the ash tree played an equally important role in the lives of medieval Englishmen, providing food for deer in autumn, while the tough elastic wood was ideal for making axe handles, pegs, wagons and bows and arrows. With a plentiful supply of ash trees at hand, it is not surprising therefore to find some of our Staffordshire ancestors living close by and setting up home in their welcoming shade; 1332:Richard atte asshe of Broughton near Charnes; 1289 Assizes:William atten ashe of Colton near Blithfield Reservoir, hence the doublet Ash(e)-Nash/Naish: 1875:Henry Ash (grocer), Dunrobin Street, Dresden; 1912:Timothy Ash (miner), America Street, Tunstall; 1912:Henry Nash (greengrocer), Bank Street, Tunstall. A locative source for the surname Ash(e) is Ash Bank, Bucknall; 1332:Henry de Asshe, taxed at Fenton Culvert and Bucknall. The imported Norman word for an ash tree - "fraisne, fresne", as in 1271 Pleas of the Forest:Richard del frene of Morfe, results in the modern surname Frain/Frane/Frayn(e)/Frean; 1907:Martin Frain (labourer), Vernon Square, Burslem; 1907:Robert Frain (engineer), Oxford Terrace, Wolstanton.

Smallthorne, midway between Burslem and Chell Heath, occurs spelt thus in 1532, and probably refers to a settlement originally built by a small thorn bush. The surname Thorn(e)/Thornes/Thorns implies a similar idea, that is, a dweller by a thorn bush or thorn bushes, as in 1360, Richard atte thorne (clerk) of Pipe, near Lichfield; 1666:Francis Thornes of Great Haywood; 1912:Charles Thorne (fitter), Highfield Cottage, Wolstanton.

A veritable gatecrasher on the Staffordshire surname scene is Hawthorn(e);

ETRURIA, 1732.

BEMERSLEY FARM, 1880

PENKHULL.

FREE SCHOOL, COBRIDGE.

BROWNHILLS TOLL-GATE.

THE "BELL AND BEAR" INN, SHELTON.

1685:Richard Hawthorn, buried at Audley; 1713:Ann Hawthorne of Norton in the Moors; 1717:Olive Hawthorne of Burslem. Spelt in this way, it is obviously a toponymic for a dweller by a hawthorn or from some place called Hawthorn, such as Hawthorn near Cannock, or Hawthorn near Easington in Durham. Yet at Norton in the Moors, Thomas Hordern signs his name in the register as Thomas Hawthorn in 1817, whilst in 1809, in the same register, Ellin Hordern puts her name down as Horthon. In fact, the overwhelming spellings of the name up until the latter decades of the seventeenth century range from 1532:John Hordorne of Stafford; 1539:Laurence Hordern of Penkhull to 1617:Thomas Harderne of Rushton Spencer and 1670:Maria Hardhorne of Audley. Several locatives are involved here - Hordern Farm in Rainow (north east of Macclesfield), Horderns in Chapel en le Frith, Derbyshire, Hordron near Penistone (Yorkshire), Little Hordern in Bolton le Moors and Hardhorn in Poulton le Fylde (both in Lancashire). All localities preserve the Saxon "hordern" - "store house". The actual fluctuation between forms such as "Hordern" and "Hawthorn", where the letter "d" is transformed into "th" is based on the local pronunciation of words such as "fodder" and "powdery", which are turned into "fother" as in "fotherbin - "trough in front of cows in a stall, from which they feed", still prevalent at Biddulph Moor, and "puthery" - "close, sultry" used of the weather. Also noteworthy in this respect is that the hospital of St. Mary of Bethlehem in London, converted into a lunatic asylum in 1547, came to be pronounced "Bedlam" and the word entered our language as a colloquial term for "uproar", "noisy confusion", with reference to the disturbed behaviour of the inmates.

Surnames in "-ley"

The shape and size of the wood are self evident in places such as Bradeley adjacent to Smallthorne, Bradley Green in Biddulph and Bradeley near Cheadle (1836 Ordnance Survey map) - "broad wood", all of which must be reckoned as prime movers towards the spread of the local surname Bradley/Bradeley/Broadley. The fourth contender - Bradley in the Moors south west of Alton Towers - is a wood where boards were obtained. In the southern sector of the county, the origin is most likely to be Bradley and Lower Bradley near Bilston, supplemented by Bradley near Penkridge; 1851:Emma Bradley (confectioner), High Street, Hanley; 1887:John Bradley (draper, hosier, smallware dealer, boot and shoe dealer), Market Square, Tunstall. Around Penn near Wolverhampton, the name alternates with Bradney; 1613:Thomas Bradeney otherwise Bradeley, a switch of letters already witnessed in Betteney-Betley. If the original name is Bradney, then this is from Bradney in Worfield, Shropshire - "broad island".

Bradeley (Smallthorne) looks towards Chatterley in the west and Baddeley Green in the east. Chatterley - "wood by a hill fort" - hardly budges at all from its starting point before the advent of the Industrial Revolution, apart from several families around the Swynnerton area in the 1700s; e.g. James Chatterley of Acton, who weds Sarah Ditchfield of Stoke in 1735. One of the monuments at the chancel end of Hanley Church (1843) was inscribed to Ephraim Chatterly of Shelton, who died 7th May 1811, aged 66 years. In 1841 Sarah Chatterly, aged 38, was in charge of the girls' burnishing room at Zachariah Boyle's China and Earthenware Factory at Stoke, and in 1887 Emanuel Chatterley was running a greengrocers and fruiterers stall in Hanley Fish Market.

The meagre showing of Chatterley contrasts sharply with the name of Baddeley/Baddiley/Baddley/Badley, from Baddeley Green - "wood of Badda's people". This branches out in all directions, assisted no doubt by immigrant families from Baddiley near Nantwich, Cheshire - "wood of Beada or Beadda", especially in the neighbourhood of Audley, Betley and Madeley on the Staffordshire-Cheshire border, where the surname ramifies most of all. A lost Baddiley Grange in Nantwich Hundred and Badley in Suffolk - "Bad(d)a's wood" might just squeeze in as outside bets. In 1628, William Baddiley who served as apprentice dyer with Richard Harrison, was admitted to the liberties of the borough of Newcastle under Lyme, paying 33s.4d. for the privilege. The Quaker burial ground at Basford, Cheddleton, recorded the names of 139 persons who were buried there from the 15th September 1667 until the 30th November 1828. The last burial recorded was Mary Baddeley, wife of John Baddeley (potter). In 1875, William J. Baddeley was landlord of the Dog and Pheasant in Mount Street, Tunstall. Hanley, where the Potteries' most famous novelist Enoch Arnold Bennett was born on March 27th 1867, gets its name from its high situation, for it means literally "the place at the high wood (clearing)". During the reign of Henry III the vill of Hanley was held in fee-farm by William de Hanley at the rent of six shillings, payable at Newcastle, and by service of Castle guard. By the 1600s the lordship of Hanley had passed into the hands of Sir Thomas Colclough under the honour of the Duchy of Lancaster.

Hanley is the most recognised spelling of the surname; 1539 Muster:William Hanley of Abbey Hulton, equipped with body armour and a leather jerkin with pieces of iron attached for protection; 1619:Roger Hanley, sergeant to the mayor at Newcastle under Lyme; 1666:Widdow Hanley, paying tax on one hearth at Stadsmorlow. Additional origins here might be four localities in Worcestershire, namely, Hanley Castle and Hanley Swan near Great Malvern, or Hanley Child and Hanley William north west of Worcester. Occasionally the letter "d" sneaks in and we have Handley; Audley parish registers 1540:William Hanley (1554:William Handeley), but Handley on its own can also be derived from Handley near Clay Cross, Derbyshire, Handley west of Beeston Castle, Cheshire or Handley Green near Chelmsford, Essex. All these are identical in meaning with Hanley; 1907:Hamlet Handley (potter) of Tellwright Street, Burslem.

By the close of the seventeenth century Buckley is abundant in all parts of north Staffordshire. Instrumental in the propagation of the surname is a location called "Bukkeleg" in the foundation charter of Hulton Abbey (1223) - "a glade where bucks (deer or goats) used to roam", but also on the agenda are places such as Buckley in Rochdale parish, Lancashire and Buckley Green near Henley in Arden, Warwickshire - "Bucca's wood" or "deer wood". Thomas Buckley who lived at Dunwood in Endon registered his

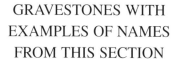

GRAVESTONES WITH
EXAMPLES OF NAMES
FROM THIS SECTION

house as a meeting place for non-Conformists in 1693. In the Endon area the name is mixed up with Bulkeley; 1532:Humphrey Bokeley of Longsdon is probably the same Humphrey Bulkley who married Johanna, daughter of William Egerton of Wall Grange in 1523. The Bulkleys were in possession of land at Stanlow near Longsdon in the fifteenth century, and probably came from Bulkeley, north of Cholmondeley Castle, Cheshire. In fact the place occurs as "Buckley" in the Middle Ages; 1851:John Buckley (corn miller) of Weston Coyney; 1887:Joseph Buckley (wheelwright), Williams Street , Hanley.

In a fourteenth century deed from the Chartulary of St. Thomas Priory, Stafford, one of the witnesses is William le wodeward de Greneley. Today we would know him better as William Woodward of Grindley near Drointon. The place refers to a green clearing or green wood and must rank as firm favourite as the ancestor of many of the North Staffordshire Grindleys, whilst in the running also are Grindley near Blythe Bridge and perhaps Grindley Hill near Penkhull. Cheshire families called Grindley could trace their ancestry back to Grindley in Tushingham cum Grindley; 1907:Henry Grindley (miner) of Heathcote Street, Hanley. In the Standon parish registers there is frequent vacillation between Grindley and Grimley, as evidenced by 1673:Thomas Grimley, who is entered in the record as Thomas Grindley in 1698. If the surname Grimley was brought into our county from elsewhere, the most likely focal point is Grimley near Droitwich in Worcestershire - "wood haunted by a ghost"; 1907:Henry Grimley (gravedigger) of Newlands Street, Shelton. By some strange quirk of fate, this gentleman's surname and occupation complement each other in the most macabre kind of way.

This sombre mood is maintained by Blakeley/Blackley/Blacklay, which is either for a dweller by a black (dark) wood or clearing: 1338:Roger atte blakeleye of Wrottesley or from any one of a number of locatives. These comprise Blakeley near Bucknall (Yates map of 1775), Blakeley (Farm) north of Moneystone Quarry (Whiston), Blakelow near Swynnerton, which occurs as "Blakeley" on Bowen's map of 1777, Blackley in Manchester parish, Lancashire, pronounced as "Blakeley", and Blakeley near Wombourne, all most probably for "dark wood (glade)". 1875:William Henry Blakeley (hatter), Stafford Street, Hanley; 1907:James Blakeley (bricklayer), Ricardo Street, Burslem.

Unlike many of the surnames in "-ley" discussed so far Chell - "glade of Ceola" or "glade on a ridge" - is far more scattered in its distribution: 1599:Edward Chell, elected as one of the eight officers of the borough of Newcastle under Lyme; 1750:Mary Chell married William Hulm of Kingsley parish at Cheddleton; 1851:Thomas Chell (blacksmith) of Back Lane, Stone; 1875:George Chell, landlord of the Bennett's Arms Inn, Dunkirk, Chesterton. James Brindley, the celebrated engineer, died at Turnhurst, an ancient house and estate in Great Chell, but he was born at Tunsted in 1716, a hamlet in the parish of Wormhill in the Derbyshire High Peak district, situated between Buxton and Tideswell. Where his surname originated is open to conjecture. Along with the north Staffordshire families called Brindley the principal sources are Brindley between Lapley and Haughton (Kip's map of 1607/1610), Brindley Heath near Rugeley and two participants from

Cheshire - Brindley west of Nantwich and Brindley Green near Sandbach. All designate woodland cleared by burning. The stronghold of the surname has always been Stoke-on-Trent, Newcastle under Lyme and the Leek and Moorlands area: 1619:Lawrence Brindley (blacksmith) of Milne Street, Leek; 1666:Randle Brindley, taxed on two hearths at Talke; 1691:George Brindley otherwise Brundley of Stoke-on-Trent; 1851:John Beavis Brindley (clock manufacturer) of Lad Lane, Newcastle under Lyme.

The surname Rowley occurs in great numbers in the Tunstall manor court rolls throughout the Middle Ages, spelt as "Rowlegh, Rowelegh, Roweley(e), Rouley" etc - "rough glade (clearing) in a forest or wood". The exact locality is elusive, although at a 1622 session of the manor court we find William Rowley of Rowley (Burslem). If we compare this recording with 1591:John Rowley de Rowley alias Turner of Norton in the Moors, then it looks as if there is a lost location in the neighbourhood of Burslem or Norton in the Moors. Additional places to be examined include Rowley Wood near Seabridge, Rowley Gate north of Longsdon, Rowley Park west of Baswich, Big Rowley in Norbury, Rowley Moor in Acton Trussell, Rowley Hill in Stretton near Brewood, Rowley Farms in Hamstall Ridware and Rowley Regis south of West Bromwich. John Rowley of Heycar was Constable of Tunstall Court in 1622, and Hugh Rowley was one of the Overseers of the Poor at Betley in 1732. In 1851 Stephen Rowley had a butcher's shop in Drayton Street, Newcastle under Lyme.

In 1539 one of the able-bodied men called to arms at Norton in the Moors was a certain William Rowley of Heykeley. This is the modern Heakley Hall Farm on the Caldon Canal between Norton in the Moors and Stockton Brook. In the sixteenth century Tunstall manor court rolls the place occurs as "Hekeley, Haickley, Hecley", but these spellings are meaningless without earlier forms. Anyway, this locality could well be the origin of local surnames such as Hackley/Hackerley, and, minus the initial aspirate, Ackley and Ackerley; 1702:Peter Hackerley of Fenton Vivian; 1800:Sarah Hackerly of Stoke-on-Trent; 1875:Ann Ackerley (grocer), Anchor Terrace, Longton; 1907:Samuel Ackley (miner), Jervis Street, Fenton.

Beasley and Beesley are normally traced back to Beesley in Kirkham parish, Lancashire -"Bisi's glade" or Beesley in Willington near Repton, Derbyshire - "clearing overgrown with bent grass". Yet there is the local Beasley between Chesterton and Bradwell. If this is an ancient site, then this is surely the chief progenitor of the names hereabouts; 1725:Royall Beezly of Norton in the Moors; 1875:Louisa Beasley (greengrocer), Herbert Street, Burslem; 1887:Charles Beasley (shopkeeper), Hall Street, Newcastle under Lyme.

Surnames in "-ton"

Placenames derived from the points of the compass such as Aston (Easton), Norton, Sutton and Weston, occur so regularly in virtually every single English county, that it is almost impossible to keep track of any family bearing one of these names without paying scrupulous attention to every scrap of information which comes to light. The surname Norton, for example, is derived in the main from the three Staffordshire localities Norton in the Moors, as in the case of Henry de Norton of Tunstall in the manor court rolls of 1298, Cold Norton near Yarnfield and Norton Canes near Cannock, all referring to a homestead or village situated north of another; 1851:William Norton (blacking maker) of Piccadilly, Hanley. Before legislation in 1754 abolished irregular marriages such as those systematically performed at the Fleet Prison in London, the village of Norton in the Moors was looked upon as a kind of local version of Gretna Green, where impatient couples were joined together in matrimony without undergoing the usual round of formalities, such as having the banns read and producing marriage licences.

Norton's opposite - Sutton - "southern farmstead" or "settlement situated south of another" is chiefly to be traced to Sutton not far from Aqualate Mere, with supplementary help from Sutton Lane Ends south of Macclesfield, Sutton in Middlewich, and two localities in Derbyshire - Sutton on the Hill north east of Tutbury and Sutton near Bolsover. In 1547, Richard Sutton, described as a husbandman of Endon, left in his will sixteen pounds worth of goods and chattels, declaring that he should be buried at "Saint Edwards churchyarde of Leke" and that "I will that Jane my wife and my child son shall have all my lands during the space of three years jointly together, and then to be at his rule and order. I will that my said wife shall have after the third year the third part of my goods and the other two parts be divided amongst my children equally." 1851:Nathaniel Sutton (tailor), Market Street, Newcastle under Lyme; 1851:George Sutton (carrier) from the Black's Head in Leek to Hartington and Longnor on Wednesdays and Saturdays; 1875:John Sutton (sexton), Congleton Road, Talke.

Weston has multiple origins, chief amongst which are Weston Coyney in Caverswall parish, held by Johannes Koyne in 1242 - Anglo French "coigne" - "a die for stamping money" or "a piece of money", hence an occupational term for a coiner or minter; Weston upon Trent near Stafford, Weston near Standon, Weston Jones near Norbury, named after John de Weston who held land here in 1316, and Weston under Lizard on the border with Shropshire, where the suffix refers to Lizard Hill. All the locations designate a farmstead facing west or village west of another; 1851:James Weston, owner of a beerhouse in Furnace Road, Longton; 1875:Benjamin Weston (forge manager), The Avenue, Kidsgrove; 1887:William Weston (fishmonger), Sneyd Street, Tunstall. The local pronunciation "Wesson" also survives as a surname, but it is extremely rare; 1851:William Wesson (stationmaster) of Cheddleton.

Aston surpasses all three of the preceding surnames in its distribution. Place names involved here are Aston near Seighford, Aston and Little Aston (both near Stone), Aston near Mucklestone, Wheaton Aston west of Penkridge and Aston in Shenstone - "eastern hamlet": 1570:Robert Aston, rector at Standon; 1666 Hearth tax returns: John Aston, one hearth at Abbey Hulton, Robert Aston, two hearths at Hanley, Humfrey Aston, exempt at Penkhull; 1851:Thomas Aston, licensee at the Roebuck, Chesterton. Now and then a toponymic for a dweller by a stone comes into the picture; 1539 Muster Roll:John a Stone of Aldridge and Great Barr. Easton is not evidenced but Eason could be a local variant, based on Aston - Asson; 1887:Henry Eason (draper), Chatham Street, Hanley; 1912:William Eason (labourer), Lonsdale Street, Hanley. North of the border Eason and Easom represent "son of Adam", so Scottish families bearing these surnames must be from this source.

Villages in prominent positions with commanding views over the surrounding countryside afforded better protection for our Saxon ancestors than settlements built out in the open. To this class belong our Hiltons and Hultons - "homestead on a hill" - as in Abbey Hulton, once the site of a flourishing community of Cistercian monks, based principally on agriculture, that is growing corn and raising herds of cattle and sheep. Abbey Hulton, along with several places called Hulton in Greater Manchester, is a West Midland dialect form of Hilton as in Hilton near Wolverhampton, Hilton in Shenstone and Hilton near Marston on Dove, Derbyshire, all of which must be involved in the modern surnames Hilton and Hulton, backed up by Hilton near Bridgnorth, Hilton near Yarm in north Yorkshire, Hilton near Bishop Auckland, Hilton not far from Coupland in Cumbria and Hilton south of Huntingdon, Cambridgeshire. Nowadays the name Hilton is the normal variant, with Hulton a poor second: 1666:Raph Hulton, certified as not chargeable for hearth tax at Leigh near Checkley; 1875:Joseph Hilton (clogger and beerseller) Market Street, Fenton; 1907:Charles T. Hilton (mouldmaker), Grove Street, Cobridge.

The various Sheltons and Shiltons up and down the country represent villages built on a bank or ledge, and this meaning is also inherent in the two Sheltons in Staffordshire - Shelton between Hanley and Stoke and Shelton under Harley not far from Swynnerton. This duo is responsible for a good number of local families called Shelton; 1332:Alkoc de Schelton, taxed at Swynnerton; 1907:Arthur William Shelton (hardware dealer), Hamil Road, Burslem; 1907:Thomas Shelton (potters' manager), Neville Street, Stoke-on-Trent. External sources include Shelton in Chellaston near Derby, Shelton in Shrewsbury, Shelton south of Newark on Trent, Shelton north west of Bedford, plus Shelton and Shelton Green about 10 miles south of Norwich. Shilton is much scarcer; 1907:Alfred L Shilton (grocer), Stanley Street, Tunstall. Principal origins here are Shilton near Coventry, Earl Shilton south west of Leicester and Shilton near R.A.F. Brize Norton, Oxfordshire.

The village of Blurton south west of Longton harks back to the time when it was founded in an exposed location, since the first part of the word is from an old topographical term "blure" -"blister, swelling" - employed in the transferred sense of "hill, bare spot". During the Middle Ages the Augustinian canons of Trentham Priory were in possession of land here, as well as at the nearby hamlet of Hanford and the outlying vills of Normacot, Longton and Meir. In the Stowe by Chartley parish registers for 1613 is recorded the burial of Simond Blurton, "a poore boye"; 1851:Thomas Blurton (rope and twine maker) of Greendock, Longton; 1875:Mary Blurton (haberdasher), Market Street, Fenton; 1875:William Blurton (hay and straw dealer), Duke Street, Tunstall.

Longton is simply "the long homestead" with early spellings of the place fluctuating with Langton, as in the local assize rolls for 1304 and 1305, where Matthew le clerk de Longetone is alternatively known as Matthew de Langeton. Hence the surnames Longton and Langton; 1566:Hugh Longton, buried at Church Eaton; 1907:E.H.Langton (draughtsman) of Jervis Street, Hanley; 1907:John Langton of the Old Inn, Trentham. The modern surnames may also have been brought into Staffordshire from Longton near Preston, Longtown north of Carlisle, Longtown near Ewyas Harold in Herefordshire, Langton south of Bishop Auckland, Langton north west of the medieval deserted village of Wharram Percy in north Yorkshire, Langton north of Tattershall and Langton about ten miles north west of Skegness (both in Lincolnshire), Langton by Wragby (east of Lincoln), Langton Green in Tunbridge Wells (Kent), Langton Green near Yaxley (Suffolk) or two localities in Dorset - Langton Herring west of Weymouth and Langton Matravers in Swanage. There is frequent confusion with Langdon; 1276 Assizes:John de Langeton (1272:John de Langhedone). Now Langdon itself often interchanges with Longdon, since Longdon near Rugeley -"long hill" - regularly crops up as "Langedon" in the twelfth century. In Sleigh's *History of Leek*, during the reign of Henry VIII (no date given), William Llandon, husband of Alice Rudyerd, has the alias Longden, thus providing us with the origin of the common local surname Landon; 1851:Charles Landon (clerk), Furnace Road, Longton; 1907:George Landen (sic), (potter), Wellington Street, Burslem. Normally, surnames such as Longdon and Langdon go back to Longdon near Rugeley, Longdon near Tewkesbury, Longden north east of Pontesbury Hill, Shropshire, Longdon upon Tern, north west of Wellington (also in Shropshire) or possibly Langdon Beck in Teesdale, all for "long hill"; 1851:Peter Langdon (gamekeeper), Alton Towers; 1907:Alice Langdon (widow), Waterloo Road, Burslem; 1907:Lewis Longden, licensee of the Smithfield Hotel, Bethesda Street, Hanley.

Clayey soils of varying texture are a feature of almost every region of the county except the millstone grit zone in the north east. Besides being the title of one of Arnold Bennett's novels, Clayhanger near Brownhills - "clayey slope" - is indicative of the boulder clay so prevalent in the coal measures of the south Staffordshire coalfield. In addition, medieval fieldnames like "le cleylond" in Brewood and "clay brok" in Cannock are irrefutable evidence of the strong clay or clay-loam soils along the valleys of the river Penk, whilst the locality Clayton near Newcastle under Lyme is a reminder of the clays in the basin of the upper Trent - "village on clayey soil". Hurst silk mill at Biddulph was occupied in 1834 by James Clayton, a silk throwster; it was vacated by 1838; 1875:George Clayton (mill manager) of Knutton; 1887:John Clayton (butcher), Market Hall, Newcastle under Lyme. No doubt today's Staffordshire Claytons rub shoulders with the Lancashire Claytons from Clayton Green, Bamber Bridge, Clayton le Moors, Accrington and Clayton le Woods, Leyland, and the Yorkshire Claytons, many of whose roots lie in Clayton near Grimethorpe, Clayton in Bradford and Clayton West, south east of Huddersfield.

Likewise with the local Fentons, whose ancestry is Fenton, the town that Arnold

Bennett forgot - "hamlet by a fen (marsh)". These have probably been augmented by families called Fenton from Fenton near Retford in Nottinghamshire, Fenton, west of Lincoln, Fenton near Carlisle, Fenton near Newark on Trent, Fenton north east of Huntingdon and Fenton near Flodden in Northumberland, where the Scots were defeated by the English in 1513 and where James IV of Scotland was killed. In 1615 Thomas Fenton was paying five shillings a year rent for one third of a messuage (site of a dwelling house), one cottage and diverse lands, including one half of Boothen Green at Penkhull; 1875:William Fenton (blacksmith), George Street, Sandford Hill, Longton; 1887:Annie Fenton (milliner and fancy draper), High Street, Wolstanton. Elijah Fenton, poet,was born at Shelton in 1683, the third and youngest son of the attorney John Fenton. He attended Newcastle Grammar School, published a collection of poems in 1707 entitled *Oxford and Cambridge Verses*, and befriended fellow poet Alexander Pope, for whom he translated four books of Homer's Odyssey. By all accounts he was one of the laziest of men and Dr Johnson said that he liked nothing more than to lie in bed and be fed with a spoon. Indeed, even his friend Pope, who wrote the epitaph for him, inscribed on his tomb in East Hampstead churchyard, conceded that he died of indolence.

When Hulton Abbey was founded by Henry de Audley in 1223, the vill or hamlet of Rushton Grange in Cobridge was handed over in its entirety to the abbot and resident monks. The place alludes to the fact that rushes once flourished where the hamlet was set up, and it is synonymous with Rushton Spencer north of Rudyard Reservoir. This gets its name from Hugh Despencer, who held land there in 1265. From these two spots have sprung a very high percentage of the north Staffordshire branches of the Rushton families, with minor cooperation from Rushton near Oulton Park racing circuit in Cheshire, Rushton near the Shropshire Wrekin and Rushton north west of Kettering. In 1841 Charles Rushton, aged 13, was working for Thomas Adams (dipper) at Messrs Yale and Barker's Earthenware Factory, Longton. He had been employed there since the age of eight, his first job being a muffin moulder. When interviewed by the inspectors he admitted that "...the dipping has hurt me once. It got into my belly, it griped me very much. I was obliged to take physic, mother sent for the doctor. I was bad for a week..." 1851:John Rushton (clog, patten, boot and shoe and last maker), Bath Street, Newcastle under Lyme; 1851:Samuel Rushton (licensee), Low Bull's Head, Chapel Street, Cheadle.

The placename Milton is found in almost every nook and cranny in the country, sometimes designating a hamlet with a mill, as in our local Milton near Norton in the Moors, and at others, referring to a middle farm. In 1686 Dr Plot recounts the methods of stripping oak bark, which were practised at Milton, Norton in the Moors and Baddeley Green. The bark was stripped off the trees between April 1st and June 30th, and allowed to stand naked all summer, drying in the sun, so that it became *"...as hard and sound without as within, being as it were all heart and not so subject to worms..."* The bark was then distributed to local tanneries for use in the leather trade. In 1703, at Audley, Isaac Milton is registered as a pauper, with a daughter called Maria; 1907:Mrs Catherine Milton,

Victoria Street, Stoke. Milton near Repton, Derbyshire is another likely base for the Staffordshire families called Milton.

Chesterton,whose name means "homestead by a Roman encampment", is situated on the old Roman road, called Ryknild Street in medieval times, which entered the county at Rocester. Another Roman road, ran west towards Chesterton,and then continued across the county boundary and on in the direction of Chester. It is the most important Roman site in the north west of the county and was probably occupied for a short period only during the final quarter of the first century A.D. Other localities to consider here are Chesterton south east of Warwick, Chesterton near Worfield, Shropshire, Chesterton north east of Oxford (the university town), Chesterton near Cirencester and two places in Cambridgeshire - Chesterton near Peterborough and Chesterton in Cambridge itself. At a session of the Standon manor court in 1434, Richard Chesterton was fined one penny for felling one ash tree in the lord's wood; 1680, April 26th:John and Mary Chesterton celebrated the baptism of their son John at Seighford.

Butterton, north west of Trentham - "butter farm" - is one origin of the surname Butterton, but this also goes back to its namesake Butterton on the Moors west of Wetton in the Manifold valley - "hill with good pastures yielding plenty of butter". In the 1539 Muster at Swynnerton, John Butterton was armed with a bill, that is, a staff five or six foot in length topped with a hook and spearhead; 1907:H.S. Butterton (engine man), Raglan Street, Fenton.

RAILWAY APPROACH, RUDYARD.

Mr S Wood

Sep 30 189 7

Dr. to G. T. HEATH,

TERMS CASH.   **Coal & Coke Merchant.**

PETROLEUM OIL IN CASKS.   Agent for WALLGRANGE BRICK & TILE CO.

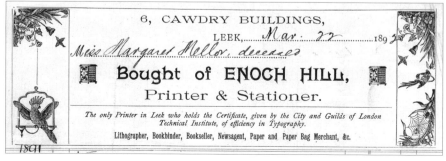

6, CAWDRY BUILDINGS,

LEEK,...*Mar. 22*...189 5

Miss Margaret Mellor, deceased

Bought of ENOCH HILL,

Printer & Stationer.

The only Printer in Leek who holds the Certificate, given by the City and Guilds of London Technical Institute, of efficiency in Typography.

Lithographer, Bookbinder, Bookseller, Newsagent, Paper and Paper Bag Merchant, &c.

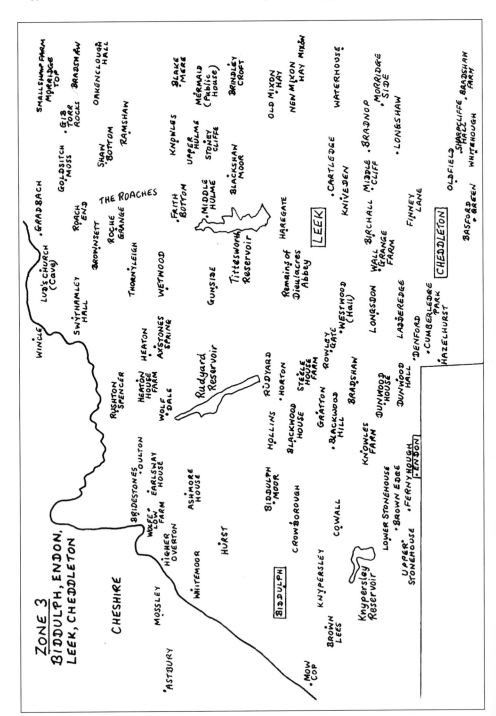

Zone Three:
Biddulph, Endon, Leek, Cheddleton

Biddulph/Biddle/Buddle 89
Dillon 89
Delf/Delves 90
Swindells/Swindell 90
Mole/Mowl/Mould/Moult 91
Rudyard/Ridyard 91
Greatbatch 94
Huntbach/Humpage 94
Comberbach 94
Bach/Batch 94
Beech 95
Bash/Baish 95
Roach 95
Rochell 95
Rockell 95
<$iBrownsword/Brownsett 95
Leek/Leake/Lake 97
Cartledge 97
Cumberledge 97
Finney 98
Beresford/Basford/Brayford 98
Oldfield/Howfield 99
Bromfield 99
Highfield/Hayfield 99
Caulfield/Corfield 101
Brookfield 101
Lichfield 101
Cowall/Cowell/Cole/Coole 101
Fernihough/Fernyhough 102

Birchenhough 102
Bradshaw 102
Blackshaw 103
Longshaw 103
Smallshaw 103
Hurst 103
Blackhurst 103
Haslehurst 103
Birchall/Bircher/Birtles/Brickles 103
Frith/Firth 105
Westwood 105
Eastwood 105
Lockwood 105
Blackwood 105
Dunwood/Downward 105
Breward 105
Underwood 106
Inwood 106
Thorley/Thornley 106
Hammersley 106
Stanley 107
Moseley 107
Shirley 107
Horton/Houghton/Haughton 107
Gratton/Gretton/Gritton 108
Bolton/Boulton 108
Heaton/Hayton 109
Eaton/Eton/Eyton 109
Stockton 109

ROCK END, BIDDULPH.

Zone Three

At the time of the Saxon colonisation Biddulph lay in a wooded valley hemmed in on one side by the great expanse of the Forest of Lyme and on the other by the bleak landscape of the Staffordshire Moorlands. The wooded character of this remote area is reflected in local place names such as Knypersley and Bradley Green, which bear witness to the forest clearances undertaken by the Saxons when they invaded the district. Later on there must have been local inhabitants who were engaged in quarrying stone or the mining of ironstone since the name Biddulph itself designates a place by a mine or some diggings. Naturally enough, the surname Biddulph survives intact. The pedigree of the Biddulph family who controlled the ownership of lands in Biddulph for over 700 years is well documented. John Biddulph, the head of the house during the reign of Charles I, was a captain in the Royalist army and contributed men and money towards raising an army which was defeated at Edgehill, the first battle in the Civil War fought on 23rd October, 1642. In the following year he was killed at the Battle of Hopton Heath, north east of Stafford, the only major Civil War confrontation in Staffordshire.

Of course, there were many ordinary families besides in the neighbourhood who had taken the surname Biddulph simply because this was where they had been born and raised in the Middle Ages. Their descendants too are all around us today; 1699:Sarah Biddulph of Horton parish, married to John Steele, also of Horton, at Cheddleton; 1851:Samuel Biddulph (corn and flour dealer), Wharf Street, Stoke. Locally, Biddulph is known as "Biddle" and it occurs in this form as early as 1471, when John Bidyll of Bidyll was hauled before the local assizes. In the Norton in the Moors parish register Hugh Biddulph (1614) is alternatively entered as Hugh Biddle de Bagnald in 1610. The name Biddle therefore, in our county, is more often than not from this local dialect variant; 1851:John Biddle (farmer) at Beech, Swynnerton, but in other parts of the country, especially in the north of England and the east Midlands, it goes back to the Saxon noun "bydel" - "beadle", who was the medieval counterpart of the modern village policeman. In Staffordshire the regular development is "budel", as in Stephen le budel, the local "beadle" at Eccleshall in 1327. This ends up as Buddle(s)/Buddell.

The ending of Biddulph - "dulf" - or some similar Saxon term for a mine or digging, forms the initial component of Dilhorne near Blythe Bridge - "house by a mine or quarry". It appears as "Dillon" in 1682 (Newcastle under Lyme parish registers) and so is the instigator of the local name Dillon; 1875:Foster Crewe Dillon (watchmaker, jeweller), High Street, Tunstall; 1907:Thomas Dillon (puddler), Etruria Road, Hanley. The Irish Dillons trace their name back to a diminutive of a Germanic personal name "Dillo". "Dulf" is allied to another Saxon word "delf" - "a digging", applied to any hole dug out of the ground, a sand pit, quarry or mine. Elias del delf of Cheadle (1320) and Peter del delves of Tunstall (1366) were more than likely quarrymen at local quarries, Elias employed at Hollington quarry, whilst Peter worked at the stone quarry at Tunstall, which was in operation in 1272. These are the origin of the surname Delf, Delve(s). In 1794 Thomas Delves had already established a tannery at Cheddleton on land rented from the Freeholders. He came from an old Cheddleton family with Non-conformist associations; 1875:Emma Delves (lamp and oil dealer), High Street, Hanley.

Yet "delf" was also used for a coal mine, as in the Lane Delph area of Fenton, marked on the 1775 Yates map of Newcastle under Lyme and the Potteries. This represents a well-worked mining seam. In fact the word is retained in North Staffordshire mining communities in such expressions as "delf hole" - "pit shaft", "delfman" - "pitworker" and "delf rags" - "miners' working clothes". In some medieval parishes coal was so easily obtainable, that it could be dug out of the earth by hand and used to heat ovens for baking bread, salt-making and metal working. Coal was being worked at Tunstall (Stoke-on-Trent) in 1282, at Shelton near Hanley in 1297, at Norton in the Moors in 1316 and at Keele in 1333. Thus, local workers such as 1316:Richard del delves of Wolstanton and 1362:John de le delves of Tunstall, might well have been coal miners rather than quarrymen. The main centre of coal mining in Staffordshire during the Middle Ages was probably Wednesbury, where there were protracted disputes between the lord and his tenants concerning the digging of coal in the common fields of the parish. Thomas atte delfe, resident at Wednesbury in 1315, could have been involved in just such a dispute. His name lives on in The Delves in Wednesbury, the chief source of the surname Delves in the southern half of the county.

As a terminal, "delf" is found in the locality Swindells (Croft) in Over Alderley, Cheshire, recorded as "Swyndelfs" in the sixteenth century - "diggings of swine". This is one origin of the surname Swindells/Swindles, although a subsidiary source might be Swindells in Wincle - 1611:"Swynehills" - "hills frequented by swine": 1851:Samuel Swindles (button mould manufacturer), Derby Street, Leek; 1875:William Swindells (station master) of Cobridge. The singular form Swindell/Swindall/Swindle/Swindale could be from either of the above, but more feasible are places like Swinedale in Bakewell, "Swindale" 1562, and "Swyn(e)dale" 1305 in Ashford (both in the Derbyshire High Peak district). These denote a valley where pigs were turned out to forage. In addition, James Swindall of Burslem (1688) occurs as James Swindane in 1686, so we are also dealing with a local dialect change comparable to that seen in "mesel-mesen" for "myself": 1851:Isaac Swindell of Longnor (stonemason). In the latter case the origin is perhaps Swindon (near Wombourne) - "pig hill".

Biddulph's neighbour to the west, Mow Cop, which bestrides the Staffordshire-Cheshire border, has two claims to fame - the site of the ruined castle-folly, built in 1754 by the Wilbraham family of Rode Hall, and the birthplace of Primitive Methodism in 1807, the brainchild of William Clowes, champion dancer of Burslem. In actual fact, the cradle of the sect was Tunstall, but it was on the slopes of Mow Cop, where William Clowes and his kindred spirit, Hugh Bourne, a wheelwright of Stoke-on-Trent, organised open air meetings, arousing much evangelistic fervour amongst their followers. Mow Cop is important for a third reason - it is one source of the surname Mole/Moule/Mowl(l) in North Staffordshire, for early spellings of the locality in the Tunstall manor court rolls comprise "Moule" in 1348, "Mouhull" in 1362 and "Mool" in 1512, whilst in the parish registers at Wolstanton it occurs as "Moll" in 1628 and as "Mole" in 1694. These forms suggest a hill with a boundary cairn; 1605:Marie Mole of Stowe by Chartley; 1661:Ann Moule of Kingsley; 1851:Henry Mole (basketmaker), Market Square, Hanley. However, at Croxden in 1684, Mary Mole also occurs as Mary Mold. In the Middle Ages, Mold was one of the many colloquial forms for Matilda, as evidenced by John, son of Matilda, taxed at Hixon in 1327, who is written down on the subsidy roll as John Mold in 1332 (for Chartley). Queen Matilda, wife of William the Conqueror, was called both "Mahald" and "Mold" and in thirteenth century deeds from the Rydeware Chartulary, Matilda Peche is also quoted as Maut Peche and Maud Peche, hence modern surnames like Maud(e)/Mald/Malt/ Mault/Mold/Moult and Mould(s); 1666:John Mault of Mucklestone; 1851:Joseph Moult (boot and shoemaker), Oakamoor; 1887:John Mould (saddler), High Street, Longton; 1907:Marie Mould (glove cleaner), Bucknall New Road, Hanley. Finally, some bearers of the surname Mole/Mould, etc, could have antecedents who were as secretive as a mole, since in the Churchwarden's accounts at Alrewas for 1776 a payment of one pound fifteen shillings was given to John Thomas for half a years moold (mole) catching.

East of Biddulph Moor is the small village of Rudyard, which, ironically has achieved worldwide fame, not because it has been handed down as a surname, but because it has been perpetuated as a christian name by Rudyard Kipling, one of the foremost writers and poets of the Victorian era. It was by the lakeside here that Lockwood Kipling proposed marriage to Alice Macdonald, and when their son was born in India, they christened him Rudyard in memory of the enchanting beauty of this corner of Staffordshire, which had so captivated them.

The Rudyard family held the manor of Rudyard from the thirteenth century until it was sold in 1723, together with the manor of Leek, to Thomas Parker, Earl of Macclesfield. Apart from this single landowning family, the surname Rudyard/Ridyard and Ridgard is very scarce locally; 1687:Thomas Ridyard of Norton in the Moors; 1708:Titterton Ruddyard of Alstonefield; 1907:John Ridgard (miner), Albert Street, Tunstall. The place means "enclosure with the red soil".

The practice of giving locative surnames as christian names to children, as in Rudyard and Titterton above, is not a new phenomenon. The oldest historical example is possibly Guildford Dudley, fourth son of the Duke of Northumberland and husband of Lady Jane Grey, with whom he was executed in 1554. The Canterbury register for 1601 records the baptism of Tunstall, son of Mr William Scott, son-in-law to the worshipful Mr Tunstall, prebendary of the church there. We have already seen how the marriage of Margaret Burslem and Gilbert Wedgwood resulted in a son whom they called Burslem Wedgwood. In fact other instances include, 1703:Burslem Hancock of Wolstanton and

1783:Burslem Daniel of Newcastle under Lyme. For a fuller list of locatives employed as christian names see the accompanying table. The motives which compelled parents to use these locatives instead of the ubiquitous names like John and William, for instance, are not easy to define. It may have been just a straightforward reaction against current popular vogues, or in the case of Raphe Walker of Preston near Penkridge, who named his son Preston Walker in 1601, to commemorate the place where his offspring was born.

YEAR	NAME	SOURCE
1766	Acton Fox(farmer) of Eccleshall	Stoke-on-Trent parish registers
1851	Ashton Travis(bleacher) of Tean Mill	White's Directory
1816	Bagnall Astbury	Norton in the Moors parish register
1613	Barton Dewerst	Ellastone parish register
1724	Beardmore Plant	Swynnerton parish register
1729	Blurton Bagnall	Newcastle under Lyme parish registers
1774	Broadhurst Harding (potter)	Stoke-on-Trent parish registers
1649	Doxie Hulme	Leek parish registers
1658	Dudley Butter	Audley parish registers
1618	Egerton Snow	Tunstall Manor Court Rolls
1759	Fenton Bill of Madeley	Newcastle under Lyme parish registers
1677	Handley Meeson	Keele parish registers
1809	Langley Allgood	Norton in the Moors parish register
1601	Lawton Vernon	Audley parish registers
1591	Littleton Cockes	Seighford parish register
1821	Milton Hewitt	Norton in the Moors parish register
1730	Moreton Backhouse of Doxey	Seighford parish register
1669	Norton Taylor	Audley parish registers
1691	Oldcott Eardley de Groby Ash	Audley parish registers
1802	Preston Howrobin	Bucknall cum Bagnall parish registers
1659	Stafford Ranalls	Betley parish registers
1760	Standley Bennitt	Wolstanton parish registers
1782	Stanton Eld	Seighford parish register
1787	Weston Bayley	Betley parish registers
1907	Whitehurst Cartlidge (blacksmith)	Potteries Trade Directory
1614	Wingfield Wetton de Hilderston	Milwich parish registers
1792	Woodhouse Bullivant	Norton in the Moors parish register
1667	Wotton Vise	Standon parish registers

Currently enjoying various degrees of popularity amongst the modern generation are Lee, Ashley and Bradley for boys and Hayley and Kimberley for girls. The process is going on all the time in the English-speaking world.

About four miles north east of Rudyard Reservoir is Gradbach, which itself is not far from Swythamley, the setting of the great medieval epic poem "Sir Gawain and the Green Knight". Of this there can be no doubt, since so many of the descriptions of the scenery in the poem correspond almost exactly with natural features in the neighbourhood that it is difficult to envisage that it could have been written by anyone other than a poet with an intimate knowledge of the local landscape. The cliffs, for instance, are called "the rocheres" - The Roaches," "the flosche", which refers to a marshy spot, can be no other place than Flash, and the mysterious "'Green Chapel", the forbidding cleft in the rock where the tale reaches its climax, is definitely Lud's Church in the valley of the River Dane.

The other side of the valley leads to Gradbach. Early spellings of the place are lacking, but it might designate a great, that is to say a wide stream valley, lying as it does on the junction of Black Brook and the River Dane. At the local assizes of 1413/1414 appearances are made by Adam de Gratebach of Leek and William Gretebache of Bramshall. The later forms are invariably Greatbach or Greatbatch; 1695:Churchwarden's accounts for Stoke-on-Trent - *"Paid to Thomas Greatbatch for building ye fframes and clockcase, mending ye church pules (pews) and makeing a safeguard in ye bellhouse from ye clock stones, and for mending Ffowley Bridge which appears by note and ffor shutts (shutters) to ye steeple windows £7.5s.6d"*; 1851:Daniel Greatbach (engraver) of Penkhull; 1851:Mark Greatbatch (licensee) of the Windmill, Werrington.

The second half of Gradbach, Old English "baece" - "stream, valley", is also the final constituent of Humpage Green near Wootton, Eccleshall, found as "Huntenebache", etc, in the Middle Ages - "valley or stream of the hunters". In 1281 Hugh de Hakedon (the modern Acton Hill, south of Eccleshall), and William de Bredelegh were charged with having unjustly dispossesed Lucy the wife of Reginald de Huntenbach and Avice the wife of William de Horseleye of four acres of land in Hakedon. In the Eccleshall parish registers both variants turn up as surnames; 1601:Symon Huntbatch; 1602:Anne Humpage. Trade directories list; 1887:Joseph Huntbach (draper), Tontine Square, Hanley; 1907:Thomas Humpage (collier), Prospect Terrace, Newcastle under Lyme.

Another compound - Comberbach/Cumberbach/Cumberbatch/Cumberbirch and Cumberburch - is traceable to Comberbach near Northwich, Cheshire - "stream or valley of the Welshmen"; 1636:Margaret Cumberbatch of Stoke-on-Trent, married to James Percy; 1875:William Cumberbach (grocer), Vale Pleasant, Silverdale; 1907:Elisha Cumberbatch (cashier), Clyde Street, Fenton. Other sources on the periphery are "Comberbach" (1570) in Rugeley and Cumberbatch in Crich, Derbyshire, but "Cumberberches" (1690) and "Comberbaches" (1794) in Helsby, east of Ellesmere Port, Cheshire, were named after Roger Comberbach, recorder of Chester in 1719.

"Bache", when used alone, is the basis of the surname Bach(e)/Batch; 1298:John atte bache of Betley, who dwelt by a stream or close to some valley. However, during the Middle Ages, this same word had a side form "bece", often written as "beche" and thus easily confused with "beche" - "beech tree". Hence an example like John del beche of

Alstonefield, tenant on the Audley estates in 1307, is ambiguous and could denote residence by some beech tree or near some stream or valley. The same applies to the locality Beech near Swynnerton in the Hanchurch Hills, recorded as "Beche" in 1240. It is usually explained as a settlement by a beech tree, but the locality is situated in a steep valley running into a hillside, and the root could just as well be "bece" in the side form "beche". Trade directories list; 1851:Joseph Bache (dispenser), Stafford Infirmary; 1907:Henry Bache (lodgekeeper), Newcastle Road, Hanley; 1887:Eliza Beech (stationer), Navigation Road, Burslem; 1887:William Beech (joiner), Greengates Street, Tunstall.

Families of Welsh descent bearing names such as Bach(e)/Batch/Beach/Beech derive from "'bach'" - "little", whilst the rare Bash/Baish is from "basch", another side form of "bache"; 1199 Assizes:Robert de basche (no locality specified) - "dweller by the stream or valley".

South of Gradbach lie Roach End, Roche Grange and The Roaches, all of which contain the Middle English "roche'" - "rock", ultimately from Old French. The surname Roach/Roch(e) signifies a person whose dwelling was near to some prominent rock in the vicinity; 1336:Robert de la roche of Creighton near Uttoxeter; 1539 Muster:Thomas and John Roche, enlisted at Bishton near Colwich; 1912:W. Roach (draper), Borough Market, Stoke-on-Trent. The imported name Roach/Roch(e) was probably brought by immigrants from Les Roches in Normandy and this goes for the surname Rochelle/Rotchell/Rockel too - dweller by some small rock, or from La Rochelle in Aquitaine, originally "Rupella'" - "little cave"; 1851:Hannah Rochell (shopkeeper), Tontine Street, Hanley; 1875:Emma Rochell (owner of an eating house), Market Street, Longton.

The curious surname Brownsword has baffled experts and laymen alike for many years and a number of theories have been put forward as to its derivation, all well wide of the mark. In his *Dictionary*, Canon Bardsley quotes several entries from the Prestbury Church register in Cheshire, variously spelt Brownsworth(e) and Brownsorde, and ascribes the surname to an unknown placename Brownsworth or Brownsward, possibly meaning "broom-covered sward". This is 'cloud cuckoo land'. In Earwaker's *History of East Cheshire*, John Brownsword is mentioned as headmaster of Macclesfield Grammar School in 1561, and Randle and Ellen Brownsword are resident in Eaton near Congleton in the latter part of the sixteenth century. Earwaker, alas, does not concern himself with surname origins. The real origin of the name lies in our own county, in the locality known as Brownsett near Roche Grange, found as "Brownsett" on the 1840 Ordnance Survey map. The place is recorded in a bewildering array of forms in the Leek parish registers during the 1600s, ranging from Brownsford, Bromsott, Braunsott, Brounsote to Brownsort and eventually to Brownsword. In the Stoke-on-Trent parish registers, Radulph Brownsword (1633), also occurs as Randolph Bromsford in 1636, and is buried as Randolph Brownsord in 1675. The spellings of the actual placename Brownsett are very late and any attempt at an accurate etymology is sure to be pure guesswork, although the form "Brownsford'" of 1634 certainly infers "Brun's ford". Both Brownsett and Brownsword occur with great

LOCAL
BILLHEADS
WITH NAMES
FROM THIS
SECTION

regularity right across North Staffordshire from the Reformation onwards. The churchwarden's accounts for Stoke-on-Trent for the year 1657 relate that Randall Brownsword was paid 14 shillings and six pence for helping Roger Tams to carry out the pointing work to the church and the steeple. In 1870, Joseph Brownsett, a collier of Brown Edge, had a daughter named Mary Ann baptized on Boxing Day at the local miners' chapel; 1875:Jane Brownsword (dressmaker), Lord Street, Etruria.

The Scandinavian influence in this zone is manifest in the ancient market town of Leek, which comes from an Old Norse word "loekr" meaning a brook. Two small tributaries of the River Churnet rise near the summit of the hill on which the original settlement was founded, making it a more practicable site than neighbouring hilltops. Sharing the same derivation as our local Leek are Leake near Boston, Lincolnshire, East and West Leake north of Loughborough, and Leake north east of Thirsk in north Yorkshire. All five locatives are probably implicated in modern surnames such as Leak, Leake and Leek(e); Wolstanton parish registers, 1806:William Leek, aged 38 years, who, according to the coroner's warrant, being lunatic, hung himself; 1851:Elisha Leak (saddler), Church Street, Longton; 1851:Richard Leek (mason), Smallthorne; 1875:William Leake (builder and grocer), Elizabeth Street, Hanley. In certain cases,the modern surnames may go back to an occupational name for a grower or seller of leeks. In addition, since the town is affectionately known by locals as "Leyk", this raises the possibility that the surnames Leek and Lake in North Staffordshire may occasionally be variants of the same name. There is no absolute proof, but in the parish registers for Lapley near Wheaton Aston, Edward Leeke (1576) is entered as Edward Leike a year later. Normally the surname Lake(s) denotes habitation by some stream, water course or lake, as typified by John atte lake, taxed at Penkhull in 1327; 1907:James Lake (engine driver), Lovatt Street, Stoke; 1887:Samuel Lake (local agent for Ind Coope and Co. Breweries), Glebe Street, Stoke.

On the eastern boundary of Leek is Cartledge, just north of Kniveden. A Staffordshire deed, dated 1284, gives details of land in "Cartelage" by Kniveden, granted to the Abbot of Dieulacres Abbey by Robert son of Ralph de le gygt. In his *History of Leek*, Sleigh defines this as Cartledge Brook, also known as "Lodebroc", which flows down between Easing and Colts Moor, turns off by Edge and through Tittesworth Hollow into the River Churnet between Hareyate (Haregate) and Hillswood, near Tittesworth Reservoir. The initial component of Cartledge is apparently a Saxon word "ceart", pronounced "chart" - "rocky or stony ground", which has been replaced by Old Norse "kartr", hence the place means "a boggy stream flowing through stony terrain," because the terminal is the Saxon "laec", Middle English "lache, leche" - "stream", a word probably akin to the Old Norse "loekr", inherent in Leek. From this insignificant spot has emanated many a local family called Cartledge/Cartlidge/Cartlich, but the surname is far too endemic to have sprung from this single locality, and other origins must be examined, chief amongst which are three places in Derbyshire - Cartledge on the outskirts of Holmesfield, Cartlidge in Edale in the High Peaks, and Cartledge Wood in Mellor. The Cheshire possibilities which cry out for attention are "Cartelache" (circa 1301) in Macclesfield, a place called "'Cartelache hurst" (1363) in Poynton with Worth, Cartleach in Marple, Cartledge in Norbury, "Cartelache" (1301) in Alsager, Cartledge Field near Knutsford and "Cartlache Moss" (1503) in Cuddington. Some of these, however, may have acquired their names from previous owners called Cartledge. In a deposition respecting the ancient township of the manor of Norton in the Moors, dated 1498, there are fourteen seals affixed at the foot of the document, one of which belongs to a certain Stevyn Cartelage. In the 1539 muster roll, some relative of his, Thomas Cartlech, enlists in the local militia at the same township. 1875:Theophilus Cartlidge (nursery gardener, seedsman and fruiterer), Finney Gardens, Bucknall and Broad Street, Hanley; 1907:George Cartlidge, restaurant proprietor at an establishment in Liverpool Road, Burslem, licensed for music and billiards.

Two miles south west of Cartledge lies Cumberledge Park, not far from the Caldon Canal at Denford. In the 1781 Land Tax returns for Cheddleton, James Tomkinson occupied land in "Cummerlidge", owned by Mrs Hollins. The ending of this locality is most likely that seen in Cartledge, but the first syllable is obscure. It is obviously at the root of the surname Cumberledge/Cumberlidge. Cumberlidge in Eckington near Dronfield, Derbyshire, where George Cumberlidge lived in 1714, is perhaps a red herring, and need not detain us any longer. The wedding of John Cumberlidg (sic) and Maria Clewley was celebrated at Swynnerton on May 26th 1705. 1851:William Cumberlidge (cow keeper), Buxton Road, Leek; 1875:Maria Cumberlidge (tripe dresser) of Rathbone Street, Tunstall.

Finney Lane, east of Cheddleton Heath, home of Philip del fyneye (1320), is the focal point of a high proportion of the local Finneys/Fynneys. The location could refer to a water meadow, where coarse grass flourished. By the end of the seventeenth century the surname is also making inroads around Stafford, Stone and Betley, and here, in the north western sector of the county, bordering on Cheshire, immigrant families bearing the name Finney/Fynney could well have brought it from Finney in Weaverham, Finney in Mobberley, Big Finney, Long Finney, Square Finney and Gawsey Finney (all in Smallwood), Finney near Kingsley, and so on. However, Finney Green near Wilmslow takes its name from John Finney, who married the heiress of the Wittonstall family in 1608, and this must be discredited as a possible source. The local Finney Green near Leycett is also doubtful for the time being. The Lancashire involvement centres around Finney near Croston, five miles south of Preston. Amongst those summoned to the Court of Star Chamber in 1547 was William Fynney of Cheddleton, who was accused, together with other local inhabitants, of causing an affray and cutting down hedges in Cheddleton Park. 1851:George Finney (shopkeeper), Meir Heath; 1851:Mary Finney (licensee), 'Admiral Jervis', Oakamoor.

The surname Beresford/Berisford/Berresford/Berrisford is generally accepted as being from Beresford near Alstonefield - "the beaver's ford" - a crossing of the River Dove in the north eastern sector of the detached portion of Fawfieldhead. Indeed, Beresford was the home of the Beresford family by at least 1232, when John de Beresford was paying 8 shillings a year to John Fitzherbert for an estate there. But also essential to our quest is Basford Green near Cheddleton, which boasts the spelling "Berrisford" in 1612. In the Middle Ages this locality occurs as "Barclesford" - "Beorcol's ford". The forms Basford and Beresford are frequently used of the same person, as in the Ellastone parish registers, where John Basford is also written down as John Berisford in 1668. It is uncertain whether Basford near Newcastle under Lyme is implicated in the modern surnames, although Basford (Hall) near Crewe is feasible. Basford in Nottinghamshire can probably be eliminated from the enquiry since the place is pronounced "Baseford". In 1838, two orphans at Brown Edge, James Berrisford, aged 7 and his sister Elizabeth, aged 4, were allowed 5 shillings per week from the Guardians of the Poor; 1887:Alice Beresford (grocer), Albert Place, Hanley. The name is often converted into Barisford; 1563:Mathew Berysford of Ford, near Grindon, who crops up as Mathew Barisford in 1583. This then loses the medial "s", as in 1539 Muster Roll:John Baryford of Tixall. In the Wolstanton parish registers, Baryford finally crystallizes into Brayford; 1789:John Brayford, 1795:Mary Baryford, with the common shift of "r"; 1851:Daniel Brayford (maltster), Trent Vale; 1875:Charles Brayford (shoemaker), Keele.

Oldfield is basically a toponymic for a dweller by some ancient open stretch of land or cultivated ground, but in North Staffordshire the name could also go back to such locatives as Oldfield just north of Basford Green, Cheddleton, Oldfield near Waterfall and Oldfield near Whiston not far from the old copper works (both the latter appear on the 1836 Ordnance Survey map). On June 4th 1611, the burial took place of one Anne Ouldfeild, *a poore lame begger* (sic) at Stowe by Chartley; 1851:Thomas Oldfield (proprietor), Red Lion, Goldenhill. In the Penkridge parish registers, Edward Oldfield of Stretton (1632), appears as Edward Owefeild in 1639. With the addition of initial "h" this gives the modern surname Howfield, but also relevant here is a fieldname like "Howfeild alias Howfeld" (1611) in Holbrook near Duffield, Derbyshire - "open land by a hill".

Bromfield/Broomfield and Brumfield usually designate a person who resided by some broom-covered open land, but this same notion is conveyed by locatives like Great Broomfield in Castlechurch, "le bromfeld" (1441) in Brewood, Bromfield near Ludlow, Shropshire, and Bromfield, west of Wigton, Cumberland. These are the major sources of the surnames in North Staffordshire; 1875:John Bromfield (milk seller), High Street, Tunstall; 1907:Joseph Bromfield (miner), Park Street, Fenton; 1907:John Broomfield (engineman), Wood Street, Stoke. Richard Bromfield, curate of Stoke-on-Trent in 1631, is alternatively quoted as Richard Brounfield in 1625, hence the variant Brownfield; 1851:George Brownfield (market inspector) of Hanley.

The prominent location of the "field" is to the fore in Highfield, Heafield; 1851:Thomas Highfield (grocer and tea dealer), Red Lion Square, Newcastle under Lyme; 1887:Charles Highfield (licensed victualler), Artillery Arms, Etruria Road, Hanley. Yet there is inevitable conflict with Hayfield, which is applied to residence by open land where

St Edwards Church, Leek, early 1800s

The Abbey Inn, Leek, 1800s

Biddulph Old Hall

haymaking was carried out; 1677:Thomas Heifield of Standon (1697:Thomas Highfield). Caulfield and Corfield are open to doubt, but are perhaps for a dweller by a cold (exposed) stretch of open land, based on a doublet like Cauldwell-Cordwell, q.v. 1851:John Corfield (boot and shoe maker), Waterloo Road, Burslem; 1907:James Caulfield of Bright Street, Fenton. On the other hand, Brookfield is simply for a dweller by the field near a brook; 1875:Edward Brookfield (boot and shoe manufacturer), Market Street, Longton and Taylor Street, Dresden. Lichfield, with its cathedral of three spires - "The Ladies of the Vale" - gets its name from the Roman garrison of Letocetum, sited at Wall one mile to the south west on Watling Street. It is a Celtic word, meaning "grey wood", and only later was the ending "field" attached, hence "open land near a grey wood". The surname derived from the place invariably gains an extra "t" in the middle; 1851:William Litchfield (seedsman), High Street, Longton; 1875:Henry Litchfield (crate maker), Fenton Park, Fenton.

Longsdon, which was once part of Leek parish, was divided into two parts - Over Longsdon and Nether Longsdon - and was named after its situation on a long hill. In 1252 it was held by James de Audley. The place shares similar early spellings with Great and Little Longstone north of Bakewell, but Nether Longsdon on its own occurs as "Longson" in 1615, thus supplying us with the modern surname Longson; 1532:Agnes Longysdon syngull woman of Warslow; 1887:John Longson (silk mercer), St. John's Square, Burslem; 1907:William Longson (grocer), Wolseley Road, Stoke.

Four miles west of Longsdon is Cowall, south of Crowborough not far from the head of the Trent. In the Tunstall manor court rolls (1348-1369) the locality occurs as "Couhale, Cowale, Kowale, Couwale" and so on, and probably refers to a cow nook, that is a sheltered spot where cattle grazed. This develops naturally enough into Cowall/Cowell. The Gentleman's Magazine of April, 1811, states that on a plain tomb at the west end of the north aisle near the entrance door of the church at Wolstanton, there used to be an inscription "Here lyeth the bodies of John Cowell, sometime of this parish, yeoman, and Christabell his wife....."; 1907:William Cowell (signalman), Carlton Road, Shelton, Hanley. Another variation is Cool(e); 1525:Ralph Coole of Tunstall, but this is probably a local form of Cole, mimicking the local pronunciation "cool" for "coal". Normally names like Cole(s)/Cowles/Coales are to be traced to two personal names, depending on whether they were introduced by the Saxons - "Cola" - or by the Scandinavians - "Koli". In an inquisition, made at Stafford on Sunday next after the Feast of St. Margaret the Virgin (July 20th) 1298, concerning the lands and tenements belonging to Edmund, Earl of Lancaster, in Newcastle under Lyme, John Cole is paying an annual rent of eight pence for holding a cottage at Shelton. Trade directories list; 1887:Samuel Cole (glass manufacturer), Norfolk Street, Hanley; 1907:Arthur Coles (tailor's cutter), Hamil Road, Burslem.

Adam de Fernihaleugh, assessed at twenty one pence in the lower band of taxpayers at Endon in 1327, is entered by the tax collectors on the 1332 rolls as Adam de Fernyhough. The place where Adam originated is noted on the 1836 Ordnance Survey map for the county as Fernyhough, adjacent to Sandy Lane, Brown Edge, a mile or so south of

Cowall. It alludes to "a fern-covered nook", but evidently it has been expunged from modern maps. Be that as it may, this small locality is behind one of the most distinctive of all north Staffordshire surnames - Fernyhough/Ferneyhough/Fernihough.   One Fernyhough who carved out an illustrious career for himself was John Fernyhough, who was servant to the right worshipful Ralph Sneyd esquire in 1610, and, as a result of the good opinion the town had of him, he was freely given his burgess rights at Newcastle under Lyme in the same year. He served in four of the minor offices, including bailiff and receiver, and was elected mayor on two occasions, in 1621 and in 1629. At Leek, Thomas Fernyhough was town crier there at the time of his death in 1742; 1851:Josiah Fernihough, Navigation Inn, Frog Hall; 1907:George Fernyhough (car driver), Park Lane, Fenton. If the name arrived here from Cheshire, then there is a lost "Fernihalgh" in Macclesfield Hundred to be taken into account. Lancashire families bearing the name may have ancestry in Fernyhalgh in Preston parish, whilst the Derbyshire connection boils down to Fernyhough in Charlesworth, Fernyhough in Ludworth, Fernyhough in Brampton near Chesterfield and Fernyhough Close in Biggin near Idridgehay. Now and then there is some interplay between Fernihough and Fernihall, as in Milwich parish registers; 1603:Ales Fernihall (1617:Alice Fernialgh vidua (widow)).   These should be taken with Birchen(h)all-Birchen(h)ough; Bucknall cum Bagnall parish registers, 1792:Thomas Birchenuff of Stoke parish, who signs his name as Thomas Burchenell. This is possibly from Birchenough in Mellor in the Derbyshire High Peaks - "birchen nook", "nook overgrown with birches". In 1805 John Birchenhough was one of the witnesses to the registration of a meeting house for Wesleyans at Brown Edge.

Woodland

If there is one theme which permeates North Staffordshire nomenclature it is the immense corpus of surnames connected with woodland. Of this vast mass of names Bradshaw is undeniably in the vanguard, for it occurs in great profusion at all periods, especially around Cheddleton, Endon and Ipstones. No wonder, really, because it radiates outwards from three distinct spots - Bradshaw near Hollinsclough Moor, Bradshaw in Ipstones and Bradshaw (Farm) in Endon parish. All places refer to a broad copse, thicket or grove. An estate existed at Bradshaw Farm by 1371, when Roger of Bradshaw issued a charter there. William Bradshaw was the sacristan at the religious house of Augustinian canons at Stone in 1518, and in 1793 Moses Bradshaw of Endon was sent to the House of Correction at Stafford "for getting Sarah Hollinshead with child and a bastard to be charged on the Poor Law". In 1851 Teresa Bradshaw was the proprietor of the Golden Lion in Market Square, Longton. One Bradshaw who brought everlasting disgrace to the family name was the lawyer and regicide John Bradshaw, sometime resident at Greenway Hall, a mansion and estate in the immediate neighbourhood of Hulton Abbey. He was actually a native of Marple near Stockport but he was Recorder at Newcastle under Lyme in 1656. Seven years earlier he had been President of the Court which had tried and sentenced Charles I to death.

John himself died a natural death - about six months before the Restoration, when his bones were dug up and suspended at Tyburn! The compound Blackshaw is either a toponymic for habitation by a black wood, or from Blackshaw Moor near Tittesworth, but there is a fieldname in Penkridge recorded as "le blakes(c)hawe" (1467, 1505), which might also have given rise to the surname. In 1877 Thomas Blackshaw, a local chemist, was amongst the list of nominees put forward as trustees for the Wesleyan Chapel at Sandy Lane, Brown Edge; 1851:George Blackshaw (baker and flour dealer) of Old Hall Street, Hanley; 1875:Edward Blackshaw (wheelwright) of Chell.

Longshaw designates residence by a long wood or comes from Longshaw near Bradnop or Longshaw south of Ramshorn Common; 1875:Charles Longshaw (grocer and confectioner), Cannon Street, Hanley; 1875:George Longshaw (tobacconist), Piccadilly, Tunstall. The self-explanatory Smallshaw most likely goes back to Smallshaw south of Flash; 1907:James Smallshaw (electrician) of Heron Street, Fenton.

Hurst and Hirst signify a dweller by a wood or wooded hill, as in Adam del hurst, taxed at Cheddleton in 1327, or derive from some locality such as Hurst near Biddulph Grange. Spellings containing "u" are the norm; 1907:David Hurst (wardrobe dealer), Caroline Street, Longton; 1907:Thomas Hurst, publican at the Stag and Peasant, Regent Street, Hanley. One origin of Blackhurst may be a place recorded as "Blakehurst" between Horsley and Bishop's Offley in the Bishop of Lichfield's Survey, dated 1298. It means "black wooded hill," or "dark wood", but also acceptable is a toponymic for a dweller by such a landmark; 1875:Richard Blackhurst (earthenware manufacturer), High Street, Tunstall; 1875:John Blackhurst (builder), Newcastle Street, Burslem.

Hazelhurst/Hazlehurst/Haslehurst is mainly derived from Hazelhurst west of Cumberledge Park - "hazel wood" or "hazel copse", but, again a subsidiary source is a topographical name for a person who resided by such a feature; 1851:Samuel Haslehurst (hairdresser), Liverpool Road, Stoke; 1907:George Hazelhurst (waggoner), Princes Square, Longport.

Birchall near Leek - "Bircholt" (13th century) - "birch wood" - lies at the heart of a whole string of complex surnames. Of course, there are the easily recognisable Birchall, Birchill, Burchell and Burchill; 1466:John Berchill hosteller of Stafford; 1666:William Burchall of Betley; 1851:William Burchall (Birchall) (fruit, vegetable and potato dealer), Marsh Street, Hanley; 1875:Thomas Birchall (farmer) of Talke. With shift of the letter "r" we arrive at forms such as Brichill/Brichell and Britchell; 1337:Robert de Birchull of Barlaston, noted as Robert de Brichull in 1336. On the analogy of Tunstall-Tunster, it was simply weakened to Bircher or Burcher; 1614:Richard Bircher of Betley; but here other origins must be scrutinised, including Birchall Bridge near Hankelow, Cheshire, Birchover south of Haddon Hall, Derbyshire, which is pronounced as "Bircher", or Burcher in Titley, Herefordshire, all denoting a ridge overgrown with birch trees. Another line of

Leek Parish Register
1834

1634-5]   *Leek.*   9

1634-5, Sept. 18.	Marg. Brinley, of Leeke, spinster	..	bur.
,, Sept. 20.	Anne f. Humphrey & Clarice Ride-		
	hurst, of Oncott	..	bap.
,, Sept. 21.	W. f. W. & Eleanor Smyth, of Cowhay		bap.
,, Sept. 21.	John Redfearne, of Leeke, infant	..	bur.
,, Oct. 2.	Catherine, wife of Henry Brockwell,		
	of Leek	..	bur.
,, Oct. 3.	W. Nicholas, of Tetisworth..	..	bur.
,, Oct. 4.	Mary f. Joseph & Marg. Tomkinson,		
	of Leek	..	bap.
,, Oct. 4.	Eliz. f. W. & Eliz. Rowley, of Bale-		
	fields	..	bap.
,, Oct. 4.	John f. Lionel & Eliz. Harrison, of		
	Parklane	..	bap.
,, Oct. 6.	Richard Clulow & Alice Brinley	..	mar.
,, Oct. 9.	Tho. Royle & Joan Robinson	..	mar.
,, Oct. 11.	Rich. f. Rich. & Anne Smyth, of		
	Knivedon	..	bap.
,, Oct. 15.	Tho. f. Hugo & Dorothy Nixon, of		
	Frith	..	bap.
,, Oct. 17.	Dorothy f. Simon & Marg. Preston,		
	of Leeke	..	bur.
,, Oct. 18.	Henry Pette & Jane Tracy..	..	mar.
,, Oct. 18.	Tho. f. Tho. & Marg. Plant..	..	bap.
,, Oct. 20.	John Tomson	..	
,, Oct. 23.	Tho. Ireland, of Leeke	..	
,, Oct. 28.	Joan Rattcliffe, of Bradnop, wid		
,, Oct. 28.	Eliz. f. Edmund & Alice Brough		
	Waterhouse	..	
,, Nov. 1.	W. Plant, of Low, sen.	..	
,, Nov. 1.	Ellen f. W. & Joan Wardle, of Lee		
,, Nov. 3.	Sarah Willet, of Mill Street..		
,, Nov. 3.	Widow Anne Ainsworth, of Beme		
,, Nov. 8.	Robt. f. Rich. & Alice Daine, of		
,, Nov. 9.	John Norbury, of Hillilees ..		
,, Nov. 13.	Robt. Ffisher, of Barneford		
,, Nov. 15.	Joan Cuncliffe, of Leeke, widow		
,, Nov. 22.	Isabel f. Ed. & Alice Craddock		
	Leeke	..	..

development became Birtles via Birkle/Birkel, which, in turn, with shift of the "r", ended up as Brickell/Brickle(s), as in The Brickhills near Adbaston, identified as "The Birtles" on nineteenth century maps; 1851:Mary Ann Birtles (milliner), Custard Street, Leek; 1875:Henry Birtles (hay and straw dealer), Albert Street, Burslem; 1887:William Brickel (stationer and bookseller), Market Place, Longton. The surname Birtles is also traceable to Birtles in Prestbury near Macclesfield, or The Birtles in Cholmondeley, both of which preserve the Saxon "bircel" - "little birch tree".

Among the earliest settlements in the wooded countryside in the parish of Leek were the granges in the township of Leek Frith, established by the Cistercian monks at Dieulacres Abbey. The "Frith" element alludes to an original tract of woodland and it occurs in Chapel en le Frith and Duffield Frith (both in Derbyshire). This word has given us the modern surname Frith or Firth as it often becomes. Leek Frith itself is found as "The Fyrthe" in 1532. At Betley during the eighteenth century many children of pauper parents were assigned to employers as parish apprentices. Under one such scheme Elizabeth and Ann Frith were bound out to Samuel Hall in 1737 to learn "the Art and Mystery of Housewifery". Other modifications of the surname include; 1633:John Freake of Stafford; 1912:Charles Freeth of Caverswall Lane, Blythe Bridge, besides the more regular Frith: 1851:James Frith (mason and quarry owner) of Stanton.

As early as 1246 Dieulacres Abbey had established a grange at Westwood near Leek, where the monks undertook arable farming. The place apparently got its name simply because it was situated west of Leek. Fortune Westwood married Richard Meate at Wolstanton on October 28th 1666; 1875:William Westwood (bootmaker), London Road, Stoke. Its exact opposite is an invader from Eastwood (Todmorden), flanking the Pennine Way, Eastwood near Southend on Sea (both for the eastern wood), Eastwood near Nottingham, birthplace of D.H. Lawrence - eastern thwaite (meadow), or for someone who set up home east of some wood or other; 1907:Robert Eastwood (motor man), Clarence Street, Stoke; 1907:Mrs Ann Eastwood, Etruria Road, Hanley.

Staffordshire families bearing the surname Lockwood have a lineage going back to Lockwood near Kingsley Holt or Lockwood in the ancient parish of Almondbury, Huddersfield, both meaning an enclosed wood; 1327:Alice de Locwode of Ellastone; 1912:P. Lockwood, Hillside, St. Edmund's Avenue, Wolstanton. Nicholas de Blacwode, tenant on the Audley estates at Horton near Rudyard in 1298, lives on in the surname Blackwood and the locality Blackwood Hill near Gratton - "black(dark) wood"; 1907:John Blackwood (pawnbroker and clothier), Parliament Row, Hanley. Dunwood, south east of Blackwood Hill, is perhaps identical in meaning with Downwood in Herefordshire - "wood on a hill", and thus could well be the origin of Downwood and Downward with the common interchange in the terminal, also exhibited by Brewood-Breward, south of Watling Street - "wood on a hill". Here the initial part "bre" is from a Celtic word; 1907:Frederick Downward (labourer), Station Street, Longport; 1907:Herbert Downwood (labourer), Garner Street, Stoke; 1434:John Brewood of Standon; 1875:Joseph Breward (grocer), Wood Street, Longton.

During the seventeenth century the surname Underwood is fairly numerous around Standon, Swynnerton, Yarnfield, Chebsey, Millmeece and Eccleshall and refers either to a dweller below a wood on a hillside or within a wood (probably for shelter); 1327:Richard Underwode of Kibblestone. During the Tudor and Stuart periods it was usually the gentry who were responsible for transacting land deals, but during the early days of the reign of James I, two men of yeoman stock, natives of Oulton near Kibblestone, namely Thomas Hall and Thomas Underwood, were concerned in one such land deal, where Thomas Hall remitted all rights to Thomas Underwood of a messuage, a cottage, ten acres of land, two acres of meadow and twenty acres of pasture in Oulton, for which Underwood gave Hall 41 pounds; 1851:Henry Underwood (stationmaster) at Norton Bridge; 1875:John Underwood (grocer), Gilbert Street, Kidsgrove.

The rare Inwood relates to residence by the "in-wood", the home-wood, as opposed to the "out-wood"; 1907:Mrs E. Inwood, Seaford Street, Shelton.

Surnames in -ley

Easily the most widely diffused surname of this type in Zone 3 is Thorley (variants Thornley, Thorniley), traced primarily to Thornyleigh near Roche Grange - "clearing overgrown with thorn bushes". External sources comprise Thorny Lee in Chapel en le Frith, two locations in Cheshire - Thorley Lane in Ringway and "Thornleigh" (1353) in Dunham Massey, Thornley in Chipping parish, Lancashire, Thornley north west of Bishop Auckland, Durham. Less compelling are Thorley near Bishop's Stortsford, Hertfordshire and Thorley, Isle of Wight. Jokes Thorley was vicar at Biddulph in 1578; 1851:Emma Thorley, owner of a beerhouse in Bucknall Road, Hanley; 1887:Sarah Thornley (draper), Heathcote Street, Kidsgrove; 1851:William Thorley (wheelwright) of Caverswall.

The Hammersleys have a long and distinguished pedigree in the Cheddleton area, and trace their ancestry back to the locality known as "The Hammersleys", as stated on the 1781 Land Tax returns for the district (Basford Quarter), the proprietor being John Sneyd esquire and his tenant Joseph Tatton. Hammersley Hayes in Cheadle looks like a good second bet, although it could be named from some previous owner named Hammersley. The actual meaning of the place is vague, but it might be a clearing in a wood, used by a hammer-man (the local blacksmith). 1667:Thomas Hammersley granted to Quaker trustees a piece of land 20 yards in length and 10 yards in breadth on the west side of his garden at Basford (Cheddleton), for use as a burial ground; 1851:Isaac Hammersley (tailor), Gower Street, Longton; 1887:James Hammersley (yeast importer), Smith Street, Hanley; 1907:Frederick Hammersley (engraver), Woodhead Road, Birches Head.

The surname Stanley rivals both Thorley and Hammersley in its abundance. It is chiefly from Stanley -"clearing on stony ground" - a former township in Leek parish, but which was later incorporated into part of a civil parish that included Endon and Longsdon. Circa 1200, Adam de Audley, lord of Horton, gave Stanley to William, son of Adam de

Stanley, and the estate was handed down through the succeeding generations of Stanleys, until it was sold in 1660 by William Stanley to Thomas Fernyhough. Places called Stanley in other counties have also contributed towards the name's productiveness - Stanley near Ilkeston, Stanley near Wakefield, Stanley in the Severn Valley (Shropshire) and Stanley near Mansfield. In the same way that Hanley is often supplanted by Handley, so Stanley is frequently transformed into Standley; 1666:Josiah Standley, exempt from hearth tax at Stafford: 1841:James Stanley, dipper at Charles Meigh's Earthenware Factory, Bucknall Road, Hanley.

Moseley, plus variants Mosley, Mossley and Mousley are generally tracked down to Moseley, not far from Wolverhampton, "Moll's glade", Moseley north west of Worcester or Moseley near Balsall Heath (both probably meaning "glade infested by mice") and thus synonymous with Mowsley south of Leicester. Yet there is no reason to reject such localities as Moseley near Hollinsclough (of unknown origin), Mosslee Hall Farm south of Basford Green, Cheddleton (possibly "mossy glade"), Mossley in Greater Manchester, Mossley in Congleton and (Little) Mosseley in Odd Rode, all either for "mossy glade" or "glade infested with mice"; 1851:Edward Mousley (grocer and tea dealer), Market Square, Hanley; 1851:John Moseley (surgeon), Dogcroft, Norton in the Moors; 1851:George Mosley (corn miller), Cookshill, Caverswall.

By the later 1820s John Shirley of Rewlach in the Manifold Valley, south east of Fawfield Head, had a mill on Blakebrook and at the end of the nineteenth century Roland Shirley was farming land at Lower Stone House Farm at Brown Edge. In all probability both of these local gentlemen were descendants of someone whose roots lay in the village of Shirley near Foxt - "wood or glade which belonged to the shire" or "wood where the shire moot was convened". Less accessible origins comprise Shirley near Osmaston in Derbyshire, Shirley near Solihull and Shirley near Southampton; 1887:Elijah Shirley (spur and stilt maker), Moorland Road, Burslem. The first instance of its use as a christian name is the heroine of Charlotte Bronte's novel "Shirley" (1849), but its present vogue is attributable to the child film-star, Shirley Temple. It was also formerly used as a male christian name, as exemplified by Shirley Crabtree, real name of the wrestler Big Daddy.

Surnames in "-ton"

When we study in closer detail the surname Horton, we see once more the north-south divide in action, glimpsed in Bagnall, for in North Staffordshire the name goes back to the village of Horton near Rudyard, whereas south of Stafford the origin is generally Horton in Tamhorn. Both locations allude to an original hamlet built on muddy land, and consequently are identical in meaning with the myriads of other localities called Horton all over the country; 1851:Joseph Horton (chair maker) of New Street, Longton; 1875.Vyse Horton (greengrocer) of Bethesda Street, Hanley. Horton often fluctuates with Haughton; 1735:William Horton of Millmeece (1739:William Haughton). This is reminiscent of the couplet Norton-Naughton; Penkridge parish registers, 1617:George Norton; 1684:Richard

Naughton. Whenever Haughton is the pristine form; 1887:Enoch Haughton (licensee), Inkerman Inn, Broom Street, Hanley and the Traveller's Rest, Chell Heath, this is traceable to Haughton near Gnosall - "village by a nook of land or in a remote valley", or to any other place known as Haughton, especially Haughton Moss, north west of Nantwich, Haughton Green in Greater Manchester, or any of four locations in Shropshire, Haughton near Telford, Haughton north of Bridgnorth, Haughton north east of Shrewsbury or Haughton near Bagley. Haughton, in its turn, alternates with Houghton; 1599:Thomas Houghton of Wolgarston (1600:Thomas Haughton). Here we must consider places such as Little Houghton and Westhoughton in Greater Manchester and Great Houghton and Little Houghton east of Barnsley, which, oddly, share the same meaning as the Haughtons.

Gratton, south of Horton (Rudyard), "Grytton" - 1273, "Gerton otherwise Gratton" -1572, "Gretton" - 1608,"hamlet on gravelly terrain" - is doubtless the main source of our local Grattons/Grettons and Grittons. Sharing this same derivation are Gretton north of Corby, Gretton near Winchcombe, Gloucestershire, Girton north of Newark on Trent and Girton near Cambridge, but Gratton near Elton, Derbyshire means "great hill", whilst Gretton near Church Stretton, Shropshire, is obscure. At the inaugural welldressing ceremony at Endon in 1845, it is recounted that Thomas Gratton the tailor, along with Philip Rogers (shoemaker), Joshua Stubbs (carpenter) and Thomas Walker procured "homemade pikelets, soaked in butter, bread and butter, cured ham and other good things, a cup of tea with cream if desired and rum to celebrate the first "dressing"; 1851:George Gretton (schoolmaster and parish clerk), Stowe by Chartley; 1875:Maria Gritton (beerseller), Brownhills, Tunstall. Grattan is an Irish variant.

Villages and towns called Bolton are exceedingly commonplace in the north of England, encompassing the counties of Cumberland, Westmorland, Northumberland, Lancashire and the three Yorkshire Ridings. They all consist of an old Saxon "bothl" - "dwelling (place)", plus the familiar suffix "-ton", inferring that this was a name given to a village or estate that was the centre of a comparatively large settlement, in essence, the mother village, as opposed to the daughter settlements or outlying farms. Some of these localities, such as Bolton and Bolton le Sands in Lancashire, and Bolton near Bradford, Yorkshire, must be put under the microscope, when we are weighing up possible origins for the widespread North Staffordshire surname Bolton/Boulton. Yet there is a ready made solution right next door in the neighbouring county of Derbyshire - Boulton near Derby - "Bola's village". Indeed the surname often see-saws back and forth between the two forms, but nowadays the spelling Boulton far surpasses its companion Bolton. William Bolton, capital burgess at Newcastle under Lyme in 1619, is noted as William Boulton in 1625. Bolton Farm in Foxt and Bolton Gate near Weston Coyney are somewhat untrustworthy, for they may have acquired the prefix from some former owner named Bolton. In the aftermath of the Diglake Pit disaster on Monday, 14th January 1895, one of the rescuers recommended for his bravery for the Royal Humane Society award was John Boulton; 1851:James Bolton (fishmonger), Pall Mall, Hanley.

Heaton, too, is confined to the northern counties, but only Lancashire, Northumberland and Yorkshire play host this time. Each locality is situated on high ground, and this is a perfect description of Heaton near Rushton Spencer, which stands at 800 feet above sea level in millstone grit territory, and which is unquestionably the primary source of the local surname Heaton. In 1854 Charles Heaton owned the house and garden occupied by the incumbent of Endon parish, the Reverend Daniel Turner, for at that time Endon had no vicarage; 1875:Richard Heaton (solicitor), Brickhouse Street, Burslem. Just as Healey is prone to alternate with Hayley, so Heaton becomes Hayton; 1610 lawsuit:"Heyton otherwise Heaton otherwise Hayton"; 1588:Margaret Cooke alias Heyton of Rocester. On rare occasions the initial aspirate goes missing; 1571:Thomas Heaton otherwise Eyton of Cheddleton. Nevertheless, Eyton, along with Eaton and Eton are from Church and Wood Eaton, north of Wheaton Aston - "hamlet in an island or in land by a river" - or Water Eaton near Rodbaston - "farmstead by a river", in this case, the River Penk. Folklore tells of a witch, Joan Eaton, who was burned at the stake at some spot south west of Church Eaton, marked by the Joan Eaton Cross on modern maps; 1875:John Eaton (grocer), Navigation Road, Burslem.

There are two separate nominees for the origin of the surname Stockton in our county - Stockton Brook near Endon and Stockton in Baswich. The latter was a farmstead which once belonged to the Priory of St. Thomas - here the initial element is the Saxon "stoc" - a religious place. Whether Stockton Brook contains the same component is unclear. If it does, then it must have been owned by Dieulacres Abbey, but if not, it denotes here a farmstead built of logs. If the surname found its way here from other counties, then the sources include; Stockton near Malpas, Cheshire, three places in Shropshire - Stockton near Newport, Stockton south east of Ironbridge, Stockton about 10 miles west of the Long Mynd, plus Stockton on Teme in Worcestershire, Stockton on Tees, and Stockton on the Forest near York; 1875:Samuel Stockton (greengrocer), Waterloo Road, Burslem; Mary Stockton (grocer), Knutton.

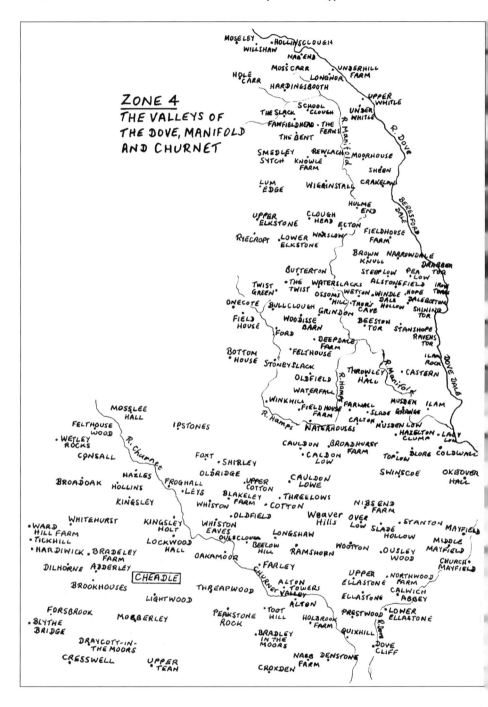

ZONE 4
THE VALLEYS OF
THE DOVE, MANIFOLD
AND CHURNET

Zone Four: The Dove, Manifold and Churnet Valleys

Blore/Bloor(e) 113
Blower(s)/Bloomer 113
Low(e) 115
Warrilow 115
Clewlow/Clewley 115
Critchlow/Critchley/
Crutchley/Cratchley 116
Torr/Tarr 116
Nabbs 116
Knobbs/Knibbs 116
Knapp(er)/Knapman 117
Napier 117
Peake 117
Pickin 117
Tootall 117
Wardle 117
Tickle/Tittle 117
Windle 117
Farnell 117
Fearns 118
Redfern 118
Banks/Fairbanks 118
Greatbanks 118
Firbank 118
Downe(s)/Downer 118
Hough/Huff 118
How(e) 119
Hulse 119
Side 119
Stiles 119
Steele 119
Wint/Went 119
Edge/Liversedge 119
Dunnicliff/Tunnicliffe 120
Ratcliffe 120
Cunliffe/Condlyffe 121
Getliffe 121
Cragg/Craig 121
Combridge 121
Brownsill/Brownbill 121
Stone(s)/Stonehouse 122
Kings(t)on 122
Ellison/Elson 122
Snelson 122
Denson/Densem 124
Brans(t)on 124

Guns(t)on 124
Featherstone/Fatherston 124
Pixton/Pickstone 124
Buxton 125
Axon 125
Clough/Cluff/
Clowes/Clews 126
Fairclough 126
Barrowclough 126
Hope 126
Stanshope 127
Alsop 127
Glossop 127
Lindop 127
Millichip 127
Harrop 128
Cowpe/Cope 128
Bottom(s)/Botham 128
Bottomer 128
Higginbottom 128
Shufflebottom 130
Rowbottom 130
Sidebottom 130
Longbottom 130
Winterbottom 130
Dale 131
Udall/Yewdall 131
Ravensdale/Ransdale/
Ramsdale 131
Slack 131
Gill/Gilson 132
Wray/Wroe/Ray/Rea 132
Winkle/Wintle 132
Dingle 132
Dell 132
Slade/Greenslade 132
Combs/Comber 132
Manifold 133
Blythe 133
Waterfall 133
Waterhouse 133
Water(s) 133
Attwater 133
Bywater(s) 133
Twiss/Twist 134
Hol(e)brook 134

Forsbrook 134
Cauldwell/Calder/Caldwell 134
Farrell 135
Fowell/Fower 135
Sitch/Sykes 135
Moor(e)/Morse/Mower 135
Dillamore 136
Morland 136
Moorhouse/Morris 136
Moorcroft 136
Morrall 136
Morrey/Murray 136
Beardmore 137
Barnes 137
Latham 137
Boothman/Booth 137
Scholes/Scales 137
Whitehurst/Whitehouse 138
Broadhurst 138
Greenwood 138
Prestwood 138
Woodhouse 138
Widdows 138
Wiltshire/Wilshaw 138
Swinscoe 140
Cheadle/Cheatle 140
Checkley 140
Farley 140
Loxley/Lockley 140
Mobberley/Mabberley/
Mabley 141
Housley/Ousley 141
Woolley 141
Newton 142
Middleton 142
Overton/Orton 142
Creighton/Crichton 142
Pointon/Pountain/Painting 142
Alton 143
Whiston 144
Cotton/Cottam 144
Wootton 144
Stanton 144
Wetton 145
Beeston/Beeson 145
Clifton 145

Zone Four

If the overriding theme of our investigation so far has been the profusion of surnames connected with woodland, then we are now entering an altogether different and exciting phase in north eastern Staffordshire. For now we find ourselves in a realm dominated by hills and crags, valleys, brooks and streams, panoramic views over wild moorland, interspersed with lush meadows, but above all, wide open spaces with a scattered population living out their lives in isolated farms and compact hamlets, a scene that would not have looked out of place in the Middle Ages.

Indeed, it is this very isolation and separateness from those far off days, which are fundamental to any real understanding of the variety and uniqueness of the surnames in this particular region. Hill names highlight this individuality only too well. Blore, for example. One source of the surname Bloor(e), Blore, lies in a remote locality north of Swinscoe and west of Dovedale. Its very name betrays its seclusion, for it is from an unrecorded Saxon word "blor", identical in meaning with a later "blure, bloure" -"blister, swelling", used here in the topographical sense of "hill", because of its exposed, remote situation. Compare the place Blurton. In 1532 there are families called Blore well established around Blore itself, Ilam and Waterfall. Yet the surname is also common at the same time on the opposite side of the county, in Madeley, Betley, Audley and Newcastle under Lyme,and here the origin is Blore south of Mucklestone, which shares the same meaning as its namesake in the north east. It was at the Battle of Blore Heath in 1459 that James Touchet, the 7th Baron Audley, commanded the Lancastrians against the Yorkists, and was mortally wounded. The records of the Guardians of Leek union for 1838 show that Jane Bloor, aged 36, born at Leek, married with five children, and described as a washer and with a husband in prison, was allowed twenty pounds of bread. 1907:William Bloor (clogger), Normacot Road, Longton.

In the seventeenth century both places are spelt as "Blower" in local parish registers, and are thus the major source of the surname Blower(s); John Blore, enrolled in the Audley militia in 1539, is taxed at Audley as John Blower in 1563. The "Blore-Blower" interchange parallels "four-fower" in the dialect. In other counties Blower(s) is either an allusion to a worker who blew the bellows in a bloomery (smelting forge), or is descriptive of an entertainer in the minstrelsy who blew a musical instrument of some sort. Thomas Whieldon of Fenton Low, a potter of distinction, wrote the following entry in his memorandum book: "June 2nd, 1749. Hired a boy of Ann Blowers for treading lathe - per week two shillings"; 1907:Mrs William Blower (grocer, general dealer), Wedgwood Street, Longton. Incidentally, the Staffordshire name most associated with "blowing", that is, making blooms (ingots of iron), is Bloomer, the craftsman who actually made them and forged them into bars, rods and plates. Richard le blomare, tenant on the Audley estates at Betley in 1298, could well have worked alongside Jordan le fevere (smith), the resident village blacksmith; 1907:Thomas Bloomer of Stockton Brook.

Ancient burial mounds or lows are found in every part of the county, but they are far more frequent in Zone 4 than elsewhere, as typified by Lady Low and Top Low in the neighbourhood of Blore, Pea Low and Steep Low near Alstonefield, Musden Low south west of Ilam and Over Low not far from Stanton. But the prolific surname Low(e) does not necessarily indicate residence by such a mound or tumulus - it could signify quite mundanely a person who dwelt by a hill; 1327:William atte lowe of Crakemarsh; 1396:John del lowe of Quarnford; 1887:John Lowe (tea merchant), Piccadilly, Hanley; 1907:Robert Lowe, licensee of the Market Tavern, St. John's Square, Burslem.

One very familiar compound which is already widely dispersed throughout north Staffordshire by the close of the seventeenth century is Warrilow/Warrillow/Warrellow/Warilow. These all go back to a locality in Combridge, recorded as "Lytle Warrelowe" in the Croxden Abbey Chronicle for 1528, or to Near and Far Warrilow in Acton Trussell and Bednall, cited as "Warelowe" in 1574. Both places stipulate a mound, hill or barrow where felons were hanged, a gruesome reminder of the lawlessness of medieval England. Also noteworthy is Warrilow Brook, which runs into the River Dove - a stream on whose banks criminals were executed. If Warrilow Head Farm, north of Macclesfield Forest dates back to the Middle Ages, then this may also be involved in some of the Staffordshire Warrilows. In 1841 George Brough, aged 10, was a jigger turner for Job Warrilow at the China Factory in Longton, owned by Bailey, Goodwin and Robey. Job Warrilow himself was apprenticed to a master as a saucer-maker. 1851:Thomas Warrilow (boot and shoe maker), Church Street, Stone; 1907:William Warrillow (clothier, outfitter), Newcastle Street, Burslem.

Two controversial surnames in "-low", which have made their homes in Zone 4 are Clewlow and Critchlow. Clewlow Sprink near Whiston Eaves (1836 Ordnance Survey map), has been submitted as the origin of Clewlow/Clulow/Cluloe, but there is no hard evidence to back up this claim. Therefore, an alternative solution must be sought. The surname first takes root in the Leek, Rudyard and Cheddleton area; e.g. in the 1543 rent roll of Dieulacres Abbey, James Clulow is paying an annual rent of twelve shillings for "Parkehowse" in Leek Frith. By the 1600s it is also branching out eastwards in the direction of Bradnop, Whiston and Ellastone, and it is one of these migratory families who probably gave their name to the aforementioned Clewlow Sprink. The origin of the name is Cleulow Cross, about three miles north of Rushton Spencer. It is the site of an Anglo Saxon Mercian-style cylindrical cross-shaft, which stands on a mound said to be artificial, in a prominent position at the head of a valley near the boundary of Sutton Downes and a crossroads, where the Congleton to Buxton road crosses the route from Macclesfield to Wincle. The place refers to a round, ball-shaped burial mound or barrow. 1851:Sarah Elizabeth Clewlow, licensee of the White Hart, Eastgate Street, Stafford; 1875:Ambrose Clewlow (potters' foreman), Cobden Street, Dresden. Clewlow often interchanges with Clewley, as evidenced by Thomas Clewley, churchwarden at Swynnerton in 1656, who is shelling out hearth tax at Shelton under Harley as Thomas Clewlow in 1666; 1907:Alfred

Clewley (miner), Chell Street, Hanley. Nonetheless, some local Clewleys and Cluleys could have originally come from Clewley in Somerford near Brereton, Cheshire, found as "Clouelowe" in the late thirteenth century and possibly synonymous with Cleulow Cross.

Just prior to the Dissolution of the Monasteries in the 1530s, the surname Critchlow is fairly well established in north eastern Staffordshire. For instance, in a list of families in the Archdeaconry of Stafford for 1532/1533 we find Oliver and Richard Crichelow at Longnor, Ellen Crichelo at Sheen, Ralph Crychelow at Wetton and James Crychelow at Alstonefield. It has been recently pointed out that these local families must stem from the locality known as Crakelow south of Sheen, but there is one drawback to this assumption - no early spellings of the place have yet come to light. The obvious theory is that the surname was brought into our county by migrant families from Croichlow (Croichley) Fold, south west of Holcombe Brook, near a hill in Bury parish, Lancashire - "a mound on a hill summit". At the Court of Star Chamber in 1552, Ralph Crychelow (the same gentleman mentioned in the 1532 list) was charged with conspiring to overturn a stone wall and a hedge at "Grene Beistone" in the manor of Wetton; 1851:Richard Critchlow licensee of the White Lion, Hollins, Talke on the Hill; 1851:Charlotte Critchlow (milliner), Spout Street, Leek; 1875:Alfred Critchlow (baker and grocer), Prospect Place, Longton.

The vacillation between Clewlow and Clewley is mirrored in Critchlow-Critchley/ Crotchley/Crutchley/Cratchley: 1666:Roger Crutchley of Maer; 1750:Hannah Critchley of Burslem; 1907:Charles Cratchley (ovenman), Kimberley Road, Hanley.

The topographical term "torr" - "high rock, peak, hill", so frequent in the Peak District of Staffordshire and Derbyshire, is a Saxon loanword from Celtic. It is certainly no coincidence that the surname Torr shows up in the 1666 hearth tax returns for Grindon - John Torr, and Ecton - Thomas Torr, for this is classic "tor" country, epitomised by Beeston Tor south of Wetton, Ravens Tor and Pickering Tor in Dove Dale either side of Ilam Rock, and Iron Tors and Shining Tor not far from Alstonefield, within easy access of the Tissington Trail. The surname simply denotes residence by a rocky peak; 1851:Adam and James Torr, farmers at Bradnop. It is later modified to Tarr; Rocester, 1812:Thomas Tarr, married to Ellen Harrison; 1907:James Tarr (kiln foreman), Etruria Road, Stoke.

It has been intimated that the names Nabb and Nabbs are derived from "Nabbe", a pet form of the Germanic personal name Robert, and this certainly seems viable, judging by such specimens as 1532:Edmund Nabe of Cheddleton and 1532:Laurence Nabe of Leek Frith, alternatively found as Lawrence Nappe in 1517. The latter is another pet form of Robert. Yet more plausible is a toponymic for a dweller by a "nab", namely, a projecting peak or hill, as preserved in Nab End near Hollinsclough and probably Nabb Farm near Denstone, recorded as The Nab in 1836; 1539:Rauffe Nabbs of Ellastone; 1699:Francis Nabbs of Ipstones. The related word "knabbe" - "hill-top", contained apparently in Brier's Knob, Cannock, has probably resulted in the modern surnames Nobbs and Knobbs. Indeed, Thomas Nabbs, sheriff of Staffordshire in 1702, occurs as Thomas Nobbs in the same document. 1851:Thomas Knobbs (farmer), Draycott in the Moors; 1912:Ephraim

Knobbs (porter), Levison Street, Longton. Nibbs and Knibbs must be roped in here, too, with reference to residence near some point or peak - compare modern English "nib" of a pen and Nibs End Farm north west of Stanton; 1595:Ellen Nibbes widow of Trentham.

The Saxon "cnaepp" - "hill-top, hillock" - is behind the trio of names Knapp, Knapman, Knapper, all for a dweller by such a feature; 1851:Joseph Knapper (postmaster) at Betley; 1875:Stephen Knapper (draper and grocer), Heathcote Street, Kidsgrove. But 1736:Thomas Knapper of Hanford (brickmaker) is entered in the Trentham parish register as Thomas Napper in 1732. Usually Napper is an occupational term for the servant who was in charge of the table linen in a lord's household, variant Napier.

Residence near some peak or other is also demonstrated by names like Peak(e)/Peek and Pickin(g)/Piggin(s); 1327:Robert del pek of Audley; 1612:John Peake, sherman and dyer, of Newcastle under Lyme; 1887:Thomas Peake and son, Clayhills, Tunstall; 1591:John Pyckyn of Tittensor; 1635:Alice Pickin of Audley; 1583:Thomas Piggyne of Eccleshall; 1803:Mary Picking of Yarnfield. These surnames are characteristic of north western Staffordshire rather than the north eastern region.

Prominent hills obviously provided vantage points from which the local inhabitants could keep a watch on what was going on around them, hence the prevalence of locations such as Toot Hill - "lookout hill", typified by Toothill between Alton and Bradley in the Moors, Toot Hill near Hollington and Toot Hill south of Uttoxeter racecourse. All these end up as the modern surname Toothill/Tootal/Tottle/Tuttle: 1624:William Tothill of Bramshall. Another similar term employed by the Saxons for a lookout hill is "weard-hyll", preserved in Wardle north west of Nantwich, Cheshire and Wardle north east of Rochdale, Lancashire, both of which are probably responsible for some local families called Wardle/Wardill/Wardell. But the major influence on the diffusion of these names must be Ward Hill near Caverswall. Early spellings of the place are missing and its actual meaning remains a closed book. In 1790, Thomas Wardle (late of the White Hart), was landlord of the Quiet Woman in Leek; 1851:Thomas Wardle (ironmonger), Market Place, Burslem; 1875:John Wardle (milkseller), Stone Road, Longton.

Rubbing shoulders with Ward Hill in Caverswall parish is Tickhill (of obscure origin), one source of the surname Tickle/Tickel(l), but Tickhill near Maltby, south Yorkshire - "Tica's hill" - should not be consigned to the out-tray as a possible secondary source; 1907:John H. Tickle (lithographer), Railway Terrace, Burslem. Locally the verb "tickle" is pronounced as "tittle" and this is duplicated in the surname Tittle; 1907:John Tittle (labourer), Bucknall Old Road, Hanley. Windle/Windell refer to a dweller on a windy hill, or go back to a locality such as Windle Dale near Wetton or Windle in Prescot on Merseyside;1672, February 14th:Dorothy Windle, a poore traveller, buried at Ellastone; 1887:Herbert Windle (chief constable) of Hanley police force. If anyone chose to dwell near a hill where ferns flourished, then he or she quickly acquired a name like Farnall/Farnell/Fearnall - "dweller by a fern-covered hill"; 1887:Charles Farnell (hairdresser, perfumer), Piccadilly, Hanley; 1887:Arthur Farnell (jeweller and watchmaker), Navigation Road, Burslem. Ferns, which grow so well on the coal formations of our county, also live on in two other widespread surnames in north eastern Staffordshire. The basic Fern(e)s/Fearn(e)/Fearns is simply for residence among the ferns, as in The Ferns near Fawfieldhead. George Ferne was one of the head monks at Dieulacres Abbey in 1532. In the 1666 Hearth tax returns for Totmonslow Hundred those assessed include John Fearne at Rocester, Joan and Ann Fearnes at Crakemarsh and John Fernes at Lowe near Heaton. 1887:George Ferns (butcher), High Street, Longton.

But the most prolific compound of all in this zone is Redfern/Redfearn. It denotes a dweller among the red ferns, not surprisingly, but three locatives vie as important sources. Redfern near the River Spodden by Caldershaw north west of Rochdale probably takes precedence here, followed by Redfern in Crich and Redfern (Manor) in Kenilworth, Warwickshire. The latter however designates either a thicket in the midst of fenland or a winding marsh. In 1770 Joseph Redfern was one of five men who had stone quarries on Longnor Edge. Joseph himself had a wharf on the Manifold east of Longnor Bridge in the 1770s, which was probably used for the transportation of stone. 1851:Thomas Redfern (attorney), Daisy Bank, Leek; 1851:John Redfern (corn miller) of Wetton; 1875:George Redfern (writing clerk) of Fegg Hayes.

In the dialect of North Staffordshire "bank" is always "bonk" as in expressions such as "pot bonk" - pottery factory, and "pit bonk" - the area at the head of a pit shaft. The word "bonk" is an allusion to the numerous spoil tips near the local collieries and pottery firms. But when used topographically, "bank" refers to a dweller by a hill(side), slope or ridge; 1666:Edward Bankes of Ipstones; 1875:Nehemiah Banks (boot and shoe maker), Wise Street, Dresden. Compounds add just that little bit extra to the local scenery. Fairbank(s), for example, is for residence by the fair (beautiful) slope(s); 1792:William Fairbanks, married to Rachael Haywood at Seighford; 1851:Sampson Fairbanks (brickmaker) of Hilderstone. Firbank and Furbank denote an inhabitant by the wooded slope, or go back to Firbank near Kendal in the Lake District - "hill in a frith"; 1476:Thomas Frythbank taillour of Stafford. Greatbanks is an enigma. It is tempting to assume a meaning such as a dweller by some big slopes, or by some slopes with gravelly terrain all around, but neither sounds satisfactory; 1887:Joseph Greatbanks (innkeeper) of Church Street, Chesterton; 1907:William Greatbanks (potter's turner), Wain Street, Burslem.

The Saxon "dun" - "down, hill, slight rise, hill pasture" is the terminal of Upper and Lower Elkstone west of Warslow - "Eanlac's hill" and Cauldon north east of Cheadle - "calves' hill". It also gives us the surnames Down(e) and Down(e)s; 1666:Edward Downes of Wall Grange (Leek); 1887:George Downes (coachman), Eaton Terrace, Wolstanton. The rare Downer also refers to residence by some hill; 1623:Elizabeth Downer of Stowe by Chartley.

Ancestors of local families called Hough/Hoof(e)/Huff originally lived by a projecting ridge of land, crag, cliff or precipice, as typified by 1384:Ralph de la hogh of Newcastle under Lyme, but other families of the same name could have brought it from

Hough near Crewe, Hough in Alderley Edge, Hough Green near Widnes, or Hough Park, east of Ashbourne; 1666:Ellen Hough of Alton; 1708:Edward Hough of Cheadle; 1784:James Huff of Newcastle under Lyme. All these spellings preserve the nominative singular of the Saxon word "hoh". The dative singular results in the modern surnames Howe/Hoo/Hoe; 1618:Alexander Howe, curate at Caverswall. But Howe is also a vernacular form of Hugh; 1222 Assizes:Howe le Champeneis - the man from Champagne, the modern Champness, and in the Danelaw How(e) also goes back to the Old Norse "haugr" - "mound, hill". Plural forms such as Howse/House and Hoose normally signify a servant who was employed in some medieval religious house, but in the Bucknall cum Bagnall parish registers these coalesce with Hulse, since Stephen Hoose (1771), is also written down as Stephen Howse in 1790, and as Stephen Hulse in 1786. Nowadays Hulse is extremely prolific across the northern half of the county; 1867:Joseph Hulse, alderman, elected mayor of Longton; 1851:Thomas Hulse (cratemaker), Glebe Street, Stoke. The sources here are Hulse Farm, Hulse Heath Farm and Hulse House Farm, north east of Davenham beyond the River Dane, Cheshire and probably Hulse Heath near Rostherne Mere, also in Cheshire. Both refer to an original place meaning "the hollows".

Adam del side, taxed at Bradley in the Moors in 1327, dwelt by a slope, and his name lives on as Side/Sydes, whilst 1348:Thomas atte style of Tunstall (Stoke-on-Trent) resided by a stile or steep ascent - Stiles/Styles; 1620:Raphe Stile of Norton in the Moors. However, there is obvious confusion with Steel(e), because Steele House Farm south of Horton village on the Longsdon road (so called in 1561), was probably occupied by the late thirteenth century. Indeed, Ranulph del style is cited as a tenant of the Audleys at Horton in 1307. The surname Steel/e)/Steels is more often than not a nickname applied to someone who was as hard or as reliable as steel; 1790:John Steel (clockmaker) of Leek; 1847:Elizabeth Steel, farming 28 acres of land at Clay Lake, Endon.

The Saxon "(ge)wind" - "ascent, steep incline" is the basis of the name Wind/Wynde, which is sharpened further to Wint; 1544:Margery Wynte of Alstonefield. William Wynt husbandman of Wetton is alternatively known as William Went in the same year (1552) and as William Winch in 1553. The variant Went parallels the local pronunciation "splent" for "splint", but Went can also represent a dweller by a crossroads, whilst many a Welsh Went stems from Gwent. 1851:William Wint (farmer) of Wetton; 1907:F. Wint (coal merchant), Fountain Street, Leek.

Nothing conjures up more compellingly the stark, rugged aspect of the outcrops of limestone and the gritstone escarpments in this zone than such local landmarks as Drystone Edge, Turn Edge and Wolf Edge north of Flash. The name Edge is extremely widespread hereabouts in the 1660s and some families are probably related to John del egge, taxed at Norton in the Moors in 1332, whose name is preserved no doubt in Baddeley Edge not too far away. The Edges who acquired Horton Hall in the early decades of the fourteenth century retained possession until the estate was sold to John Alsop in 1720. In 1841 Stephen Edge was the secretary of the Wesleyan Methodist Sunday School at Burslem;

1887:Catherine Edge (tobacconist), Stafford Street, Longton; 1912:Joseph Edge (engine driver), Regent Road, Fenton. The compound Ladderedge near Longsdon is a wolf in sheep's clothing if ever there was one, for the place occurs as "Leveresheved" in the Middle Ages, e.g. William de Leveresheved, assessed for tax purposes at Leek in 1327. Now this is clearly for "Leofhere's headland" and it is converted later into such forms as 1599:John Levershurd of Mucklestone; 1666:Thomas Liverseech of Trentham and 1612:Thomas Lyversage of Newcastle under Lyme, who was paying two pence per annum rent for a porch at his house in Pencle Strett (sic). All authorities agree that the surname Liversage/Liversidge is derived from Liversedge in the parish of Birstall (West Riding of Yorkshire) - "Leofhere's edge", but the local instances totally refute this idea. A few families of this name must be from the north of England, but by and large, the local base is best; 1851:George Liversage (flour dealer, baker), High Street, Stone.

The steep rock faces that add their own dramatic overtones to the landscape incorporate Stoney Cliffe near Upper Hulme, Sharpcliffe on Ipstones Edge, Middle Cliff near Bradnop and Dove Cliff east of Quixhill. Yet not one single locality containing the ending "- cliff(e)" has produced a surname. To be sure, there are three compounds with this particular element in this zone, which have ramified to an amazing degree down the years, but all have wormed their way in from other counties. Tunnicliff(e)/Dunnicliffe, for example, stems from Tonacliffe, north of Rochdale, Lancashire - "the farmstead next to the brook by the cliff". Before the advent of the Industrial Revolution the surname is firmly established around Heaton (Rushton Spencer), Leek, Alstonefield, Fawfield Head, Okeover, Ilam and Castern, and Denstone near Rocester; 1538:John Tonaclyffe of Tittesworth; 1605:William Tonnecliffe of Berdehulme (the modern Bearda near Swythamley Hall); 1637:Nicholas Tunnecliffe of Ellastone. At Ellastone in 1640 the parish clerk informs us that *"John Tunnecliffe, who was wounded in Davis Lane with a stone falling upon him the 8th day of June, died upon the 13th day."* 1851:John Tunnicliff (shoemaker) of Fulford; 1912:Frederick Dunnicliff of Balance Street, Uttoxeter. The Tunnicliff-Dunnicliff interchange is a direct copy of Tunstall-Dunstall.

In a 1532 list of families the heads of the household comprise Thomas Ratclyff at Waterfall, John Ratclyff at Uttoxeter, William Ratclyff at Grindon and Ellis Ratclyff at Rocester. But there is much doubt as to where these local families came from in the first place. External sources are plentiful, e.g. Radcliffe in Greater Manchester, south of Bury, Radcliffe on Trent near Nottingham, Ratcliffe upon Soar, east of East Midlands Airport, Ratcliffe Culey, south of Twycross, Leicestershire, Ratcliffe on the Wreak near Leicester, Radcliffe south of Amble, Northumberland, and Radclive near Buckingham. All refer to a red cliff, that is one containing sandstone. In a lawsuit of 1282, there is an isolated reference to a field called "Radeclyve" in Denstone, Rocester. If this is trustworthy, then it will go a long way towards explaining why the surname Radcliff(e)/Ratcliff(e) has become so entrenched in this zone; 1851:James Ratcliff (farmer and limeburner) of Waterfall; 1851:John Ratcliff (victualler), Black Horse, Heaton.

Much thinner on the ground than either of the two preceding surnames is Cunliff(e)/Condliff(e)/Condlyff/Concliffe, which is from Higher or Lower Cuncliffe near Blackburn, Lancashire or a place in Knutsford, Cheshire, that occurs as "Cundeclif, Cunteclyf" in the Middle Ages. According to local folklore these two localities commemorate a rock with a hollow in it, through which people used to crawl in order to be healed of some sickness or malady. In 1704 the lords of the manor of Leek Frith licensed several local miners, including Jeremiah Condlyffe, to dig for lead and copper ore on the waste near the Roaches. 1851:Ann Condliffe (shopkeeper), America Street, Tunstall; 1875:Francis Condliffe (licensee), The Swan Inn, High Street, Silverdale; 1907:Charles Conliffe (potter) of Blake Street, Burslem.

Thomas Getcliffe, assessed for one hearth at Cheadle in 1666, is cited as Thomas Getliffe and Thomas Getly in the Cheadle parish registers for the same period. These spellings, coupled with 1618:Margaret Gatley of Rocester, are undoubtedly from Gatley near Cheadle Hulme, Cheshire, which conceals an earlier "Gateclyve" - "cliff frequented by goats"; 1851:Simon Getliffe (shopkeeper) of Market Place, Leek; 1907:William Gaitley (potter), Normacot Road, Longton; 1907:William Gately (potter), Copley Street, Tunstall.

One would expect one or two localities in this area containing the element "crag", but, apart from Darfur Crags near Wetton Mill, pointed out by Mee in his study of Staffordshire, these are conspicuous by their absence. However, the surname Cragg does show its face now and then, denoting habitation by a steep, precipitous rock or rocks: 1592 Lawsuit:William Craggs of Cheadle; 1600:Margaret Underwood alias Cragge of Eccleshall; 1770:James Cragg of Wolstanton, married to Sarah Collison on October 28th; 1907:Thomas Cragg, publican at the Rising Sun, Waterloo Road, Burslem. Craig is the Scottish variant; 1875:J.W.Craig (M.D.) of Shelton House in Snow Hill, Shelton, Hanley; 1907:D.Craig (hairdresser) of Elgin Street, Shelton.

Two locations in the neighbourhood of Uttoxeter are not all they appear. Combridge, probably "ridge with a crest", appears as "Cambrig" in 1656 (Leek parish registers), and is thus a local source of the surname Cambridge; 1907:Solomon Cambridge (collier) of Bucknall New Road, Hanley. But the name must have also been introduced by migrant families whose roots lay in the University town of Cambridge - "bridge over the River Granta", or in Cambridge, Gloucester - "bridge over the River Cam". Bramshall, west of Uttoxeter, home of William de Bromschulfe, taxed at Gratwich in 1327, designates a shelf or ledge of land covered with broom, that yellow flowered plant so familiar on heaths. In 1745 the place is recorded as "Brownshelf", which is easily transformed into Brownsill; 1907:William Brownsill (miner) of Queen Street, Tunstall. This brings to mind the unsolved surname Brownbill; 1851:William Brownbill (farmer) of Beech, Swynnerton. Bardsley lists families called Brownbell, Brownbill, Broombill and Brambell in the Prestbury Church registers during the sixteenth and seventeenth centuries. These obviously allude to residence by a bramble bush. There can be no connection with the brownbill, a kind of halberd painted brown, used by foot soldiers.

Surnames in "-ston, -stone"

To seek shelter from the bleak, inhospitable winters in the Staffordshire Peak district, our medieval ancestors were not averse from establishing their home base near some stones; 1327:Hugh del stones of Wootton under Weaver chose his site with this in mind. At Alstonefield during the seventeenth century, families called Stones were distinguished by various aliases, probably on account of their fertility; 1667:Thomas Stones alias Roger's Thomas, to differentiate him from 1658:Thomas Stones alias Joanes Tome (sic). The singular form Stone is either for residence near some boundary stone or Hundred stone, where a meeting was held; Thomas atte stone, porter at the castle of Newcastle under Lyme circa 1370; or from Stone north of Stafford. Traditionally this has been connected with a mound of stones erected to commemorate the legendary slaughter of Wulflad and Rufinus, supposed sons of King Wulfhere (659-675), after their conversion to Christianity. A more likely derivation is that the place was the site of a natural boulder or rock formation, or even a prehistoric megalith or Roman milestone; 1841:Rebecca Stone, mistress of the National Day School for girls, St. John's Church, Burslem; 1875:Samuel Henry Stone (tea dealer and Italian warehouse), Market Street, Kidsgrove.

Stonehouse is simply for residence at a stone house; 1907:John Stonehouse, Alderhay Lane, Newchapel, Kidsgrove - cf Lower and Upper Stonehouse in Brown Edge, perhaps from Ranulf del Stonhouse, taxed at Norton in the Moors in 1332.

In attempting to make sense of the many compounds in "-stone", one is soon lured into a labyrinth of inconsistencies. Kingstone, for instance, near Bagot Forest, south west of Uttoxeter, was originally a royal manor, that is a settlement belonging to the king. It has given us the names Kingston/Kinston/Kingson and Kinson; 1616:Maude Kingston, a poore woman, buried at Stowe by Chartley; 1658:Edward Kinston of Barlaston; 1851:John Kingston (boot and shoe maker), County Road, Stafford; 1887:Edward Kinson (greengrocer) of Newport Lane, Burslem. Kingson and Kinson are also patronymics for son of someone called King, from a Saxon personal name "Cyng', or for son of a person who played the part of king in a pageant or who served in a royal household but these do not apply here.

In the 1642 Quarter Session Rolls, Mr Hill is quoted as vicar or pastor of Ellison namely Ellastone, a village which looks into Derbyshire across the River Dove with the Weaver Hills looming in the background - "Eadlac's homestead". This is a sign that the surname Ellison is often from the locative source in our county rather than a patronymic for "son of Elie", the Old French form of the old Hebrew prophet Elijah; 1912:John Ellison (potter's placer), Lower Mayer Street, Hanley. Elson is either an abbreviated version of Ellison or from Elson near Ellesmere, Shropshire - "Elli's village or hill"; 1448:William Elson of Alton; 1907:George Elson (carter), Longfield Terrace, Hanley.

Practically opposite Ellastone on the other side of the River Dove lies the Derbyshire village of Snelston - "Snell's hamlet; "Ralph Snelston was elected prior of the Augustinian abbey at Calwich near Ellastone in 1507 after the resignation of Thomas Dawson alias Dakyn, who had been an inmate of Trentham Priory at an earlier stage in his career. Three

CROXDEN PARISH REGISTER

Croxden Parish
Register 1771

1771, July 19.　Joseph Cadman & Hannah Evans,
　　　　　　　　Banns　..　　..　　..　mar.

1774, Jan. 31.　John Wright, parish of Collwich, &
　　　　　　　　Mary Kent, Banns　..　　..　mar.

1783, Nov. 3.　William Carrington & Elizabeth Shaw,
　　　　　　　　parish of Doveridge, *Lic.*　..　mar.

　,, Dec. 30.　Thomas Swinson & Sarah Bentley,
　　　　　　　　Banns　..　　..　　..　mar.

1784, Feb. 9.　Phillip Morrey, parrish of Checkley, &
　　　　　　　　Mary Saunders, Banns ..　　..　mar.

　,, June 14.　William Whieldon & Sarah Barnet,
　　　　　　　　Parish of Mayfield, Banns　..　mar.

　,, Sept. 30.　Thomas Milner, parish of Checkley, &
　　　　　　　　Ellen Harvey, *Lic.*　..　　..　mar.

　,, Oct. 11.　William Robinson & Hannah Swinson,
　　　　　　　　Banns　..　　..　　..　mar.

　,, Dec. 4.　William Robinson, Widower, & Martha
　　　　　　　　Hinckley, Widow, Banns　..　mar.

1785, May 16.　Joseph Woolley & Ann Holinsworth,
　　　　　　　　Banns　..　　..　　..　mar.

1786, Feb. 19.　Francis Godrich, parish of Alveton, &
　　　　　　　　Mary Saunders, *Lic.*　..　　..　mar.

　,, July 14.　Thomas Bloor & Ellen Higgs, Banns..　mar.

　,, Aug. 28.　George Harvey, parish of Alton, &
　　　　　　　　Mary Keeling, *Lic.*　..　　..　mar.

　,, Dec. 6.　William Saunders & Dorothy Wood,
　　　　　　　　Lic. ..　　..　　..　　..　mar.

　,, Dec. 26.　William Deaville & Jane Holmes,
　　　　　　　　parish of Alveton, *Lic.* ..　　..　mar.

1787, Feb. 1.　Thomas Evans, parish of Rocester,
　　　　　　　　Widower, & Hannah Hinkley,
　　　　　　　　Spinster, *Lic.* ..　　..　　..　mar.

　,, Apr. 5.　Thomas Holmes, parish of Bradly,
　　　　　　　　Farmer, & Martha Wood, Spinster,

　,, Sept. 6.

Croxden Abbey
late 18th century

years after Ralph's death in 1530, Calwich Priory was the first religious house in Staffordshire to feel the full force of Henry VIII's suppression of the monasteries. Snelston is identical in meaning with Snelson in Over Peover Chapelry, Cheshire, and this duet lies at the root of the majority of local families called Snelson; 1703:Joseph Snelston, married Mary Boden at Seighford, and was buried as Joseph Snelson in 1750; 1875:W. Snelson (accountant), Penkhull Terrace, Stoke. A rare alternative might be the patronymic "son of Snell", from a Saxon word meaning "quick, active".

Denstone near Rocester in the Churnet valley - "Dene's farmstead", first loses the final "e"; 1666:Stephen Denston, taxed on one hearth at Ashley; 1912:E.Denston (labourer), Hyde Terrace, Kidsgrove. Then the "t" disappears, since the place is cited as "Denson" in the Croxden parish registers for 1755, hence the modern surname Denson and its later variant Densem; 1666:John Denson of Yoxall. A supplementary source is a patronymic for "son of the dean (head of the chapter of a cathedral)" - 1295 Assizes:Henry le denesone of Stramshall.

The "t" also goes absent without leave in Branson/Bronson, which are derived from Branston near Burton on Trent - "Brant's village"; William de Bronston, abbot at Burton Abbey died in 1474; 1851:James Branson (shoemaker), Bradley Green, Biddulph; 1912:John Branson of Oldcott Green, Goldenhill. Our local Branston is identical in meaning with Branston south of the Vale of Belvoir, Leicestershire, Braunstone in Leicester, Branston and Branston Booths near Lincoln, Brandeston, north east of Ipswich, Brandiston, north west of Norwich, Braunston near Daventry, Northamptonshire and Braunston near Oakham in Rutland. All are further sources of the surname.

Gunstone, south of Brewood - "Gunni's homestead" occurs as "Gunson" in 1754 (Codsall parish registers), and is consequently the origin of both Gunston and Gunson; 1907:John Gunston (clerk), Bower Street, Hanley; 1907:William Gunson (draper), Etruria Road, Stoke. Yet Gunson is also a patronymic for "son of Gunn", where the latter is either from Old Norse "Gunnr" or "Gunne", a pet form of the female name "Gunnhildr"; William Gunne, taxed at Bradnop in 1327 and Henry son of Gunnild of Alrewas (1259). Four miles to the east of Gunstone is Featherstone, which represents a cromlech made up of three upright stones and a headstone, an arrangement also seen in Featherstone near Pontefract. Both localities have contributed towards the surname Featherstone; 1907:Reverend P. Featherstone of Baddeley Street, Burslem; 1907:Robert Featherstone (chemist), South View Terrace, Station Road, Tunstall. Fatherson is a curious perverted spelling of the name; 1629:Margery Fatherson of Wolstanton.

One theme much used by the Anglo-Saxons in the formation of personal names is "stan" - "stone", which inevitably clashes with placenames ending in "-stone". For instance, an unrecorded Saxon name 'Picstan' has been postulated as the origin of the surname Pickston(e)/Pixton, but in Staffordshire a local source cries out for attention, namely, Peakstone Rock, not far from the Highwayman Inn, Threapwood. It occurs as "Pixton otherwise Peakestones" in 1618 and refers to some pointed stones. Walter de

Pecston, assessed at Alton in 1332, clearly hailed from this locality. In 1907 Maud Pickstone is listed as a milliner in Newcastle Street, Burslem.

Two undocumented Saxon names - Bucstan and Burgstan - have been implicated in the surname Buxton, but such assumptions are not to be taken seriously regarding the Staffordshire Buxtons, for these are exclusively from Buxton in the Derbyshire Peak District, which vies with Cumbria' s Alton as the highest town in England. The place gets its name from some logan stones or rocking stones, poised boulders that were easily rocked from side to side. Up to the beginning of the nineteenth century the surname fluctuates between Buxton (Buckston) and Buckston(e)s; 1398:Richard and Thomas Couper of Buxstones, resident at Quarnford; 1532:Nicholas Buxton of Longnor; 1610:Jane Buckestones of Ellastone; 1666:William Buckestones of Ilam, Castern and Okeover; 1666:William Buckston of Grindon; 1782:Samuel Buxton of Cheddleton, married to Ann Mellor. Today the customary spelling of the family name is Buxton; 1851:John Buxton (saddler and shoemaker) of Wootton under Weaver; 1851:Louisa Buxton (schoolmistress) of Ipstones. Buxton north of Norwich - "Bucc's farmstead" - is probably too remote to have played any part in the proceedings.

Axstones Spring in Heaton (Rushton Spencer) poses a dilemma - is it a locative name in "-stone" or is there some association with the surname Axon? This arrives on the scene locally comparatively late for an accurate assessment, but in any case, there are several conflicting hypotheses as to its actual meaning. Spellings such as 1611:Ellen Acson of Norton in the Moors, and 1756:Richard Ackson of Madeley near Newcastle point to "son of Acke", from the Saxon personal name "Acca". On the other hand, widdow (sic) Axam, exempt from hearth tax at Maer and Aston in 1666, could be traceable to Askam in Furness, Cumbria, Askam Bryan or Askam Richard near York, Askham south east of Retford, Nottinghamshire or Askham near Penrith. All localities were originally villages built amongst some ash trees. Here the initial part of the placenames "Ask-" becomes "Aks-" by analogy with the dialectal "aks" for "ask", spelt later as "Ax-". The change from "-am" to "-on" probably comes about because of the similar modification displayed in Denson-Densem. Another plausible solution centres around the patronymic Hackson; 1400:Robert Hackson of Bramshall - "son of Hake", from a Scandinavian personal name "Haki" or "Hake" - "hook, crook", an original byname for a hunchback. Minus the initial aspirate this gives us Ackson. Trade directories list; 1875:Joshua Axon (store keeper), Chatterley Iron Company, Tunstall; 1907:James Axon (collier) of Gill Street, Hanley.

Valleys

The isolation of the limestone crags and windswept plateaus contrasts sharply with the spectacular ravines and gorges and wooded valleys, carved out of the landscape over the ages by the Dove, Churnet and Manifold. The terrain is now ruled by "cloughs", "dales", "bottoms", "hopes" and "slacks". Our new surroundings are encapsulated in Hollinsclough near Glutton Bridge in the valley of the Dove, Oulsclough north of Oakamoor in the

Churnet valley and School Clough near Fawfield Head in the Manifold valley. Clough is an old Saxon word for a ravine or deep-sided valley, as already outlined in our treatment of Colclough. Benedict del clough, incorporated in the top band of taxpayers at Leek in 1332, dwelt by such a topographical feature, and his descendants are with us today as Clough, Cleugh or Cluff; 1428 Feudal Aids:Richard Cluff (no locality specified); 1670:Thomas Clough married Sara Symson at Audley on May 20th. Thomas del clou, assessed in 1327 at Heatonlow near Rushton Spencer, results in the modern forms Clow(es)/Clews)/Clew(es)/Clue(s)/Cluse and Close. Lawrence Close, who is being charged an annual rent of eleven shillings for "le Grenes" in Leek Frith in 1543 by the monks of Dieulacres Abbey, is also quoted as Lawrence Clowes in 1538. Clowes is the preferred spelling of the surname in Zone 4, and this situation applies as well to north Staffordshire in general. Elsewhere across the county, the forms Clews and Clewes have the ascendancy, whilst Close and Cluse pale into insignificance; 1842:Thomas Clewes had a lime kiln (rateable value ten pounds) at Stanley Moss, Endon; 1851:Elisha Clews (shoemaker) of Onecote, Leek; 1851:James and Richard Clowes (timber merchants and builders), Basford (Cheddleton); 1851:Michael Clowes (shoemaker) of Ipstones; 1851:Thomas Cluse (baker) of High Street, Uttoxeter; 1907:Richard Close, proprietor of the Roebuck Inn, George Street, Newcastle under Lyme. It has been shown for other counties that Clowes and Cluse can occasionally be derived from "cluse, clowse" - "enclosure, narrow passage, sluice, flood gate", with reference to a person who was in charge of the mill dam, but there is no sign of this in the Staffordshire material.

Of the compounds, Colclough (see Zone 2) is far and away the most prolific in north Staffordshire and the rest are way behind. Fairclough is for a dweller by the fair (beautiful hollow or from a locality in Hope Woodlands in the Derbyshire Peak district, recorded formerly as "Fairecloughe"; Eccleshall parish registers 1603:Oliver Fayrcloughe (a stranger); 1907:William Fairclough (bricklayer), Podmore Street, Burslem; 1907:Richard Fairclough (grocer), Market Street, Stoke. Barrowclough, too, is struggling to make the grade; 1578:Robert and William Barrowcloughe of Kingsley; 1851:Reverend Jonathan Barrowclough of Uttoxeter; 1907:John Barraclough (Inspector for the N.S.P.C.C.) Bucknall New Road, Hanley. The exact origin is uncertain, but worth looking at is Barrow Clough on the border of the West Riding of Yorkshire and Derbyshire, just north of Hope Forest, near to Howden Moors.

The Saxon "hop" signified a small enclosed valley or a smaller valley that branched out of the main one, the sense conveyed by the northern dialect word "hop", preserved in the local placename Hope in the parish of Alstonefield. Henry del hope, taxed at Alstonefield in 1332, obviously came from this locality, and many a Staffordshire Hope must also have his or her roots in the same region; 1678:Jacob Hope of Ellastone 1851:Thomas Hope (paper maker) of Winkhill; 1851:Edna Hope (milliner and dressmaker), Queen Street, Burslem. Some, however, could trace their family tree back to Hope near Castleton in the Derbyshire Peaks or Hope Green near Poynton in Cheshire

Hopes with Lancashire connections might derive their name from either of two places in Greater Manchester - the Hope in Swinton or the Hope in Pendleton, whilst the Shropshire Hopes owe their name to localities such as Hopesay not far from Aston on Clun, Hope north east of Mitchell's Fold Stone Circle, Hope Bowdler near Church Stretton, or Hope east of Ludlow.

Stanshope, less than a mile away from Hope to the south - "stony valley", or "Stan's valley" - probably lives on as Stanhope; 1714:Maria Stanhope of Stoke-on-Trent, married on August 28th to John Smith; yet we ignore at our peril such locations as Stanhope Bretby near Burton on Trent, Stanhope several miles south west of Consett, Durham and Stanhope in Upper Tweeddale, Scotland, all probably for "stony valley".

About two miles distant from Hope on the Derbyshire side of Dovedale is the village of Alsop-en-le-Dale - "Aelle's valley". It lies beside the Tissington Trail, that runs from Ashbourne up to Heathcote near Hartington and joins the High Peak Trail between Needham and Monyash. During the Middle Ages there are frequent references to persons designated as "de Alesop, de Alsop(p)", etc in the Okeover Deeds and the Charters of Burton Abbey, and, not surprisingly, it is in this very area, where the surname evolves, before it radiates outwards in every direction, encroaching on village after village all across the county. By the close of the seventeenth century it has conquered every territory bar the south west of the county. In the case of Starter versus Kynnersley at the Court of Star Chamber(1530), Richard Alsop of Loxley near Uttoxeter, aided by some of Kynnersley's henchmen, was charged with herding 60 head of cattle into some pasture in Crakemarsh, where the stampeding beasts destroyed good grazing land. 1851:Thomas Allsop (brickmaker) of Upper Cotton near Cauldon Lowe; 1907:George Allsop (solicitor's clerk), Princes Road, Hartshill.

Two other Derbyshire interlopers have made their mark on local nomenclature - Glossop in High Peak Hundred - "Glott's valley" and Lindop Wood in Edensor, aproximately two miles south of Chatsworth House - "valley with a lime tree"; 1532:John Glosop of Waterfall; 1690:Ellen Glossop, buried at Ellastone. Lindop and Lindup are relative newcomers to our county, not making any impression until the late sixteenth century, when Margaret Lindop (1593) and Anne Lyndop (1598) occur in the Eccleshall parish registers. Thereafter it gradually creeps northwards, taking in Standon, Whitmore, Onneley, Keele and Newcastle under Lyme, reaching Stoke-on-Trent in the latter decades of the seventeenth century; 1663:William Lindupp of Stoke. Abraham Lindup, the Wesleyan preacher, was born at Mow Cop in 1738. 1851:Benjamin Lindup, owner of an eating house in High Street, Hanley; 1875:John Lindop (tailor) of King Street, Burslem.

One Shropshire infiltrator is Millichope on Wenlock Edge - "the valley by the hill where a mill was erected". However, the surname is subject to much mutilation and has produced some weird modern variants; 1907:Mary Eliza Melenship of High Street, Stoke; 1907:Elizabeth Mellenchip of Penkhull New Road, Stoke; 1907:Frank Millership (clerk) of Grosvenor Avenue, Oakhill; 1907:James Millichip (coachman), The Stable, Cliffe Vale,

Hartshill Road, Stoke; 1907:E. Mellorchip (miner), Nelson Street, Fenton.

Cheshire chips in with Harrop near Pott Shrigley and possibly Harop Green east of Jodrell Bank, perhaps for a valley populated by hares, synonymous with Harehope north west of Alnwick, Northumberland, a third source of the surname Harrop/Harrup; 1875:William Harrop (parian manufacturer), Tinkersclough, Hanley; 1907:John Harrop (waggoner) of Trubshaw Street, Burslem. Two locations in Lancashire - Harrop Dale on Saddleworth Moor and Harrop Fold near Grindleton, are less amenable as sources.

Cowpe south of Rawtenstall, Lancashire, is found as 'Couhop" in the Middle Ages - "cow valley", and is the architect of such local names as John Cowhop of Ipstones (1481), Thrustane Cowapp of Rocester (1581) and Raph Cowap of Woodlands, Uttoxeter (1666). Inevitably these spellings mingle with Cope, the midlands form of Cape - a maker or seller of capes or long cloaks; Castlechurch parish registers 1581:Anne Cowpe cited as the daughter of John Coppe; the latter is also known as John Cowappe in 1589, and as John Cope in 1620. 1851:William Coup (corn miller) of Cauldon; 1875:Henry Cope (milk seller), Shooter's Hill, Lightwood.

Bottom(s), Botham and compounds

It has long been a favourite standby of comedians to inject a slight hint of risqué humour into their monologues and routines with amusing anecdotes about grotesque mothers-in-law and seaside landladies, blessed with such surnames as Broadbottom, Longbottom, and so on. This is the essence of the cheerful vulgarity of the McGill seaside postcards, and is not intended to cause offence in any way. Yet many families called Shufflebottom, Sidebottom, etc are embarrassed by their own names, and have resorted to variations in spelling in order to deter other insensitive people from making jokes at their expense. The alteration of their names to Shufflebotham, Sidebotham minimizes their predicament. In all fairness, they need not have bothered, because the fact remains that the Saxon word "botm, bothm" refers to the "bottom" of a valley, that is, the lowest part of a deep valley, and the surname Bottom(s)/Botham merely signifies residence there, and has no anatomical connotation at all. This is evident from Hugh de Bothom in a thirteenth century deed from the Staffordshire Chartulary, who could have come from Bottom House, 2 miles north east of Ipstones, or from "Bothom" in Chell, or from "the Bothom" in Cheddleton. The term also survives in Shaw Bottom near the Roaches, Frith Bottom at the north end of Tittesworth Reservoir and in the remarkable Dale Bottom near Hope, which combines three valley words into one. In 1532 the heads of the household consisted of Henry Bothom at Combridge, Thomas Bothom at Wootton under Weaver, Robert Botham at Prestwood near Quixhill and Richard Bothom at Warslow.1851. James Botham (farmer) of Houghton Cross, Cotton. Bottomer could also be a toponymic, identical in meaning with Bottom; 1851:James Bottomer (tailor) of Bramshall.

In this zone two compounds are head and shoulders above their companions - Higginbottom and Shufflebottom. Higginbottom/Higginbotham/Heginbotham/ Hickinbottom are from Oaken Bottom on Bradshaw Brook near Tonge Fold, Lancashire -

LOCAL
BILLHEADS
WITH
EXAMPLES OF
NAMES FROM
THIS SECTION

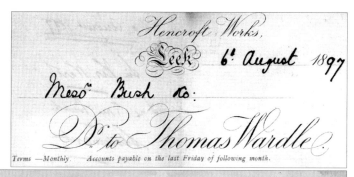

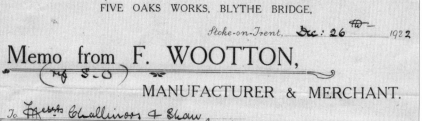

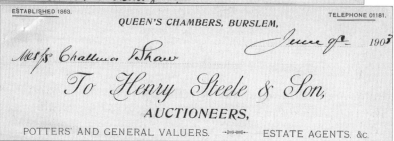

"oaken valley", backed up by Higginbotham in Bredbury near Stockport, Cheshire and Higginbottom Piece in Mellor, Derbyshire. The two latter localities refer to a wicket-gated place in a valley. 1532:Ralph Hegenbothom of Ellastone and John Hegynbothom of Rushton Spencer; Bucknall cum Bagnall parish register 1801:William Hickinbotham (signs Hickinbottom) of Stoke parish; 1851:Charles Hickenbotham (boot and shoe maker), Chapel Street, Cheadle; 1875:Edwin Higginbotham (beer seller,tobacconist), Piccadilly, Hanley.

Following the Restoration of Charles II, the surname Shufflebotham/Shufflebottom multiplies considerably around Horton, Leek, Cheddleton, Rushton Spencer and Alstonefield, but, unlike Higginbotham, it spreads out westwards towards the Potteries conurbation and over to Audley, Betley and southwards to Swynnerton. All these different branches go back to Shipper Bottom Farm near Shuttleworth in Bury parish, Lancashire - "the valley with a stream, where sheep were washed." This small, insignificant spot is a perfect example of how a surname can sometimes proliferate over a wide area out of all proportion to its humble beginnings; 1768:John Shufflebotham of Alstonefield married Hannah Smith at Cheddleton; 1810:Daniel Shubotham of Gratton, Endon; 1851:James Shufflebottom (coal dealer), Hanover Street, Hanley; 1875:Abraham Shufflebotham (fruit and vegetable dealer) of Sneyd Green.

Rowbotham/Rowbottom/Robotham/Rubotham fails to make the same impact as either of the two previous surnames. The main sources are two locations in Cheshire - Rowbottom near Poynton and Rowbothams in Offerton near Stockport - "rough valley" that is "a valley with rough, impenetrable vegetation" or "difficult to penetrate"; 1851:Joseph Robottom (gamekeeper) of Ilam; 1851:Samuel Lowe Rowbotham (cow leech) of Blore (Ilam); 1851:George Rowbotham (farmer), Woodhouse Field, Denstone.

Other compounds are very infrequent. Again, two Cheshire localities are potential origins of the surname Sidebotham/Sidebottom - Sidebottom Fold in Stalybridge and Sidebottom Farm in Utkinton, both designating a wide (spacious) valley: William Sydebothome wed Elizabeth Whytall at Audley in 1622, and by a will, dated 1744, Mary Sydebotham left the interest on £11 for distribution to poor widows in Rushton Spencer. Families called Longbottom perhaps have links with Longbottom in the West Riding of Yorkshire or Long Bottom in Heath near Chesterfield - "long valley"; 1887:Luke Longbottom (engineer) of Fenton Villa, High Street, Fenton. Winterbottoms could trace their ancestry back to any one of a trio of locatives in Cheshire - Winterbottom not far from Tatton Park, Winter Bottom in Matley near Macclesfield or Winterbottom Farm in Goostrey (Holmes Chapel) - a valley used only in the winter months, presumably as shelter for a herdsman and his animals; 1907:William Winterbottom (painter), Regent Road, Fenton; 1907:Walter Winterbottom (coal cutter), Frank Street, Stoke.

Dales - miscellaneous terms for valleys

The dales in Zone 4 proclaim their presence with self-explanatory names like Deepdale

Farm near Grindon and Narrowdale east of Ecton, compared with the natural wildness inherent in Wolf Dale at the northern tip of Rudyard Reservoir. The basic surname Dale(s) remains pretty constant at all periods after the end of the Middle Ages, particularly in north Staffordshire, and is a straightforward reference to residence in a dale; 1332:Henry in le dale of Chartley. In August, 1509, John Whytney of Swythamley sued Robert Dale and other riotous persons for assaulting, wounding and illtreating him in a warlike manner, as he was returning home to his place of residence at Swythamley. The defendant, Robert Dale, declared that he was not guilty of the offences, and alleged that the Whytneys bore a longstanding grudge against him. The outcome of the lawsuit is not on record. People called Dale seemed to make a habit of falling foul of the law in days gone by, for in the Corporation Minutes at Newcastle under Lyme for the 7th August, 1599, Thomas Dale (alderman) was found guilty and fined five marks because he "...sayde at sondrye tymes and in severall places that the nowe maior of the towne of Newcastle is a skurvye rouge (sic), a knave, a raskell Jacke and a vyllayne, and wyshed alsoe that the sayd Mr Maior were hanged in a halter...." 1851:Ambrose Dale (butcher), Market Square, Tunstall; 1907:Enoch Dale (secondhand book seller), Burslem Market Hall.

During the seventeenth century the Udalls appear out of the blue at Ellastone; 1642:Ann Udall; 1664:John Udel; 1699:Sarah Udal. The immediate reaction is that these were Scottish immigrants from Udal in Inverness, Udal in North Uist, or Udale in Ross and Cromarty. But this is jumping the gun somewhat, I fancy. The surname is still found at Ellastone in 1851 - William Udale (tailor), with a variant form Yewdall/Yewdell also frequent; 1779:Ebenezer Yudall (collier) of Stoke. Ewe Dale in Pennington parish, Lancashire - "valley of the wolves" - is a much more acceptable base for the names.

Another compound in "-dale" typical of this zone is Ravensdale/Ransdale; 1332:Robert de Ravenesdale, taxed at Cauldon; 1532:Margery Rannsdall widow of Cauldon; 1666:James Ransdale of Whiston. Major sources include Ravensdale in Carsington and Ravensdale near Mickleover (both in Derbyshire) - "Hrafn's valley" or "valley of the ravens", although Ravensdale near Westport Lake, Tunstall, if an old name, must certainly be classed alongside these two; 1851:Thomas Ravensdale (farmer) of Ford, Grindon. Ramsdale is probably a variant of Ransdale or from Big, Little and Long Ramsdale in Odd Rode, Cheshire - "valley where rams grazed" or "valley where wild garlic flourished"; 1907:William Ramsdale of Liverpool Road, Kidsgrove.

The Scandinavian impact, touched upon earlier in Hulme, Toft and Leek, is also noticeable in The Slack near Fawfield Head, Stonyslack close by the River Hamps north of Winkhill and Waterslacks in the Manifold valley north of Ossoms Hill. All contain the Old Norse word "slakki" - a shallow valley or dell, the sense conveyed by the surname Slack for someone who dwelt there. In the hearth tax returns of 1666 there are 15 people with the surname Slack and they are all present in zones three and four, namely, at Horton near Rudyard, Rushton Spencer, Heaton, Longsdon, Ipstones, Sheen, Alstonefield, Stanton and Cheadle. At Leek in 1730 Richard Slack is described as a tallow chandler, and in 1765

James Slack of Knotbury took out a lease on a coalmine there for 21 years at a rent of £10. l5s. per annum from Sir Henry Harpur. 1851:William Slack (shoemaker) of Hollinsclough, Alstonefield; 1851:Joseph Slack (clock and watchmaker) of Kingsley. A nickname for a slack, lazy individual is also possible but not evidenced in the Staffordshire material.

In the Lake District a ravine or narrow glen is still called a "gill", from the Norsemen who settled there before the Conquest. This word has a hard "g" sound as in "give" - a dweller in a narrow glen; 1611:Grace Gill of Forsbrook; 1869:Eliza Gill, head teacher at Oulton School, Kibblestone. Old Norse "Gilli" - "servant", also results in Gill with a hard sound, but if Gill is spoken with a soft "g" as in "ginger", then this is from "Gille", a pet form of Gillian (Juliana); 1572:Matthew Gille of Bemersley. The variant Gell/Jell from Gelion (Jelion), another form of Juliana, is also extant; 1666:Francis Gell, exempt from hearth tax at Okeover, Ilam and Castern. The corresponding patronymic Gilson is for "son of Gill" or "son of Giles"; 1347:Juliana Gillesone of Fenton Vivian.

Old Norse "vra" - "nook, corner", hence a remote valley or isolated place, normally gives us Wroe/Wray; 1327:William in le wro of Penkhull; 1685:Anne Wray of Croxden; 1875:Hartley Wroe (beer seller), Sneyd Street, Tunstall. But this often loses the initial "W", becoming Rea; 1685:Thomas Wray of Stanshope (1682:Thomas Rea), or Ray(e); 1586:Thomas Wray of Hanchurch (1613:Thomas Raye); 1841:Moses Ray of Wynne and Ray's China Manufactory, Daisy Bank, Longton; 1907:John Ray (furnaceman) of Holly Place, Fenton. The series of surnames spelt Ray(e)/Rey/Rae/Rea/Ree/Rye also denote habitation by a stream or low lying land near a stream, or are nicknames from Old French "rei" - "king", appertaining to someone of a regal bearing. The Irish Rea is often equivalent to MacRea, Reagh or Reavy.

The Saxon "wincel" - "secluded nook" - is one origin of Winkle/Wincle/Winckle; 1685:Joan Winkle of Cheddleton, married to William Goold of Uttoxeter; 1851:Samuel Winkle (victualler), The Crown, Rushton James. Locatives involved here consist of Wincle south of Cleulow Cross - "Wineca's hill" and Winkhill near Waterfall (of doubtful meaning). In our county Winkle develops into Wintle because of the local tendency of pronouncing "wrinkle" as "wrintle"; 1532:John a Wyntull of Biddulph; (1539:John Wyncoll); 1907:George Wintle (labourer) of Cotton Street, Newcastle under Lyme.

The Dingle south west of Rushton Spencer (1842 Ordnance Survey) and the modern Dingle Brook and Dingle Lane in the same neighbourhood all preserve the Middle English "dingle" - "a dingle, deep dell or hollow"; 1327:Robert Dyngel of Stafford. This name is synonymous with Dell; 1616:John Dell of Checkley, and Slade; 1732:John Slade, vicar of Biddulph. The topographical term occurs in Slade House near Calton and Slade Hollow, north of Scrip Low, Stanton. The unattested compound Greenslade is either for a dweller in a green valley or a green glade between woodlands, as in "Greneslade" (1300) in Hilton near Shareshill and Green Slade in Mickleover, Derbyshire.

Old English "cumb" - "valley" is behind the basic "Combe(s)/Coombs/Coombes and Comber/Coomber/Cumber(s)/Coomer, all referring to residence in a small valley, although

Comber could also be derived from The Compa in Kinver, recorded as "Coumbere" in 1332 (of unknown origin) or might even be an occupational name for a maker of combs; 1887:Abel John Coomer (blacksmith) Marsh Street, Newcastle under Lyme; 1907:Henry Comer (bricklayer) of Pleasant Street, Burslem; 1907:Thomasina Coombes (sewing woman), Bath Street, Burslem; 1907:Harry Combs (fishmonger and greengrocer), High Street, Cheadle.

Rivers, streams, brooks

Surnames derived from the names of rivers are the exception rather than the rule. In North Staffordshire there are no families called Churnet, whilst Trent is unrecorded and Dove is a nickname for someone of a gentle disposition. On the other hand, Manifold is in good supply from the mid-sixteenth century; 1532:Nicholas Moneffold of Longnor; 1599:Robert, the supposed childe of George Warner, gentleman and Grace Manifoulde of Ellastone; 1851:George Manifold (farmer) of Wigginstall (Alstonefield parish); 1851:Ralph Manifold (shoemaker) of Sheen. The river name means literally "with many folds", an obvious allusion to its winding course, and hence, the surname Manifold is rather a nickname transferred from the river name, defining an individual whose personality was endowed with as many twists and turns as the river itself. Furthermore, Blyth(e) has no connection with the River Blithe, but once more is a nickname for a pleasant, happy-go-lucky person or from Blythe Bridge near Caverswall, Blythe End near Coleshill, Blyth north of Worksop or Blyth on the coast of Northumberland, a few miles up from St. Mary's Lighthouse; 1907:Charles Blyth, publican of the King William Inn, Bagnall Street, Newcastle; 1907:Jonathan Blyde of Queen Street, Goldenhill. Bligh and Blight are two additional modern variants.

Waterfall, north of Waterhouses, origin of the surname Waterfall, is actually the place where the River Hamps disappears in the ground; 1699:John Smith alias Watterfall, John (sic), in contradistinction to 1662:John Smith junior alias Whytehead (Alstonefield parish registers); 1851:William Waterfall, proprietor of the Izaak Walton Hotel in Dovedale. Waterhouses is one source of the surname Waterhouse, but the major origins are Waterhouse near Onecote and Waterhouse Farm, south of Longnor in the Manifold valley, or a toponymic for anyone who dwelt at a house by the water or at a moated house; 1632:Robert Waterhouse (sherman), buried at Ellastone. In 1881 the improvement Commissioners took over rooms in Union Buildings, Market Street, Leek, built as a concert hall in 1878 to the design of Alfred Waterhouse and others.

Water(s), At(t)water and Bywater(s) all designate residence by some stretch of water; 1400:William atte water of Bramshall; 1651:Robert Bywater of Cheadle; 1725:Cornelius Waters of Betley. Yet Water was a common medieval pronunciation of the Germanic personal name Walter; 1327:William Walters of Pillatonhall (Penkridge), cited as William Waters in 1332.

In North Staffordshire the surnames Twiss and Twist are traceable to three distinct locations. In Zone 4; 1395:Richard Twys of Bradnop and 1424:Gilbert de Twysse of Ilam are more than likely from the modern Twist (Green) in Butterton on the Moors, whilst 1685:James Twisse of Audley most probably had ancestry around Twiss's Wood in Rostherne or Twiss Brow in Great Budworth (both in Cheshire). These all contain a hypothetical Saxon word "twis", meaning a fork or junction where two streams met. In the case of Twist, Butterton on the Moors, Hoo Brook is not all that far away, and this at one time must have joined up with another nearby brook or stream.

Hoo Brook occurs as "Holebrook" in 1586, identical in meaning with Hole Brook, and Holbrook Farm near Alton, a stream that flows through a deep hollow in the vicinity before running into the River Churnet. Many indigenous Staffordshire families called Holbrook undoubtedly had ancestors who resided by one of these brooks, but Derbyshire migrants could have transplanted the name from Holbrook in Eckington or Holbrook Farm in Staveley, whilst William de Holdebroock, tenant of the Audleys at Betley in 1307, might well have come from "le holdebrok" (13th century) in Acton Grange near Nantwich which survives as Holdbrook; 1851:Richard Holbrook (school teacher and parish clerk) of Weston on Trent; 1851:Joseph Holebrook (plumber and glazier), Carter Street, Uttoxeter.

Forsbrook near Blythe Bridge - "Fot's brook" - has the variant Fosbrook(e); Wolstanton parish registers February 7th 1804:Mary Fosbrook, aged 2, daughter of Thomas and Ellen Fosbrook, buried.

Another compound with "-well" like Cresswell q.v., which is answerable for a wide range of unusual offshoots, is Caldwell. This form, along with Cauldwell, Coldwell and Couldwell are simple enough to interpret, for they signify a dweller by a cold spring (stream) or are derived from Coldwall near Blore in Dovedale, a lost "Caldewall" (1275) in Blurton, Cold Well between Gentleshaw and Goosemoor Green, or Caldwell near Swadlincote, just south of Burton upon Trent. 1587:George Caldwell (schoolmaster) of Leek; 1610:Mary Cauldwall of Standon. Caldwell/Cauldwell often become Caud(e)well, as testified in thirteenth century deeds from the Trentham Chartulary, where Robert de Caldewelle is also quoted as Robert de Caudewell. This is transformed into Cordwell; 1766:John Caldwell of Barlaston (1763:John Cordwell). Cordwell in Holmesfield, Derbyshire, was originally "Caldewell" in 1327, thus reinforcing the forms. In the Penkridge parish registers (1695-1733), Moses Caudwell (Cordwall) is variously written down as Cawdall, Cawdell, Cawdle and Caudal, with loss of "w" through lack of stress. Hence other variants like Cordell and Cordall belong here as well, together with Cardwell/Cardall; 1652:Margrett Cardewill(sic) of Norton in the Moors; 1778:William Cardall of Wolstanton. In certain cases, Calder represents an earlier "caldwell" as in "Calder croft" in Norbury near Gnosall, but Calder/Caulder are primarily north country surnames going back to Calder Bridge near Gosforth in Cumberland or Calder or Cawdor in Caithness; 1875:F.W.Calder (solicitor), High Street, Longton; 1875:John Cardall (second hand clothes dealer), Church Street, Burslem; 1907:Joseph Cordall (potter), Wain Street, Burslem; 1907:John Caudwell (butcher) of Middle Madeley; 1907:Frederick

Cardwell (potter), Ward Street, Hanley.

Farewell, near Lichfield, derives its name from its spring of fair, clean water, which comes from the red sandstone. A Benedictine Priory was founded here c. 1140 by Roger Clinton, Bishop of Coventry. The place is recorded in 1618 as "Farewell, Farwall, Farrall" and is the principal base of the surname Farrall/Farrell and Farwell, although Farwall near Calton (early spellings may also be involved at some date) is also implicated. However, there must be a number of post-Industrial Revolution Farrall/Farrell families in Staffordshire of Irish descent, from "O'Fearghail" - "man of valour"; 1851:James Farrall (farmer) of Stallington; 1851:Samuel Farrall (victualler), Hare and Hounds, Bradnop.

Fole on the River Tean in Leigh parish was the birthplace of William de Fowall, assessed for tax purposes at Tean in 1332. The meaning of the locality is uncertain - either stream used by cattle or multi-coloured stream. At any rate it has given the modern surnames Fowle(s)/Fowell(s) and Fowle, which are concentrated in Zones 3 and 4 up to the end of the seventeenth century; 1539:Elizabeth Fowall of Leek; 1666:Richard Fowell of Huntley (Cheadle); 1907:William Fowell (grocer), Elm Street, Cobridge. At Croxden Fowell mutates into Fower; 1717:William Fowell, is buried in 1729 as William Fower, whilst his daughter Jane, baptised as Jane Fowell in 1723, is known as Jane Fower on her marriage to Thomas Hulme of Butterton in the Moors in 1748. Outside our county the surname is for a hunter who pursued fowling or birdcatching for a living or a nickname for a person as elusive as the quarry he hunted, and Fower denotes a hearthkeeper.

The locations Goldsitch Moss east of Gradbach Hill and Smedley Sytch by Boosley Grange contain the Saxon 'sic" - a small stream, especially one flowing through flat terrain or marshy ground. It was also used in the sense of "gully, dip, hollow". The word developed into "siche" in the south and the midlands, giving the modern surname Sich/Sitch/Seach and became "sik(e)" in the north, resulting in Sykes/Sikes. Both forms survive as surnames in our county, but only Sykes is recorded for North Staffordshire; 1666:John Sikes, chargeable on one hearth at Weston Coyney; 1736:Edward Sykes (button merchant) of Leek.

Moorland

The Staffordshire Moorlands is a high tract of barren uncultivated land of considerable extent, covering large areas of Zones 3 and 4, and preserved in such names as Bradley in the Moors, Draycott in the Moors, Norton in the Moors, etc. More/Moor(e)/Moors/Morse define any person who dwelt by a moor or waste upland; 1391:Robert atte more of Ellastone; or who came from a place called More or Moor(e) such as 1284 Feudal Aids: "More juxta Weston (upon Trent)". Also pertinent is a personal name from Old French "Maur", Latin "Maurus" - "a Moor", or a nickname for someone who was as swarthy as a Moor; 1370:Robert More of Stafford (Dean of the free chapel of St. Mary). Just as Blore is pronounced locally as Blower, so More follows suit, turning into Mower; 1532:John More of Little Stoke near Stone (1539:John Mower). If the original name is Mower, as in

1332:William le mower of Cauldon, then this refers to a mower or cutter of crops or grass. 1907:Ann Moore (pork pie and sausage maker), Trentham Road, Longton; 1907:Edward Morse of the Spread Eagle Inn, Hope Street, Hanley. The rare Dillamore is either from Delamere, south west of Northwich - "the place by the lake", or an importation from any one of a number of villages called La Mare (the pool) in Normandy; 1907:William Dillamore, London Road, Chesterton; 1912:S. Delamere (carter), Derby Street, Hanley.

The basic Mor(e)land too is few and far between; 1851:John Morland (wharfinger, keeper of a wharf), Weston on Trent. Rather more substantial is Moor(e)house/Morehouse - "dweller at the house on the moor"; 1875:Edwin Moorhouse (superintendent of the public baths), Lichfield Street, Hanley. Moorhouse is regularly contracted to Morris; 1699:Joseph Morehouse of Kingsley (1701:Joseph Morris). On the whole Morris and Maurice are derived from the Classical name "Mauritius" - "Moorish, dark and swarthy like a Moor". According to legend, St. Maurice was an officer in charge of a Roman legion stationed in Switzerland, who was put to death along with all his men for refusing to sacrifice to the gods. 1841:Sarah Morris, one of the overseers in the apprentice girls' painting department at Wood and Brownfield's Earthenware Factory, Cobridge; 1851:John Morris, licensee of the Spotted Cow, Cellarhead.

Instead of a house, the person in question may have dwelt at a croft on the moor; 1532:William Marcroft of Warslow; 1691:Millisent Morecroft of Rocester; 1851:John Moorcroft (farmer) of Cheadle Mill, or at the hall on the moor; 1436:Henry Morehall of Bagnall; 1584:Joanna Morrall widow of Norton in the Moors. The variant Murrall/Murrell as in 1666:John Murrall of Cheadle is also, on occasion, from the Celtic name "Muriel" - "sea bright"; 1327:John Muryel of Kingstone, near Uttoxeter. One gruesome legend concerns William Murhall of Bagnall, the county magistrate (died 1762), who had a Scottish Jacobite skinned over a signpost at Leek and then had the hide sent to the tanyard at Endon to be made into leather for a drum head!

The vacillation between Morrall/Murrall is repeated in Morrey/Murrey/Murray. This denotes habitation at the enclosure on the moor or is from Morrey near Yoxall, Higher Morrey near Shavington in Salop or Middle Morrey near Wilkesley on the Shropshire/Cheshire border; 1589:John Morrey of Oulton (Kibblestone) was granted a licence at the Quarter Sessions to run an alehouse. In the Swynnerton parish registers, William Morry (1809) of Sandyford, appears as William Murray in 1812. However other local Murrays are of Scottish ancestry with roots in Moray; 1875:Edward Murray (sponge merchant) of Church Street, Longton; 1875:John R. Murray (ironmonger and tinman), Newcastle Street, Burslem.

One compound in this zone which is very difficult to pin down is Beardmore/Beardsmore. It is quite clear that the surnames congregate around the Cheadle/Alton area from the Middle Ages up to the middle of the sixteenth century; 1311:Richard de Berdmor of Whiston; 1448:John Berdesmore of Froghall; 1532:Thomas Berdmore of Alton; 1532:John Berdemore of Kingsley. These names must be preserved in Broadmoor Wood, Hollington. With the familiar shift of "r" the original "Berdmore" became "Bredmore" and then "Breadmore" before attaining its final form. At the Staffordshire Assizes, on 13th June, 1836, John Beardmore, aged 30, was transported for life for stealing two rams at Caldon, the property of Thomas Mellor. 1851:Thomas Beardmore (iron and brass founder) of Liverpool Road, Burslem.

Barns, huts, shelters

Strictly speaking "barns" are storehouses where barley was once kept and the surname Barn(e)s, as in 1334:Robert del bernes of Uttoxeter designated habitation near or employment at some barns; 1532:Randal Barnes, monk at Dieulacres Abbey; 1542:Alice Barns of Crakemarsh; 1666:Richard Barnes, ineligible for hearth tax at Cheadle; 1851:Elizabeth Barnes, licensee of The Unicorn, High Street, Stone. The Scandinavian equivalent is Latham/Lathom/Lathem/Laytham, which go back to Lathom near Skelmersdale, Latham in the West Riding of Yorkshire or Laytham north east of Selby in the East Riding. All refer to a place at the barns; 1666:Katherine Lathame, chargeable on two hearths at Draycott in the Moors; 1851:Darius Latham (gardener, fruiterer, seedsman), Kilncroft, Burslem; 1907:John Latham (checkweighman), Ellgreave Street, Burslem.

Booth comes from a Scandinavian word for a cowhouse or a herdsman's hut, as in Hardingsbooth west of Longnor, and in John de la both, tenant of the Audleys at Alstonefield in 1307. This John lived in such a shelter, and was perhaps in charge of the herds of cattle on the lord's manor, and consequently identical in meaning with Boothman in the sense of "cowman, herdsman"; 1887:Reverend E.D. Boothman (M.A.), rector of St. Mark's, Rectory Road, Hanley; 1907:W Boothman (foreman), Potteries Electric Traction, Selwyn Street, Stoke. According to Guppy's survey, the surname Booth is concentrated in the Danelaw counties of Cheshire, Derbyshire, Lancashire, Lincolnshire, Nottinghamshire and Staffordshire. Indeed in our county it ramifies extensively across the whole of North Staffordshire from the 1600s onwards; 1624:Edmund Boothe of Leek Frith; 1666:Francis Booth of Rushton Spencer and Cloudwood; 1666:William Boothe of Butterton on the Moors; 1851:Eliza Booth (hosier), Newcastle Street, Burslem; 1907:Miss Fanny Booth (New Crown Dining Rooms), High Street, Hanley.

The allied name Scales/Scholes is also from a Scandinavian term for a hut or shed, found in Scholar Green near Mow Cop and Schoolclough, south east of Hardingsbooth. Again this is very much a surname typical of the northern Danelaw shires, derived from localities such as Scales near Aldingham, Scales in Ribbleton, Newton with Scales, Scholes near Wigan and Scholes in Sefton parish (all in Lancashire), plus several places in Yorkshire - Scholes near Rotherham, Scholes east of Holmfirth, Scholes north west of Cleckheaton, and Scholes on the north eastern outskirts of Leeds, with the Cumbrian involvement focussed on Scales near Threlkeld. 1851:William Scales (superintendent of the carriage department of the North Staffs Railway), Stoke; 1907:Archie Scoles (clerk), Honeywall, Penkhull.

Woodland

The woodland saga continues with Whitehurst, which is not far from the Godleybrook terminal on the Foxfield Light Railway, Dilhorne; 1332:Richard del whytehurst of Dilhorne and Forsbrook. The place may refer to a copse or wooded hillock on chalky soil, but this is far from certain. 1851:John Whitehurst (sawyer) of Darlaston, Stone; 1851:Jacob Whitehurst of the Roebuck, Brookhouses, Cheadle. There may be some confusion with Whitehouse; 1787:Richard Whitchurst (sic) of Tittensor (1790:Richard Whitehouse). In this case the name would denote residence at a white (stone) house; 1875:Sampson Whitehouse (butcher), John Street, Longton.

The widespread Broadhurst is either for a dweller by the broad wood or from Broadhurst near Caldon Low quarries (1836 Ordnance Survey map), Broadhurst in Brewood or Broadhurst Green on Cannock Chase; 1851:Henry Broadhurst, licensee of the Churnet Valley Hotel, Station Road, Leek; 1851:Joseph Broadhurst (hairdresser and fancy dealer), Church Street, Silverdale.

What surname is more evocative of the pristine woods and forests of medieval England than Greenwood, where, according to folklore, Robin Hood and his fellow outlaws had their hideout, and were engaged in a war of attrition against the Sheriff of Nottingham. The surname Greenwood, alas, is imbued with no such fanciful illusions, for it is simply descriptive of a dweller in the green wood; 1583:Julyan (Juliana) Grenewoodde of Ellastone; 1851:Reverend Henry Greenwood, incumbent at Aston, Stone; 1875:James F. Greenwood (clothier and pawnbroker), Piccadilly, Hanley. Prestwood and Priestwood are essentially South Staffordshire surnames, derived either from Prestwood near Stourton (Kinver) or Prestwood in Wednesfield - wood originally belonging to some priests. Yet John de Prestwode, taxed at Ellastone in 1327, is to be traced to Prestwood about one mile away to the south west, the wood here belonging to the Augustinian canons at Calwich Abbey; 1907:John Prestwood (bricklayer), Gordon Street, Fenton; 1907:Mrs Eliza Priestwood of High Lane, Burslem.

The compound Woodhouse, Wodehouse - "dweller at the house in the wood" is early and widely scattered; 1327:Adam de Wodehous of Mayfield in the valley of the Dove, contrasting with 1416:John Jolye del wodehouse of Newcastle under Lyme. The ending is often clipped, forming such modern variants as 1851:Edmund Woodisse(farmer), Old Rakes, Sheen, and 1887:Joseph Woodus (hotel manager), Piccadilly, Hanley. These recall the dialectal "coalus" for "coalhouse". Woodhouse also fluctuates with Widdowes; 1594:Oliver Seckerson alias Widhouse of Stafford, quoted as Olyver Wodhouse alias Seckerson in 1595. Widdow(e)s normally alludes to a widow or widower as in 1327:Avicia le wydowe of Waterfall, and 1420:Hugh Turnour wydowe of Ipstones.

One highly unpredictable compound in "-shaw" which has made its home in this zone is Wilshaw/Wilsher and its numerous variants. All authorities derive it unhesitatingly from the county of Wiltshire, and an isolated instance such as 1414:Robert Wilteshire of Normacot apparently corroborates this theory. However, with regard to the North Staffordshire Wilshaws several other avenues are far more promising. First and foremost

LOCAL GRAVESTONES WITH
EXAMPLES OF NAMES FROM
THIS SECTION

is the locality Willshaw near Hollinsclough (no early forms), although 1307:William de Walshawe of Alstonefield could have come from the place, or this may go back to Wilsher Place in Wildboarclough, north east of Cleulow Cross, since the latter is found as "Walschawe" in the Middle Ages - "copse by a stream". In addition, our attention must be drawn to Wilshaw House in Newbold Astbury, recorded as "Wilshawe" in the sixteenth century - "wild wood", whilst also noteworthy is Wilshers in Croston parish, Lancashire, which occurs as "Wlfschahe(sic)" in the Middle Ages - "copse frequented by a she-wolf". All in all, a derivation from the county of Wiltshire seems a very remote prospect in the light of all the above possibilities; 1851:William Willshaw (beerhouse), Bradley Green, Biddulph; William Wiltshaw, a coal dealer of Sandy Lane, Brown Edge, was appointed one of the trustees of the Wesleyan Chapel in 1894.

Akin to the Saxon "shaw" is the Scandinavian "skogr", which forms the ending of the locality Swinscoe between Stanton and Blore - "pig wood"; 1875:David Swinscoe (grocer), Rathbone Street, Tunstall; 1907:Arthur Swinscoe (potter), Scotia Road, Burslem.

Surnames in "-ley"

In medieval times the little market town of Cheadle - "glade in Chetwood" - stood on the ancient salt route, linking Nantwich and Derby, along which pack horses travelled, carrying loads of salt; 1600:Symond Chedle husbandman of Stowe by Chartley; 1875:Frances Cheadle of the Eagle and Child Inn, Audley Road, Chesterton; 1907:E.D.Cheatle (grocer's manager), St. John Street, Hanley. Cheadle Hulme in Cheshire (same meaning) is a secondary source of the surnames.

In 1204 William de Checkley escaped from the donjon at Newcastle, thereby being outlawed. His family most likely stemmed from Checkley just over the Staffordshire-Cheshire border near Blakenhall, rather than from Checkley in the valley of the River Tean. Both places probably mean "wood of Ceacca". 1887:John Checkley (maltster) of Sutherland Road, Longton.

On the death of Thomas de Fournival in 1339, who held the Castle and manor of Alton with its members and appurtenances, one of the signatories called upon to swear on oath the actual extent of the deceased's possessions was Richard de Fernelay of Alton, who obviously came from Farley near the modern Alton Towers pleasure park - "fern-covered clearing." This location is without doubt the prime source of the Staffordshire surname Farley/Farleigh, yet there are places so called in many counties too numerous to mention, which could well have become integrated with the local Farleys.

Some folklorists maintain that Loxley near Uttoxeter - "Locc's glade" was Robin Hood's stamping ground, but the legend is so shrouded in mystery that any historical basis has all but lost its credibility and the benevolent character of the popular imagination has taken over. Leaving this aside the surname Loxley, together with Locksley and probably Lockley, all derive from the aforementioned Loxley, synonymous with Loxley near Stratford on Avon, or from Lockley Wood near Cheswardine, Salop - "glade with an enclosure"; 1532:Robert Lokeley, rector at Tixall; 1851:Thomas Lockley (farmer), Hill

Farm, Croxton; 1887:Alfred Locksley (commercial traveller), Leek Road, Smallthorne.

Mobberley south of Cheadle and Mobberley near Knutsford, Cheshire - "glade by the mound where assembly moots were held" - have joined forces to bring us the surname Mobberley; 1572:Margaret Mobberley of Kingsley; 1907:G. Mobberley (potter's painter), Hazlehurst Street, Hanley, and Mabberley; 1588:William Mabberley of Cheadle. The latter also hints at Mabley/Mably, but these are shortened forms of the female name "Amabilis" - "lovable"; 1327:William son of Mabille of Ellastone; 1332:Robert Mably of Leek.

Housley/Ouseley is an awkward customer. The modern Ousley Wood and Ousley Lane south of Rangemoor Wood, Upper Ellastone, are presumably implicated in some of the surnames. Ousley Brook which runs into Rangemoor Brook has been taken as referring to a glade by a muddy place or marsh. At Ellastone in 1682, Edward Langford is stated as being from Ouseley Crosse, whilst on the 1836 Ordnance Survey map there is a locality known as Housley Barn in Bradley in the Moors. This body of evidence, supported by such instances as 1637:Richard Housley of Leek and 1666:Thomas Housley of Alstonefield, confirms that the surnames evolved in this zone. Nevertheless at Leek the name alternates with Horsley; 1683:Thomas Howsley (1685:Thomas Horsly). If Horsley is the original form, then this is derived from Horsley near Eccleshall - "pasture for horses". Finally, a case is also to be made out for Houseley, east of Tideswell, Derbyshire, of obscure meaning; 1907:Thomas Housley (carter), Oxford Street, Longton; 1907:George Ouseley (potter), Windmill Street, Tunstall.

With Woolley, too, there is more than meets the eye. First impressions favour Woolley (The Woolley) near Brewood - "wood or glade of the wolves", incontrovertible proof that wolves once roamed wild in the county. Indeed, they were not exterminated until the end of the thirteenth century. In 1281, for instance, a licence was granted to Peter Corbet to take wolves by man, dog or traps wherever they could be found in Staffordshire, Shropshire, Worcestershire, Herefordshire and Gloucestershire. Alternatives consist of Woolley in Brackenfield, Derbyshire, about 15 miles from Warslow, Woolley Bridge east of Mottram in Longdendale and Woolley, north west of Barnsley, all sharing the same derivation as the Staffordshire locality. Wolfe Low Farm near The Bridestones has been tentatively put forward as a base, but this has not yet been verified. In 1588, William Wooley of Alton bequeathed to his brother John in his will *"my spurs, my saddle and bridle and my best cote, to my mother Alis Wolley my cloke, to Godfrey Nedham my medley hose and jerkin, to the son of Thomas Bayley my blue cote and to Elen Sherrat a pere of nether stocks"* (stockings). 1851:Edward Woolley (tailor) of Mount Pleasant, Kingstone; 1875:John Woolley (electric bellhanger), Waterloo Road, Burslem.

Surnames in "-ton"

Newton - "new village" - is probably the most widespread of all English placenames, noted at least a hundred times from Northumberland to Cornwall and even over the border in Wales. The Staffordshire Newtons are principally traced back to Newton by Blithfield or Newton between Cresswell and Upper Tean; 1604:Hughe and Elizabethe Newton, poore laboringe foulkes (of Ellastone); 1851:James Newton, owner of an eating house in Market Square, Tunstall; 1875:Hannah Newton (grocer), Hope Street, East Vale, Longton.

About two miles south of Newton (Cresswell) is Middleton Green - "the middle village", which is responsible for a high percentage of local families called Middleton, but neighbouring counties must also have played their part. Of special mention are the following - the Derbyshire trio of Middleton near Winster, Middleton by Wirksworth and Stoney Middleton, whilst the Shropshire contingent comprise Middleton near Ludlow, Middleton near Oswestry and Middleton near Chirbury. At Kibblestone in 1753, Sampson Cotton was allowed 2 shillings "poor relief" "...for clothes for daughter of Vernon Middleton and to take her into service".

If we follow the course of the old Roman road from Upper Tean to Hollington, then we come to the village of Overton immediately to the south - "upper homestead" or "homestead on the bank of a brook", since Broadgatehall Brook is close by. This is one origin of the surname Overton, supplemented by Higher Overton in Biddulph and Orton near Penn which evinces the form "Overton" in the fourteenth century. Hence the vacillation between Overton and Orton; 1666:Kathren Overton widow of Tean; 1841:John Orton, aged 8, working in the oven for the oven-man Thomas Asprey at F. and R. Pratt and Company, Earthenware Factory, Fenton; 1907:Enoch Overton (miner) of Bradford Terrace, Birches Head.

Two miles south of Overton (Hollington) lies Creighton - "place by a rock or cliff", origin of Creighton and Crayton; 1728, November 28th:Mary Crayton, married to Francis Biddle (Lichfield Cathedral Registers); Isaac Creighton of Cromwell Terrace (Leek) was turning wooden bobbins for the textile industry in the early 1880s. In Scotland these spellings compete with Crichton in Midlothian - "boundary place", a name immortalised by Sir Thomas Urquhart in his account of The Admirable Crichton, otherwise James Crichton, the brilliant Scottish traveller, scholar and swordsman who won a Master of Arts degree at the age of fourteen in 1574.

North of Creighton, just beyond the same Roman road which runs from Hollington to Rocester, is a small spot called Pointhorne, recorded as "the Pinthorn" in 1779 (Croxden parish registers). Significantly, at Rocester in 1799, John Adams is quoted as living at Pointon in the parish of Croxden, and consequently the surname Pointon/Poynton in our county is often to be traced to this particular tiny place on the map. Other local Pointons and Poyntons probably owe their ancestry to Poynton near Bramhall, Cheshire, Poynton near Shawbury, Shropshire or Pointon north west of Spalding, Lincolnshire (of varying etymologies); 1851:James Pointon (wheelwright) of Biddulph; 1875:Thomas Pointon, Davenport Arms, Wharf Street, Middleport. In the Rocester parish registers three other variants are brought into focus; 1718:Joseph Pountain; 1810:Mary Paintin (sic), which obviously becomes the modern Painting. Samuel Pountain (1806), is also written down as Samuel Pounteney in 1805.

The pleasant, compact village of Alton in the Churnet valley - Aelfa's homestead" is now world famous for its unrivalled pleasure park, yet the bulk of the visitors who flock here every year are probably unaware that the hill on which Alton stands - Bunbury Hill - was once an Iron Age fort, dating back to the third century BC, and that, during the Civil Wars, Alton Castle was used as a parliamentary garrison and suffered considerable damage. Be that as it may, the surname Alton is very scarce; Brother Thomas Alton was elected prior at Ranton Abbey in 1511, and he may have traced his roots back to Alton near Wirksworth in Derbyshire - "old farmstead" rather than to the local Alton.

TOTMONSLOW HUNDRED.   753

WESTON-COYNEY & HULME.
Marked 1 *are at Adderley green;* 2, *Hulme;* 3, *Wherrington; and* 4, *at Cellar Head.*

Buckley John, corn miller
2 Bull Wm. blacksmith
Coyney Cs. Esq. *Weston-Coyney Hl*
3 Cooper Samuel, schoolmaster
Hicks Richd. Esq. guano merchant, &c. *Fox Earth*
Keen Geo. butler, & Mrs Ann Broster, house keeper, Park Hall
Parker Thos. Hawe, Esq. *Park Hall*
3 Prince John, tailor
1 Pye Thomas, coal master
3 Reeves Thomas, joiner, &c.
Slinn George, blacksmith
1 Stirrup and Pye, coal masters
2 Walker John, farrier, &c.
Walklate Mrs Eliz., *Adderley House*

INNS & TAVERNS.
1 Bird-in-Hand, Samuel Robinson
2 Coyney's Arms, Wm. Hurst
4 Hope and Anchor, Thomas Heath
3 Red Cow, L. Clarkson, butcher
1 Waggon and Horses, Jph. Simcox
3 Wind Mill, Mk. Greatbatch, miller
Beerhouses, Wm. Bentley & Jno. Lees

FARMERS.
Beardmore Thps
Bradbury Jas
Brookes John
2 Davis Joseph, and butcher
2 Finney John
1 Forrister Geo
Hassall Danl
2 Heath Geo
Heath Wm
3 Lees Gabriel
Poyser Jonathan
2 Shaw Anty
2 Shaw Jas.&Spn
2 Shaw Ralph
2 Smith John
2 Wain Mrs
2 Walklate Thos
Walters Anty. cattle dlr. *Blythe House*
Wardle John
2 Wright Thos

SHOPKEEPERS.
1 Daniel Geo
3 Downes John
3 Greatbatch Mk
3 Lees John
4 Shenton Thos

CHEADLE, celebrated for its splendid new Roman Catholic Church, is about 10 miles from Leek, Uttoxeter, and Stone, 13 miles E. of Newcastle-under-Lyme, about three miles from *Froghall and Oakamoor Stations* on the Churnet Valley line, and four miles E.N.E. of *Blythe Bridge Station*, on the main line of the North Staffordshire Railway. It is a small but neat market town, seated in a pleasant vale, between the small river Tean and one of its tributary streams ; surrounded by lofty hills, most of which have been enclosed and cultivated since 1815, and the sterile parts planted with firs and other trees. Among these hills are several valuable collieries, from which the inhabitants are supplied with coal. The *parish* increased its population from 2750 in 1801, to 5730 souls in 1841, and has now upwards of 6000. It contains about 6700 acres of land, divided into four *quarters,* for the reparation of the public roads, viz. *Cheadle, Above-Park, Cheadle Grange,* and *Huntley.* The soil belongs to a number of proprietors, the largest of whom are Sir J. B. Y. Buller, Bart., lord of the manor of Cheadle ; John Bill, Esq., lord of Cheadle Grange ; and James Beech, Wm. Allen, and John W. Patten, Esqrs. The hamlets in the parish, and their distances from the town, are BROOKHOUSES, on the river Tean, ¾ mile S.W. ; CHEADLE MILL, ½ mile S. ; ABOVE-PARK, 2 miles N.W. ; CHEADLE GRANGE, 1¼ mile E. ; HUNTLEY and MOBBERLEY, 1½ mile S. ; and OAKAMOOR, on the river Churnet, 2½ miles E. by N. ; but a small part of the latter is in Kingsley and Alton parishes. Messrs. Patten & Co., have extensive *brass and copper works* at Oakamoor, where they smelt *ingots of copper and brass,* and manufacture them into *bars, sheets, rollers, wire, &c. ;* as Messrs. Keys & Sons do at the Brass and Copper Works at Brookhouses. The latter have also similar works at Kingsley. The copper ore was formerly supplied from the mines at Mixon and Ecton, in this county, but is now

A page taken from White's History, Gazetteer and Directory of Staffordshire 1851 (second edition, first edition 1834).

Approximately four miles away to the north west, on the opposite side of the valley is Whiston, which is to be taken with Whiston not far from Penkridge. Both localities signify a settlement used as a base by some Saxon known as "Hwit" or "Witi", or possibly a homestead by a white stone and both are behind most of the Staffordshire families named Whiston, although there could also be a toponymic for a dweller by a white stone. Hearth tax contributors in 1666 include Thomas Whiston on two hearths at Bradnop, widdow (sic) Whiston on two hearths at Uttoxeter and William Whiston on one hearth at Cheadle. 1875:James Whiston (iron and brass founder), Canning Street, Fenton.

Cotton, nestling in a wooded valley, two miles away to the south east, is also steeped in history, surrounded on all sides by prehistoric burial mounds and tumuli such as Threelows and Beelow Hill. The locality means "(the place) at the cottages", and is thus identical with Coton near Milwich, Coton by Stafford, Coton Clanford in Ranton, Coton near Hopwas and Coton near Gnosall. With this abundance of sources at our disposal, it is hardly surprising,that the surname Cotton/Cotten/Coton/Coaton and Cottam proliferates in virtually every region of the county. As a result of the Bishop's visitation in 1636, Thomas Cotton of Stoke-on-Trent was excommunicated "....*for takeing the psalme out of the minister's mouth as he was in giveing it and afterward justifieing himselfe for so doinge.*" 1851:Caroline Cotton (farmer) of Hilderstone; 1912:John Cottam (printer), Balfour Street, Hanley. Charles Cotton, the poet and fishing companion of Izaak Walton, lived at Beresford Hall near Alstonefield, and was so beguiled by the landscape in north eastern Staffordshire that he celebrated it in verse: "*Oh, my beloved nymph, fair Dove, princess of rivers, how I love, upon thy flowery banks to lie.*"

No less a writer than Mary Ann Evans (pen name George Eliot) was inspired by the setting of Ellastone for her novel "Adam Bede", in which Ellastone was transposed into Hayslope. But other literary figures were less impressed. Amongst them was the French philosopher, Jean-Jacques Rousseau,who arrived in England in 1766 as a refugee, driven out of his native France because of his relentless attacks on the Church and State. He chose Wootton Hall in the valley of the Dove for its seclusion, but the peace and solitude only aggravated his manic depression. The village of Wootton in the shelter of the Weaver hills denotes a homestead by a wood, as does its namesake Wootton south of Eccleshall. From these two locations have come generation after generation of Staffordshire Woottons, Woottens and Wottons, but there are places called Wootton with distinctive additions in at least fifteen other English counties, and some of these probably drifted into Staffordshire over the years; 1841:Phillip Wootton, mould carrier at Ashwell and Cooper's Earthenware Factory, Longton; 1875:James Wootton (parish coffin maker and joiner), Chapel Street, Wolstanton; 1907:Thomas Wootton (confectioner), Leek Road, Hanley.

Stanton - "village in stony terrain" - is a tiny, isolated place on the eastern rim of the Weaver Hills, best known as the birthplace in 1598 of Gilbert Sheldon, who, at the Restoration became Bishop of London and then Archbishop of Canterbury. Stanton occurs in numerous other counties, but of special importance are a handful of Derbyshire localities, consisting of Stanton near Swadlincote, Stanton by Bridge (south of Derby), Stanton by Dale near Ilkeston and Stanton in Peak not far from Haddon Hall. On the opposite side of the county the name may have been brought in by families with roots in Stanton Long west of Bridgnorth, Stanton Lacy north of Ludlow or Stanton upon Hine Heath south east of Wem; 1851:George and Jesse Stanton (cratemakers), Lower Green, Newcastle under Lyme; 1851:John Stanton, licensee of the Roebuck, Forsbrook; 1912:H.Stanton (watch repairer), Proctor's Row, Stoke.   Staunton is a rare variant; 1592:Thomas Staunton of Great Chatwell.

Wetton in the heart of the Staffordshire Moorlands - "village on a wet hill" - certainly lives up to its name, since it is open to the elements on all sides and at all seasons. Yet it is in this very region where prehistoric man's legacy is all pervading, from the burial mounds scattered everywhere, which were excavated in the nineteenth century by Samuel Carrington of Wetton and the Derbyshire antiquarian Thomas Bateman, to the famous Thor's Cave and the later archaeological finds dating back to the Roman occupation. It is here too, of course, where the surname Wetton first ramifies before it is taken to other parts of the county by enterprising families eager to put down their roots elsewhere; 1532:William Wetton of Gratwich; 1640:Henry Wetton of Leigh (near Tean), member of the trained band in the local muster; 1851:Joseph Wetton (hairdresser) of High Street, Stone; 1851:John Wetton (tailor) of Great Haywood.

Beeston Tor close by Wetton Low is probably the base of many a local Beeston. It is recorded as "Beistone" in 1552 and its derivation has not yet been determined. But there are additional origins to ponder such as Beeston east of Tattenhall, Cheshire - "stone where commerce took place", Beeston near Nottingham, Beeston a suburb of Leeds (West Riding), Beeston south east of Bedford and no less than four localities in Norfolk - Beeston Regis, Beeston St. Andrew, Beeston St. Lawrence and Beeston near East Dereham. All these places signify a village where reed or rush grew. Beeston near Nottingham is pronounced "Beeson", hence the doublet Beeston-Beeson/Beason; 1851:Richard Beeston (station master), Madeley; 1875:Charles Beeson (Beeston), seedsman of High Street, Mount Pleasant, Fenton; 1851:Jesse Beason (chapel clerk), Kidsgrove.

Before the Industrial Revolution the surname Clifton is concentrated mainly in the southern half of the county, where the origin is Clifton Campville near the river Mease not far from the Staffordshire/Leicestershire border - "settlement on a hill, hill slope or brink of a river". However, in North Staffordshire, the principal origin is perhaps Clifton south of Ashbourne on the opposite side of Dovedale from Church Mayfield, with external assistance from Cliftons in umpteen other counties. 1421:John Clyfton was elected sub-prior at the Augustinian Priory of Trentham on the resignation of Thomas de Trentham; 1875:Sarah Clifton (infants' mistress), Catholic Schools, of Church Terrace, Cobridge.

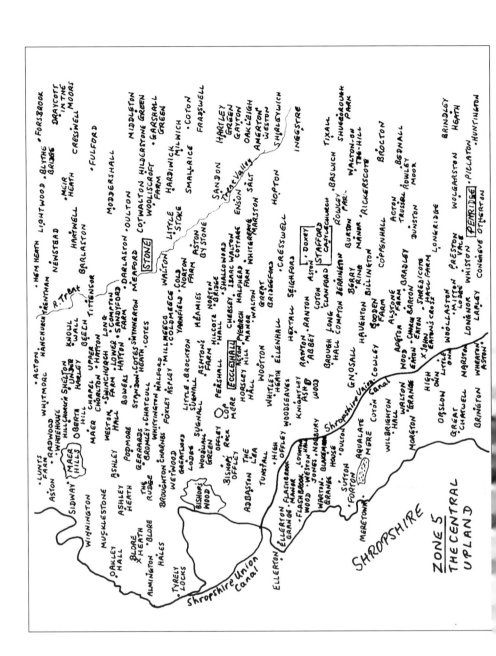

Zone Five: The Central Upland

Fenn 170
Wagg 170
Doxey 170
Slinn/Slyne/Slaney 170
Heames/Haymes/Eames 171
Pybus 171
Halfhide/Heyford/Halford/Holford/Alford 173
Hide/Hyde 173
Walford 173
Fulford 173
Stafford 173
Platt 174
Tittensor 174
Swing(e)wood/Swinswood 174
Rudge/Ridge/Riggs 175
Smalldridge 175
Eccleshall 175
Pershall/Pursell/Purcell 175
Moddershall/Mottershaw 175
Yoxall 176
Wetwood 176
Ashwood/Dashwood 176
Haywood/Hayward 176
Collingwood 177
Lunt/Lowndes/Laund/Lunn 177
Aldershaw/Oldershaw/
Eldershaw/Ollerenshaw 177
Alldersey/Alder(s) 178
Greatolder 178
Perry 178
Ashley 178
Aspley 178
Oakley 178
Barclay 178
Brierley 178
Hadley/Hateley/Heatley 178
Wheatley/Whateley 179
Barlow/Barley/Burley 180
Abberley/Habberley 180
Stockley 181
Langley/Longley 181
Shelley 181

Harley/Hartley 181
Oxley 182
Shipley/Shepley 182
Cowley/Coley/Colley 182
Offley 183
Wolseley 183
Sedgley 183
Fradley 183
Walton 183
Acton 183
Ashton 184
Parton 184
Thornton 184
Brereton 184
Hazleton/Heseltine/Hazeldene 185
Ellerton 185
Withington 185
Barton 185
Leighton 186
Hopton 186
Compton 186
Hatton 186
Mor(e)ton 187
Mars(t)on/Mitton/Mutton/Myton 187
Wharton 187
Hampton 188
Swynnerton 188
Colton/Coulton 188
Burton 189
Broughton 189
Oulton/Olton 189
Billington 189
Amberton/Emberton 189
Loynton/Laynton 189
Croxton/Cruxton/Crowson 189
Whittington 189
Winnington 190
Willington 190
Charlton/Chorlton/Carlton 190
Knighton 190
Preston/Presson 190

Zone Five

This region is mainly an undulating plain consisting of strong clay or clay-loam soils of great fertility, but very difficult to work. It is drained by the River Trent and its tributaries, the Sow and the Blithe. This central clayland was one of the most prosperous areas of Domesday Staffordshire and this is reflected in the surname Clay, which has been a permanent fixture in this region from the Middle Ages. Sibilla de Cley, mentioned in an inquisition at Stone in 1326, is called upon to give to the Prior and Convent of Stone a messuage (a dwelling house with outbuildings and land assigned to its use). Her name denotes that she dwelt on clayey ground, but the modern name Clay may also apply to workers employed in a clay-pit, who prepared excavated clay for use in making bricks or in the wattle and daub process of making walls of medieval houses. Of course, in a county famous all over the world for its pottery it is one of the most appropriate surnames for a local potter to have. 1568:Isabell Clay of Mucklestone; 1647:Francis Clay of Burslem; 1666:Widdow Claye, not chargeable for hearth tax at Stone; 1807, March 29th:Anne, illegitimate daughter of Harriet Clay of Tittensor, baptised at Swynnerton.

The rich grasslands in this zone have always supported great herds of cattle. The method of farming favoured in medieval Staffordshire was with open arable fields and meadows and the Saxon word "aecer' referred to a field or land which had been ploughed. The surname Acres/Ackers/Akers signified a dweller by a plot of arable land; 1666:Edward Akers, taxed on two hearths at Uttoxeter; 1887:William and Henry Acres (drapers), Market Square, Hanley; 1907:Mrs Lilley Acres of Leek New Road, Cobridge. Of the compounds only Whitaker/Whiteaker/Whittaker/Whitticase occurs with any regularity. It designates residence by a white field, as in 1332:Roger de Whyteacre of Sandon; 1539 Muster:Ralph Whitacres of Kibblestone, equipped with a bill; 1875:James Whittaker (beerseller), Eagle and Snake, Waterloo Road, Burslem. The Oldacre territory - "dweller by the old ploughed field"; 1532:Richard Oldacur of Colton, south of Blithfield Reservoir; 1907:William Oldacre (potter), Norfolk Street, Shelton (Hanley) intriguingly, overlaps that of Newland(s), as exemplified by 1337:Richard del Newelond of Hamstall Ridware - "dweller by the newly cleared land" or "land newly acquired". His name is preserved in Newlands about a mile and a half from Colton to the north east. 1458:Thomas New(e)land of Newlands(Colton); 1907:Henry Newland of Marsh Terrace, Marsh Parade, Newcastle under Lyme.

In the Middle Ages there were two types of meadows; the large common meadow, where all the local tenants had the right to gather hay in accordance with how much arable land they held, and freehold meadows which were not subject to village control. Habitation by meadowland is evident in a recording such as 1327:Peter del medwe of High Offley - the modern Meadow(s); October 15th 1738:Sarah Meadow, married Thomas Morey at Seighford. The singular form is later corrupted to Madew/Maydew;

1532:Richard Madew of Stafford; 1799:Thomas Maydew of Stoke-on-Trent; 1851:Thomas Madew, licensee of the Boar's Head, Halmerend.

One surname above all is a permanent reminder of medieval farming methods - Fallows - which denotes residence by ploughed or arable land, broken up, harrowed, and ready for sowing; 1539 Muster:William Falowes of Hixon; 1666:John Fallowes senior and junior, exempt from hearth tax at Milwich; 1912:William Fallows (bowlmaker), Pitt Street, Longton. Fallows is converted not only into Follows, as confirmed by Diana Fallows who signs her own name as Dianah Follows in the Bucknall cum Bagnall parish register for 1811, but also into Fellows; 1724:Joseph Fallows of Shelton under Harley, noted as Joseph Fellows in 1731. Fellows/Fellowes is either from Old Norse "felagi" - "partner, co-worker, companion", as in Richard Felawe of Lichfield (c. 1200) or from Fellhouse, a weakened form of Fieldhouse; 1677:Dannell Fellhouse of Castlechurch.

As we have already seen, the medieval croft was any piece of enclosed land used for tillage or pasture, that is, a small tract of arable land next to the peasant's place of residence where he cultivated his own crops and vegetables. Of all the compounds in "-croft" the only serious challenger to the superiority of Holdcroft is Wooliscroft/Woolliscroft and Williscroft, which goes back to Wooliscroft Farm between Cotwalton and Hilderstone. It is recorded as "Willanescroft" in a twelfth century deed from the Cartulary of Stone Priory, where "n" represents "v", giving us a croft that once belonged to a Saxon called Wiglaf. In 1605 the locality is found as "Wollascroft, Willowescroft, Wyllescroft", thus providing us with the fluctuation between Wooliscroft and Williscroft; 1532:William Wylliscroft of Great Bridgeford; 1677:John Woolescroft of Milwich, alternatively known as John Willowscroft in the same year; 1851:George Wolliscroft (licensee), Crown, Red Street, Talke on the Hill; 1851:Jesse Woolliscroft of The Black Swan Inn, Fenton. At Baswich we get the variant Ellen Woolsencroft (1695), forerunner of the modern Wolstencroft, Woolstencroft, Woolstancroft, but these are generally from a lost Wolstancroft in Lancashire, or possibly Wolstencroft Farm, east of Lymm, Cheshire; 1765:Mary Wolstoncroft of Burslem, witness to the marriage of John Lees and Sarah Phillips. This Burslem lady shares the same name as her more illustrious compatriot Mary Wollstonecraft Shelley, authoress of the classic horror story "Frankenstein".

The main crops grown on the croft included "wheat", "rye" and "barley" resulting in the obvious Wheatcroft; 1887:Mallinson M. Wheatcroft (grocer, tea dealer, Italian warehouseman), Market Street, Longton; Ryecroft/Roycroft; 1875:Henry Roycroft (agent to the Shropshire Union Canal Company), Ricardo Street, Burslem, and Barcroft; 1907:Henry Barcroft (stoker) of Derby Street, Hanley. Some crofts were surrounded by thorn bushes as in "Thornnicroft" (1377) in Tunstall (Stoke-on-Trent); 1666:Thomas Thornycroft of Acton (Swynnerton); 1851:William Thornicroft (ironfounder and millwright), Foundry Street, Hanley. The Cheshire Thornycrofts are probably traceable in the main to Thorneycroft Pools and Farm in Siddington, south west of Macclesfield. Ash trees often grew in the vicinity as in "Asshcroft" (1364) in Brewood and Ash Croft in

Kinvaston; Elizabeth Ashcroft married George Dean at Audley on New Year's Eve, 1684; 1907:Charles Ashcroft (waggon builder), Lomas Street, Hanley. Other crofts were situated by a meadow; 1875:James Meadowcroft (grocer, draper), High Street, Silverdale; 1907:Noah Meadowcroft (fitter), Salem Street, Etruria.

Roger Leycrofft, one of the novices at Stone Priory in 1521, possibly had ancestry in Leacroft near Cannock - "croft where the land was left untilled or fallow", whilst local families called Ravenscroft might stem from Ravenscroft near Middlewich, Cheshire - "Hraefn's croft"; 1851:Thomas Ravenscroft (joiner and cabinet maker), of Audley; 1907:George Ravenscroft (boiler maker) of Whieldon Road, Fenton.

Cottages and buildings

One common term much resorted to by the Saxons, wherever they settled, was "cot" - "cottage, shelter, woodman's hut", preserved in Cotes between Swynnerton Park and Millmeece Pumping Station. This is one source of the surname Coat(e)/Coates/Cote(s), but it can also be a toponymic for a dweller at the cottage(s) or an occupational term for a shepherd, who lived at a sheep cote; 1851:John Coates (boot and shoe maker), Greengate Street, Stafford; 1851:Anthony Coates (stone mason), Ball Haye Green, Leek. As a terminal it appears in some very familiar local surnames. Draycott is chiefly from Draycott in the Moors or Draycott in the Clay, but the exact significance of the localities is undetermined, although most applicable seems to be a cottage where drays were made, that is, a type of unwheeled wagon used for agricultural or forestry purposes. External sources include Draycott near Long Eaton, Derbyshire, Draycott east of Claverley, Shropshire and Draycott near Kempsey, Worcestershire; 1851:Thomas Draycott (baker, flour dealer), Foregate Street, Stafford; 1875:Samuel Draycott (butcher), Mill Street, Hanley.

Swancote/Swancott was brought into the county by migrants with roots in Swancote near Bridgenorth, Shropshire or Swancote Farm in Chaddesley Corbett, Worcestershire - "cottage of the swineherds"; 1532:Robert Swancott of Seighford; 1539:Richard Swancote of Aston and Doxey; 1907:Joseph Swancott (labourer) of Deansgate, Newcastle under Lyme. Yet another Shropshire locality - Heathcote near Stoke on Tern - "cottage on a heath" - is behind some of the Staffordshire Heathcotes, Heathcoats or Heathcotts, but others have ancestry in Heathcote near Hartington, just over the county boundary from Sheen, or two locations in Warwickshire - Heathcote Farm in Wasperton or Heathcote in Warwick St. Nicholas, all referring to a cottage or cottages on a heath; 1851:Samuel Heathcote (cattle dealer) of Wetley Rocks; 1851:Thomas Heathcote (dairyman) of Boothen Road, Stoke. There is frequent interchange with Heathcock; 1604:Richard Heathcote of Wolverhampton (1607:Richard Heathcocke). In its own right Heathcock is a nickname from the "heathcock" - a vernacular name for the black grouse; Wolstanton Parish registers 1774:August 5th, Mary Heathcock married Joseph Hassels.

Derbyshire's main contribution is Froggatt/Froggett, from the village of Froggatt in the Derwent valley - "frog cottage". In the Churchwarden's accounts for Stoke-on-Trent

(1641) Roger Machin paid five shillings to Ellis Ffroggatt "for fees of the Court at Leitchfeild"; 1887:James Henry Froggett (cashier), Sheppard Street, Stoke; 1907:Edwin Froggatt of Neville Street, Stoke. Lancashire's legacy is Prescot(t)/Preskett/Priscott, from Prescot on Merseyside - "the cottage of the priests", or "manor house", also denoting employment at such an establishment. The two Shropshire locations, Prescott near Baschurch and Prescott near Farlow, are of lesser consequence. In October, 1604, at Oulton near Kibblestone, Simon Prescott died from some sort of plague, which continued to afflict local inhabitants until Christmas of the same year; 1907:Peter Prescott of Anchor Terrace, Longton.

Caldecote and Caldecott are very common placenames, occurring in many counties throughout England, yet they seem to be absent from our own county. They all refer to "cold huts" or "a cold hut", and often appear in the abbreviated form Calcott, Calcutt or Caulcott, as in Far Calcots Leasow in Norbury, north west of Gnosall and Calcot Hill south east of Clent, which was part of Staffordshire until 1544, when it was transferred to Worcestershire. In 1703, on April 7th, Elizabeth Caulcott married Thomas Yates at High Offley; 1875:Thomas Caulcott (joiner, builder) of Fegg Hayes; 1887:Richard Caldecott (coal dealer), Sneyd Street, Tunstall; 1907:John Calcutt (potter), Queen Street, Fenton; 1907:Richard Caldicott (greengrocer) of Alfred Street, Hanley.

Another invader is Foskett; 1875:James Foskett (coal dealer) of Loftus Road, Etruria; 1907:Herbert Foskett (colliery fireman) of Clifford Street, Hanley. First in line as possible origins are Foxcote in Pedmore, Worcestershire and Foxcote in Ilmington, Warwickshire, which occurs as "Foxcott alias Foscott" in 1679. Both denote "burrow used by foxes" or "fox-infested cottages." The surname is also to be traced to Foxcote near Cheltenham, Gloucestershire, Foscote near Towcester, Northamptonshire and Foscot, south west of Chipping Norton, Oxfordshire.

Derricott/Derricutt/Dorricott is a very difficult surname to fathom; 1788:Richard Dorricot of Norton in the Moors; 1907:William Derricott (joiner) of Meir Road, Longton. One likely candidate is Dodcott Grange south west of Audlem, approximately nine miles from Aston near Radwood, where John de Dodecote is assessed in the 1327 lay subsidy rolls. Richard Dodycot was elected prior at Stone Priory in 1507 and Elizabeth Dodicote (widow) was resident at Croxton near Eccleshall in 1664. Now, according to Joseph Wright in his English dialect grammar, the change of "d" to "r" as evinced in "anybody-anybory" and "somebody-somebory" is a trait of the north west Midland dialects, especially Lancashire. Staffordshire is also classified as belonging to the same group of dialects, and so we could well have the alternation between Dodecote and Dorricott. This implies that a spelling such as 1749:Richard Dedacott of Penkridge would end up as the modern Derricott. A very striking local analogy here is Derrington near Stafford, recorded as "Dodinton" in 1242 - "the village of Dudda's people". Last but not least is Dodecote Grange, south of Child's Ercall, Shropshire, about six miles west of Aqualate Mere. Can this place too have some bearing on the surname Dorricott?

Norcup, too, is a puzzle, although there is no shortage of specimens; 1724:Lawrence Norcop of Onneley; 1775:Sarah Norcope of Woodsease (Woodseaves), High Offley; 1851:Joseph Norcup (joiner and builder), Hill Street, Stoke; 1907:Thomas Norcup (miner), Frederick Street, Fenton. However, in the Stoke-on-Trent parish registers for December 15th, 1790, Elizabeth Norcope is alternatively written down as Elizabeth Norcot. This is for a dweller at the northern cottage or from some place called Northcote, Northcott or Norcot, such as Norcot Brook (Farm) in Higher Whitley, west of Antrobus, Cheshire, which appears as "Northcotes" in the Middle Ages, or even Northycote Farm in Bushbury, birthplace of Richard de Northcote of Bushbury in 1286. 1875:Samuel Norcott (farmer) of Clanway, Tunstall.

Bowers is completely orthodox throughout its evolution. The surname is derived from Bowers near Standon, where William de Boures was chaplain in 1338. It is the plural form of the Saxon word "bur" - "cottage", hence "the cottages". A subsidiary source might be Bowers Hall in Stanton in Peak, Derbyshire. An occupational term is also worth considering, that is, for a servant who was employed at the bowers. During the Middle Ages the "bowers" were detached buildings which combined the domestic offices and served as bedrooms for the lord of the manor and his family. Consequently, such employees were highly influential members of the lord's household staff. At Wolstanton on September 17th 1807, Mary, daughter of John and Anne Bowers, aged 13 years, was buried, her death having been occasioned by her clothes becoming entangled in the machinery of a cotton manufactory; 1851:William Bowers (limeburner and dealer) of Middleport; 1851:Eli Bowers (baker and flour dealer) of Browning Street, Stafford. The singular form Bower was often a medieval spelling of Bowyer, an artisan who crafted and sold bows; 1386:Thomas le bower of Knypersley, noted as Thomas le bowyer in 1396; 1887:Jacob Bower (clogger) of Sneyd Street, Tunstall.

Derivatives of "bower" are as follows: Bowerman/Borman/Burman - a servant at the bower; 1851:William Bowerman (stationmaster) at Bramshall, synonymous with Bowring/Bowering; Catheren Bowring of Seighford, buried on November 2nd, 1618, having survived her husband John, a husbandman, by three years; 1907:George Bowering, licensee at the Coachmaker's Arms, Lichfield Street, Hanley. Burroughes, Burrows and Borrows signify habitation or employment at the bower house; 1539 Muster Roll:Hewe Burrus of Stafford; 1627:William Bowrowes of Stowe by Chartley; 1851:James Burrows (linen and woollen draper) of Market Street, Longton; 1887:William Burrows (railway accountant) of Penkhull New Road, Stoke. These are not to be confused with the singular form Burrough/Burrow/Borrow, which denote a dweller by a hill or fort; 1666:Richard Burrowe, taxable on one hearth at Rownall; 1851:John Burrow (tinner, brazier, ironmonger) of Market Street, Longton.

Although it is true that most surnames fall naturally into four groups - locality, occupation, nicknames and relationships - it should be remembered that these are neat labels used for the most part by modern researchers for their own convenience and do not accurately reflect the intentions of our ancestors at the time when the names were first created. A case in point is the surname Bold/Bould, which is both a nickname and a locative name. One of the attributes most valued by our medieval ancestors was personal bravery and hence a man like Geoffrey Bold, taxed at Fulford in 1332, would have been held in very high esteem by all and sundry in his local community. This is one origin of the modern surname Bold/Bould, but the major source is the Saxon "bold" - "house, dwelling place", as typified by Richard de la bolde, resident at Newton near Blithfield in 1327, and Robert atte bolde, taxed at Penkridge in 1332. The former locality just north of Blithfield Reservoir is now known as Booth, whilst the "bold' near Penkridge is obsolete and survives only in the place Bull Bridge in Penkridge.

As a result of these diverse origins the name Bold/Bould gains a foothold in many parts of the county by the end of the nineteenth century, but is especially common in north Staffordshire; 1539 Muster:Ralph Bold of Fenton and Longton; 1640 Muster:Walter Bould of Sandon; 1666:Chrispin Bould, exempt from hearth tax at Penkhull; 1887:Joseph Bould (saw maker), Liverpool Road, Stoke; 1912:Orlando Bold (electrician), Hamilton Road, Hanley; 1912:Ephraim Bould (kiln foreman), Milner Street, Hanley. However, the name is often sharpened to Bolt/Boult; William Bold of Salt (1332 Subsidies), appears at the local assizes in 1323 as William Bolt. Normally these denote a craftsman skilled at making crossbow bolts, or are descriptive of a short, heavily built person, or are from an Old Norse personal name "Boltr"; 1912:Charles Boult (leather dealer), Charles Street, Hanley.

The surname Bowden/Bowdon/Boden is generally derived from any one of five localities - Bowden in Wiltshire, Bowdon near Altrincham, Cheshire, Bowden Edge near Chapel en le Frith in the Derbyshire Peak district, Great Bowden near Market Harborough, Leicestershire or Bowden near Galashiels, Roxburghshire, yet none of these has much relevance to our local Bowdens, etc. Rather, the point of origin is much nearer home, centred in fact on Booden Farm in Haughton south west of Stafford. In documents covering the sixteenth and seventeenth centuries this particular location occurs as "le hall of Bolde", "Bold Hall alias Bowld Hall", "Boldhall alias Bolden", and so on, and is thus a combination of the Saxon "bold" - "dwelling place", and "hall". On the Yates map of 1775 it is spelt Boldon. This final change from Bolden/Boldon to Bowden is on a par with the dialectal "cowd" for "cold". The likelihood, that Booden Farm is the point of departure of these early Staffordshire families called Bowden, etc, is reinforced by the fact that in the 1539 Muster Roll for the county, out of eight persons enlisted for their various villages, seven were from localities within a few miles of Booden Farm, e.g. Edmond and Martyn Boden of Ronton, John Bodon of Billington, Hugh Boden of Stafford, George Bodon of Seighford, Stephen a Boden and Roger a Boden of Derrington. The 'a' in the last two names is a vestige of the old preposition "atte". A much later example, relating to sentences passed at the Staffordshire Assizes, in 1832, narrates how Joseph Boden alias Bowden, aged 26, of Endon, was transported for life, for stealing a dark brown cart mare, the property of Hannah Smith, at the parish of Leek; 1875:James Bowden (builder, contractor), Regent Street, Burslem and Endon; 1907:Thomas Bowden (engraver), Stanier Street, Fenton. A subsidiary source for the names might be Boothen near Trent Vale, since in the churchwarden's accounts for Stoke-on-Trent, it is recorded as "Booden brig (sic)" in 1683, and as "Boothen (Bowden) Bridge" in 1689.

Occasionally Boden interchanges with Boydon; 1532:Thomas Bodon of Haughton, called to arms in 1539 as Thomas Boydon. Usually the surnames Boyden/Boydon/Bodin are from the Germanic "Baudin", brought over by the Normans as "Bodin", as evidenced by "Bodin", ousted from his lands at Gailey in the Staffordshire Domesday survey. Another variant is Bawden; 1532:John Bawdon of Billington (1539:John Bodon); 1851:John Boydon (baker, flour dealer), Broad Street, Stafford.

The most commonly recurring compound containing "bold" in our county is Newbold/Newbould, as in John de Neubold of Halfhead Farm near Chebsey (1334 Assizes), who probably came from a lost Newbold near Hilcote Hall, Eccleshall, and Roger de Neubold of Leigh (1332 Subsidies), who obviously hailed from Lower and Upper Nobut between Church Leigh and Bramshall. The localities designate a new building, dwelling or homestead, a meaning shared by (The) Newbolds in Wednesfield, Newbold Manor House (Newbold Lands) near Barton under Needwood and "Newbold ende" (1585) in Rugeley, all of which may have engendered local families called Newbold/Newbould; 1851:Edward Newbold (baker, flour dealer), Cross Street, Stafford; 1875:Jane Newbold (grocer), Albert Street, Longton. When the final "d" is lost, as in 1666:Francis Newball of Brewood, it tends to become Newbon with the familiar "l-n" switch, e.g. 1798:Anne Newbold of Newcastle under Lyme, probably identical with Ann Newbon (1799). The surname Newbon, in the main, is a survival of the feudal system of medieval England, alluding to a new bond (unfree tenant or serf); 1875:Thomas Newbon (plumber, glazier, bellhanger), Church Street, Longton; 1907:William Newbon (potter), Mayer Street, Hanley.

In the Danelaw counties of Derbyshire, Lancashire, Yorkshire, Cumberland, Northumberland and Durham, the Scandinavian counterpart of Newbold is Newbiggin or Newbigging (with the same meaning). Locally, Newbuildings Farm near Newton by Blithfield Reservoir, occurs as "Newbygginge" in 1464. The second half of the compounds is preserved in the surname Biggin(s) - "owner of or worker at an outbuilding or outhouse"; Henrie Biggins, miller at Cheddleton mills circa 1628, was in charge of two mills, one for fulling and one for corn; 1875:Joseph Biggins (horse slaughterer), Toll Street, Hanley.

Surnames in "-wich, -wick"

The Saxon "wic" had such a wide range of meanings, that it is not at all easy to arrive at the exact sense implicit in the surname Wich/Wych/Weech/Weetch. For instance, Robert del wych, resident at Swynnerton in 1332, could refer to a dweller by or at some particular abode, village, town, hamlet or even dairy farm. Furthermore, 1375:William atte wiche of

Newcastle under Lyme might denote residence by a wych elm; 1532:John Wyche abbot of Hulton Abbey; 1606:Thomas Wyche of Rushton Spencer. The hardened variant "wick" lives on in Wick(e)s/Wike/Wyke(s)/Wix/Week(e)s; 1539 Muster:Ralph Weekes of Stafford; 1594:John Wickes of Stowe by Chartley; 1907:Walter Frank Weeks of the King's Head, Ashwood, Longton; 1907:Henry Wykes (miner), Ravensdale Terrace, Chatterley; 1912:Leonard Wix (stationmaster), Station Villa, Albert Road, Fenton. The mysterious Wedge could be a late form of Wich; 1875:Benjamin Wedge (grocer), Primitive Street, Smallthorne; 1887:Emma Wedge (mineral water manufacturer), Port Vale, Burslem.

The coincidence that places like Droitwich in Worcestershire and Nantwich in Cheshire were noted for their saltworks, has led many writers to assume that "wich" here means "saltworks". But in both cases "wich" refers to "sheds, buildings, dwellings" where saltworking was carried on. Droitwich and Nantwich were the two most important inland saltworks during the Middle Ages. From here the salt was carried by packhorse all across the Midlands, along tracks known as "saltways", several of which traversed the Staffordshire Moorlands, linking the county with Cheshire in the west and Derbyshire in the east. One well documented drovers' road ran from Congleton in Cheshire to Winster in Derbyshire and passed through Meerbrook, Middle Hulme, Blackshaw Moor, Stoney Cliffe near to Blakemere House (the present Mermaid Inn on Morridge), Warslow, and crossed over the River Dove close to Hartington. Another saltway, called Earlsway, also starting out from Congleton, went through Rushton James, Cauldon, (where it was known as Yarlsway - cf Eardley-Yeardley), Waterhouses and on into Derbyshire. Salters Bridge over the River Tame between Alrewas and Elford, carried the saltway from the saltworks at Shirleywich, south east of Weston upon Trent, probably linking up with Saltersford Lane via Ellastone and continuing on towards Ashbourne.

There are no references in the Staffordshire Domesday survey to saltpans, in spite of the fact that the locality Salt in the Trent valley got its name from the salt pit there. Salt, of course, was an indispensable commodity in any medieval village community, used in the preservation of fish and curing meat after the autumn killings, keeping it fresh throughout the winter months. In the reign of Henry III, Ivo de Saut "held one knight's fee in the Barony of Stafford". Hence the surname Salt/Sault, which is extremely prolific in North Staffordshire from the close of the Middle Ages. In the 1539 muster for the county, for example, local men enrolled include George Salte at Stafford, Rawfe and Leonard Salt at Coton near Seighford, and Thomas Salt at Tunstall (Adbaston). In 1604 the minister at Onecote near Butterton on the Moors, Ralph Salt is denounced as no preacher and a lewd young man who "out of all good order wears a feather in his hat." Overseers of the poor at Betley comprised John and George Salt in 1728, and Samuel Salt in 1768; 1851:Joseph Salt (victualler), Royal Oak, Dilhorne. The variant Sault is hardly in the picture at all, apart from a sprinkling here and there; July 18th 1574:Elisabeth Sault, baptised at Swynnerton; September 18th 1582:Katheren Sault and Francis Steedman, wed at Seighford.

John le salter, working on the Audley estates at Betley in 1307, was most likely employed in the salt trade as a maker or merchant. His descendants bear the surname Salter or Saulter, although an alternative origin for these is a minstrel in a travelling show, who was skilled in playing the psaltery, a stringed instrument akin to the harp; 1598:James Saulter of Norton in the Moors; 1907:Mary Jane Salter (grocer, provision dealer), Waterloo Road, Cobridge.

Many compounds ending in "-wich" undergo a trimming down process. Colwich in the valley of the Trent, not far from Cannock Chase - "farmstead where charcoal was obtained" - is written as "Collidge" on Kip's map of 1607/1610,and is also weakened to "College" and "Colledge" in the Swynnerton parish registers (1761, 1762). Christopher Colwyche, resident at Moreton not far from Colwich in 1533, is quoted as Christopher Colage in 1518. Gratwich near the river Blithe, east of Fradswell Heath - "farmstead on gravelly terrain" - is pared down to Grattidge and Grattage; Bucknall cum Bagnall parish register 1767:Margaret Grattidge of Stoke parish; 1907:James Grattage (potter), Rothesay Road, Longton; 1907:Frederick Grattidge (collier), Mount Pleasant, Longton. Milwich, four miles west of Gratwich - "farmstead with a mill" - develops into Millidge/Milledge/Millage; 1666:Widdow Willidge (sic) of Crakemarsh, exempt from hearth tax. This is clearly an error for Millidge; 1772:Thomas Baily of Millage. Bloxwich near Walsall - "Blocc's farm" - is contracted to "Blocksich" and "Bloxedge" in the Penkridge parish registers (1598, 1729); 1617:Humphrey Blocksedge of Tipton; Lichfield Cathedral Register 1748:Thomas Bloxsidge of Solihull. West Bromwich in the Black Country is reduced to "West Bromidge" in 1695, and Castle Bromwich, a north eastern suburb of Birmingham, appears as "Castle Bromage" in 1667, thus resulting in the modern surnames Bromage/Brommage/Bromige. Both localities refer to a farmstead where broom grew; 1887:Tom Bromage (builder), Newland Street, Hanley; 1912:Lydia Bromage (widow) of Alberta Street, Longton. An additional source might be a location in Church Lawton, Cheshire, recorded as "Bromegge" in 1440 - "broom-covered hillside."

Aldridge near Walsall, home of Jordan de Alrewych (1307 Assizes) was originally a village built among alders and this locative source is undoubtedly the principal base of the surname Aldridge; 1694:William Aldridge of Ellastone, and possibly Eldridge; 1633:Cassandra Eldridge of Barlaston. Subsidiary locatives to be considered include Aldridge Grove in Buckinghamshire - "Eldrigge" (13th century), an unidentified place in or near Worcester - "Elrugge" (14th century) and perhaps Alderhedge Wood in Aston by Budworth, Cheshire -"alder hedge", which would inevitably be corrupted to Aldridge by unsuspecting parish clerks. Oldridge near Foxt must also feature in the proceedings now and again; Ranulph de Oldrugge, taxed at Cheddleton in 1332 - "the old ridge" - cf. 1539 Muster:Steven Olryche of Seighford and 1637:Mary Oulridg(sic) of Standon. Yet the names Aldridge/Eldridge and Oldridge are in some cases to be traced to two Saxon personal names - "Aethelric" - "noble ruler" and "Aelfric" - "elf ruler". From the Staffordshire Domesday folios it emerges that "Aluric (Aelfric)" held land at Cooksland, Eccleshall at the time of Edward the Confessor, whilst "Alric" was a landowner at Tixall near the River Sow. 1887:Joseph Aldridge (outdoor beerseller) of Copeland Street, Stoke. One outsider here is Prestwich, north west of Crumpsall, Lancashire - "farmstead of the priests" or "parsonage". It is pronounced by local Lancastrians as "Prestage", hence presenting us with such surnames as Prestage/Prestedge/Prestige besides the original Prestwich. At Stowe by Chartley in 1635, Ellis and Ursula Prestwich had a son, whom they christened Littleton, baptized on May 7th of that year. In Staffordshire the form Prestige is transformed into Pestridge with the very common shift of the letter "r". 1912:C.Pestridge (stonemason) of Spode Street, Stoke.

The constant erosion endured by compounds in "-wich", also affects locatives ending in "-wick". Hardwick(e)/Hardick, for instance, is derived from Hardwick in Aldridge. "Little Hardewicke" (1570) in Cannock, "le herdewyke" (1333) in Shareshill or Hardiwick near Smallrice, Sandon, from whence came Robert de Herdewyke, taxed at Fulford and Saverley in 1332. All these places mean literally "farm for the herd or flock" that is, "sheep farm", but Hardiwick near Caverswall, another possible origin of the surnames, has been taken as "Heregeard's farm". There are localities called Hardwick or Hardwicke in at least fifteen other counties, but it is impossible to say one way or another whether any of these have played any part in Staffordshire families of these names; 1613:William Hardick of Seighford; 1875:Thomas Hardwick (Inland Revenue Officer), Sutherland Terrace Longton; 1907:John Hardwicke (miner), Birch Street, Hanley.

One curious anomaly of note here is that all the compounds that have attained any kind of stability as surnames have been introduced by migrants from other counties. Outstanding amongst these is Chadwick, which boasts four possible origins - Chadwick near Billinge in Rochdale parish, Lancashire, where the church is dedicated to St. Chad. Chadwick near Stourport on Severn, Worcestershire, which also preserves the saint's name, Chadwich near Bromsgrove, Worcestershire and Chadwick End in Balsall Warwickshire, both of which contain the name "Ceadel(a)", diminutive of Chad. During the seventeenth century the surname is most common in the Staffordshire Moorlands and the Churnet valley, but nowadays it has extended its range and encompasses the whole of North Staffordshire; 1851:Samuel Chadwick (linen and woollen draper), Market Place, Burslem; 1851:George Chadwick (schoolmaster) of Bradnop; 1875:Harvey Chadwick (licensee), Swan Inn, Kinnersley Street, Kidsgrove; 1907:George Chadwick (brewer's drayman), Leek New Road, Cobridge. The surname alternates sometimes with Chaddock since Gilbert Chadwicke, not chargeable for hearth tax at Audley in 1666, is entered in the Audley parish register as Gilbert Chaddock in 1663. If the original name is Chaddock then Chaddock Hall in Leigh parish, Lancashire (of obscure meaning) may be the true origin. In addition, there are some conflicting spellings in the Bucknall cum Bagnall registers, e.g. James Chadwick (1812) is variously written down as James Chadick in 1808 James Caddick in 1806, and as James Caddock in 1802. Chadwick and Chadick are easy to explain, but, again, if the genuine surname is Caddick/Caddock, this is either a nickname from Old French "caduc" - "infirm, decrepit", applied to an epileptic, or a pet form of the

Welsh saint's name "Cadfael", which occurs as "Cadog". 1887:Alfred Caddick (librarian of Stoke Free Library); 1907:John Caddick (brick and tile manufacturer), Brampton Lodge, Brampton, Newcastle under Lyme.

Another migrant from the north is Beswick/Bestwick, which is from any one of three localities - Beswick between Ardwick and Openshaw (Manchester) - "Beac's farm", Beswick north of Beverley in the East Riding of Yorkshire - "Besi's farm" or Beswick in Mobberley, Cheshire - "farm where reed or rush grew". James Wright Beswick, pottery manufacturer, was born in Tunstall in 1845, son of Robert Beswick, earthenware manufacturer and coalmaster. He began potting in Albion Street, Longton about 1890, before moving to Britannia Works, High Street, and then to the Gold Street works; 1851:William Bestwick (farmer) of Leek Frith; 1875:Robert Bestwick (pawnbroker), Watergate Street, Tunstall.

Swanwick/Swannick/Swannock also has a number of origins, chief amongst which is Swanwick in Alfreton, Derbyshire, pronounced "Swonnick", followed by Swanwick Green in Marbury Chapelry, Cheshire and Swanwick north west of Fareham, Hampshire, all for "dairy farm of the swineherds." Swanwick Hall Farm near Goostrey and Great and Little Swanwick in Stublach (both in Cheshire) may be alternative possibilities, although they could be named from some previous owner called Swanwick. Swannick as in 1764:Joseph Swannick of Ranton (1766:Joseph Swannock), is also a nickname for someone with a "swan neck", as typified by Edith of the Swan Neck, mistress of King Harold. But Swanwick is the regular spelling; 1851:Eliza Swanwick (shopkeeper), Sash Street, Stafford; 1907:Joseph Swanwick (wagoner) of Registry Street, Stoke.

Berwick and Barwick - "barley farm, outlying grange" - are indigenous to several counties, e.g. Berwick on Tweed and Barwick in Elmet near Leeds, but the nearest and most appropriate sources are Berwick Maviston and Great Berwick in Shropshire. Berwick and Barwick are compressed into Berrick and Barrick; 1666:John Berwicke of Colton; 1729:Charles Barwick of Ellenhall; 1681:Margreat Berrick (widow) of Penkridge.

` Warwick/Warrick is primarily from Warwick, the county town of Warwickshire, probably "farm by the weir"; Ronton Abbey Chartulary, 13th century deed:Roger de Warwic. However, in the northern shires and especially in Scotland the main origin is Warwick near Carlisle - "farm on the bank of the river Eden".

Another Cumbrian locality - Sedgwick south of Kendal - "Siggi's farm", provides us with one origin of the surname Sedgwick, with Sedgewick Castle in Nuthurst, Sussex very much an outsider. John Poulson, church warden at Stoke-on-Trent in 1695, reports that Sara Sedgwick was charged two pence for a letter of request; 1887:John Sedgwick (superintendent of the Prudential Assurance Company), Rushton Road, Burslem.

Southwick and Southick are characteristic of the southern sector of the county; 1613:Richard Southewicke of Wolverhampton, and go back to Southwick close by Fotheringhay, the Northamptonshire village with its ruined castle, where Mary, Queen of Scots was imprisoned and executed in 1587, or any other place called Southwick, including Southwick near Waterlooville, Hampshire, Southwick several miles south west of Cheddar, Somerset, Southwick in Sunderland, Southwick in Brighton or Southwick near Trowbridge, Wiltshire. All these denote "the southern farm".

Thomas Worswicke, bailiff at Stafford in 1611, had ancestors with roots in the parish of Worswick in Furness, north Lancashire - "farm by a lake frequented by bison or wild cattle." One final compound - Borthwick is of Scottish origin, derived mainly from the old barony of Borthwick along Borthwick Water in the parish of Roberton, Roxburghshire, but other local families called Borthwick could have ancestry in Borthwick in Midlothian or either of two lost Borthwicks in Berwick or Selkirk. The meaning of the places varies from "home farm" and "wood farm" to "farm which supplied the board or table of the lord of the district"; 1912:H.Borthwick (widow) of Cross Keys Square, Fenton.

Fortifications and defences

The Celtic tribes that invaded Britain during the third century BC left stronger imprints on the British landscape than any other prehistoric people. These took the form of great hill forts, which were originally stockaded and flanked by deep ditches. The largest and most impressive of these fortifications in Staffordshire is Castle Ring, which stands at 801 feet on the most exposed point of Cannock Chase and extends for nine acres, complete with its banks and ditches. North of Maer, the Iron Age hill fort now known as Berth Hill, consisting of a single ditch and extensive earthworks, appears as The Bruff on Bowen's map of Staffordshire (1777), and it was the home of William de le burgh of Maer, mentioned in a lawsuit of 1330. This represents the Saxon "burh" - "a defended place, fort", which evolves along several separate lines, with and without the shift of the letter "r". For example, one path leads to Burgh, Borough, Burrow and Burf, which becomes Berth on account of the dialectal confusion between "f" and "th", as evinced in the Cockney "fink" instead of "think" and in Thistley Moors in Hilton near Wolverhampton, found as "Thistlemore alias Fisle more" in 1691.

With the transposition of the letter "r" we arrive at the more common forms Brough/Brugh/Bruff, which in many instances must go back to several localities in other counties. In contention here are Brough in the Hope valley in the Derbyshire Peak district, Brough north of Newark on Trent, Brough under Stainmore in Cumbria, Brough west of Hull and Brough by Skipsea (East Riding of Yorkshire), and Brough near Catterick or Brough near Reeth (North Riding of Yorkshire). All these places are pronounced "Bruff" or "Broof", and were originally Roman encampments taken over by the Saxons. The surname often fluctuates between Burgh and Brough; 1597:Edmund Brough of Leek noted as Edmunde Burghe in 1605, but the modern spelling is invariably Brough; 1851:Thomas Brough (builder, brickmaker) of Checkley; 1887:John Brough (restaurant and dining room proprietor and tobacconist), Glebe Street, Stoke; 1907:Thomas Brough (potter's packer), Moston Street, Birches Head.

The native Burgh was changed into "Burk" by the Normans, resulting in Burk(e) and

Bourke; 1907:John Burke (furnaceman) of North Road, Cobridge; 1907:Michael Bourke of Brook Street, Hanley. But the name Burk(e) is mainly of Irish origin, numerous in all the provinces except Ulster, and derives from the family of "de Burgh" who settled in Ireland during the reign of Henry II. Therefore, some Staffordshire families bearing this surname might well be from the Emerald Isle.

The allied names Broughall/Burghall/Bruffell are to be traced to Brough Hall near Gnosall, recorded as "Burgh" in 1283, "Broughall" in 1601 and "Bruff" by Plot in 1686, with Broughall near Whitchurch in Shropshire of minor interest. At an assembly in Newcastle Guildhall on 30th January, 1635, it was agreed that *"Richard Machine and Richard Broughall shall be viewers and tenders of the towne ffeildes and shall from tyme to tyme impounde the cattell of fforenors....... and shall be paid for the impounding of every beast one penny, for a horse two pence, for ffive sheep one penny....".* 1706:Maria Burghall of Audley; 1907:Thomas Bruffell (platelayer), Keary Street, Stoke.

Another surviving hill fort, dating back to the Iron Age is on Bury Bank near Darlaston (Stone), which covers about three acres on top of a thickly wooded eminence. This particular location is to be discussed with the ancient earthwork Berry or Bury Ring near Stafford, since both preserve the dative singular of the Saxon word "burh", that is, "byrig". Here we have two origins of the modern surnames Berry/Berrey/Berrie/Bury, although we must not forget Bury in Greater Manchester, Bury north of Huntingdon, Bury St. Edmunds in Suffolk, Bury near Arundel (West Sussex) and Berry Pomeroy near Totnes, Devon. In the Middle Ages "beri, biri, buri" was employed in the sense of "manor house", and so the surnames could refer to a servant, entrusted with all the menial tasks associated with such a post there. Occasionally the forms Bury and Berry are used indiscriminately of the same person; 1615:Edward Bury(Berrye) of Wolgarston, but Berry spellings predominate from the seventeenth century onwards; 1610:Besteanus Berry of Burslem; 1640 Muster:Richard Berry of Whitgreave and Marston; 1875:William Berry (beerseller), John Street, Hanley; 1907:Herbert Berry of London Road, Chesterton; 1907:James Berry of Leek Road, Smallthorne.

Only a handful of compounds in "-bury" have ramified to any extent in north Staffordshire, and all are newcomers from surrounding counties. Bradbury/Bradbery/Bradberry is from Bredbury near Stockport, recorded as "Bradbury" in 1670, or from Bradbury near Sedgefield, Durham. Both denote a fort built of boards. In 1841, Ann Bradbury was one of the superintendents of the apprentice girls' painting department at Wood and Brownfield's Earthenware factory, Cobridge. Of the 24 females in her charge, 10 were under the age of 13. 1851:Thomas Bradbury (carrier) from the Golden Lion, Leek to Longnor; 1851:John Bradbury (coalmaster) of Bradley Green, Biddulph; 1887:George Bradbury (fishmonger), Hanley Fish Market and Piccadilly, Hanley.

Astbury near Congleton - "the eastern fort" - spawns several curious offshoots. Naturally enough we find the untouched Astbury; 1630:Randle Astbury (blacksmith) of Trentham; 1851:James Astbury (police officer) of Upper Tean; 1887:John Astbury (journalist) of West Street, Newcastle under Lyme. But William Astbury of Chebsey (1707), is entered in the register as William Ashbury in 1710, and as William Aspery in 1713, hence the variants Ashbury and Asprey; 1657:Elizabeth Ashbury of Seighford; 1789:Thomas Asprey of Bradley, south of Haughton. Furthermore, at Stowe by Chartley, George Astbury (1641) is alternatively written down as George Astaberrie in 1655, which is clearly a forerunner of the local Austerberry; 1875:George Austerberry (hosier, haberdasher, milliner, general draper), Waterloo Road, Burslem; 1887:Michael T. Austerberry (herbalist), St. John Street, Hanley. Another probable corruption is Esprey, based on the couplet Aspley-Espley, but this is not on record.

Pilsbury, which is characteristic of the north eastern sector of the county, goes back to Pilsbury on the Derbyshire side of Dove Dale, east of Broadmeadow Hall, midway between Longnor and Sheen - "Pil's fort". In 1543 John Pillsbury was paying Dieulacres Abbey an annual rent of twenty one shillings and four pence for land in Leek Frith. 1851:George Pilsbury (sergeant at mace), Backwalls, Stafford. Pilsbury often seesaws back and forth with Spilsbury; 1760:John Pilsbury of Church Eaton, registered as John Spilsbury in 1762. If the original name is in fact Spilsbury, then Spelsbury south of Chipping Norton, Oxfordshire is the most likely target, since it occurs as "Spillesbury" in the Middle Ages - "Speol's fort". 1851:Francis Spilsbury (shoemaker and owner of a beerhouse) Rushton Marsh, Rushton Spencer.

Salesbury near Blackburn - fort by a pool where sallows grew" - is the main source for Salisbury, despite its pronunciation "Sailsbury", with Salisbury in Wiltshire - "fort at Old Sarum" - a shadowy presence in the background. 1851:Lazarus Salisbury (hatter), St. John's Square, Burslem; 1851:Benjamin Salisbury (saddler), Gaolgate Street, Stafford.

Staffordshire families called Norbury trace their ancestry back to any one of several locatives - Norbury north east of Aqualate Mere, Norbury on the Staffordshire-Derbyshire border across from Ellastone, Norbury near Stockport, Cheshire, Norbury west of Church Stretton, Shropshire or Norbury, north of Croydon, Surrey, all designating "the northern fort"; 1750:George Norbury, licensee of the Packhorse alehouse, Burslem; 1841:Philip Norbury, superintendent and secretary of the Primitive Methodist Sunday School, Tunstall; 1907:William Colin Norbury (greengrocer and coal dealer), Edensor Road, Longton.

From thirteenth century deeds in the Cartulary of Stone Priory it emerges that Bury Bank near Darlaston was also known as "Wulf(e)cestre" during the Middle Ages. The name "Wulf(e)" is probably a reduced form of "Wulfhere", since Wulfhere, king of Mercia (659-674), is said to have founded a monastery at Stone, and built a fortified stronghold In this area, extending for four acres. This would certainly explain "Wulf(e)cestre", because the second part of the name is the Saxon word "ceaster", a loan word from Latin "castra" -"camp, fort". Moreover, it would also resolve the hitherto perplexing surname Walchester borne by Catherine and Josiah Walchester, who lived in the village of Endon in 1876; James Walchester (potter's packer), Eversley Road, Longton (1907); 1907:John Walchester (blacksmith) of Foley Street, Fenton. The element "ceaster" occurs as the final part of numerous placenames all over England, usually spelt as "-chester, -cester, -caster" as in Chichester, Gloucester and Tadcaster. Yet it must not be assumed,that every single town ending in this component was a Roman settlement, since the Anglo Saxons attached it freely to any enclosed place intended for habitation. Indeed, many of the places so designated had quite different names during the Roman occupation.

The surname Chester(s) is derived not only from the obvious Chester in Cheshire on the River Dee, where the 20th Legion was stationed, but also from Little Chester not far from Derby town centre, Chester le Street in Durham and Chesters in Northumberland. All of these were former Roman encampments; 1875:Joseph Chesters (confectioner), Market Square, Tunstall; 1907:Samuel Chester (potter) of Dale Street, Burslem.

The West Riding town of Doncaster - "Roman fort on the river Don" - supplies us with Doncaster/Dancaster; 1851:Martha Doncaster (milliner and dressmaker) of Waterloo Road, Burslem; 1875:William Doncaster (grocer) of Sun Street, Hanley, whilst Leicester - "Roman encampment of the people of Ligore" - survives as Leicester and Lester; 1851:William Lester (schoolmaster) of Rough Close, Meir Heath: 1875:Thomas Leicester (chemist, druggist) of Market Place, Burslem. However, these surnames may have been introduced by immigrants from Lestre in Normandy (province of La Manche) subsequent to the Norman Conquest in 1066, and there may even be some confusion with Lister/Lyster, which normally denotes a dyer of cloth; 1338:Ralph le Listere of Burton upon Trent; 1887:Martin Bernard Lyster (surgeon) of Rathbone Street, Tunstall. A very rare variant of Leicester is Lasseter; 1851:Samuel Lasseter, proprietor of the Cock Inn, Derby Street, Leek.

Rocester - "Hrothwulf's fort", pronounced "Roaster", stands on the old Roman road that ran from Little Chester in Derby to Chesterton and on to Middlewich and Chester. It lives on as Roster; 1655:Edward Roster, married to Jone Holles at Seighford, and as Rochester; 1693:Andrew Rochester of Ellastone. The latter, however, may occasionally be from Rochester in Kent or Rochester, south of Otterburn, Northumberland.

Castle(s) and Castell(s) generally denote someone who lived near a castle or who was employed in some capacity at a castle, but locally the major source is Castlechurch, five miles south of Stafford, which was originally "the castle", and recorded as "Castel" in 1332. The place is close to the hill on which stands Stafford Castle. Newcastle under Lyme may well be involved too, since, in the medieval manor court rolls we come across such specimens as 1372:John atten castell and 1373:Roger del castell. Later examples are in short supply, apart from 1590:Nathaneel (sic) Castle (Castell) of Eccleshall. The motte and bailey castles, constructed by the Normans in great numbers during the Middle Ages, consisted of the "motte" or mound, which was steep-sided, sometimes partly natural, sometimes wholly artificial, formed in part by soil from the encircling ditch. It was flat topped and roughly circular in shape, its base ranging from one hundred to three hundred feet in diameter, and its height measuring anything from ten to one hundred feet. Thus the surname Mott(e)/Mote/Moat(t) signified a dweller at one of these "mottes";

1657:Elizabeth Mott of Stowe by Chartley; 1666:Robert Mott, charged on three hearths at Blithfield and Admaston. But there again, the name is probably synonymous with Castle, that is, an occupational name for a servant or labourer there.

For defence, castles had drawbridges, whilst many towns and cities had their own walls and gates. Yet the surname Gate(s) does not necessarily imply residence by the town gate or city gate, e.g. 1358:Robert atte gate of Maer, could have dwelt by a gate to some field. 1887:Thomas Edwin Gates (clerk) of Bradwell Lane, Wolstanton. In the Danelaw shires the name Gate(s) more often than not refers to residence by some road or way. "Gate" is still used in Scotland and the north of England in the sense of "roadway" or "street" and streets bearing the suffix "-gate" survive in many of the older towns and cities settled by the Scandinavians, as in Pottergate in Norwich, Goodramgate and Skeldergate in York, Fargate in Sheffield, Briggate in Leeds, and closer to home Bridge Gate in Derby, whilst Tamworth has its Aldergate and Gungate. The soft sound in "yate" is the more normal development in Staffordshire, as in 1327. Henry atte yate of Ashley south of Maer hills, the modern Yate(s)/Yeat(e)s, prolific in all areas - "dweller by the gate", or an occupational term for a gate-keeper. 1887:Jane Yates (burnisher) of Charles Street, Hanley; 1907:James Yates (licensee) of the Dusty Miller Inn, Commerce Street, Longton.

In compounds the contrast between "-gate" and "-yate, -yatt" is revealed in Bygate - Byatt (Byott) - "dweller by the gate". Bygate is not evidenced but Byatt/Byott is fairly frequent; 1736:William Byott of Swynnerton; 1875:Hugh Byatt (carriage builder) of Normacot Road, Longton; 1907:Thomas Byatt (labourer) of Scotia Road, Burslem. Byatt alternates with Byard, although the latter usually denotes a person who resided by an enclosure. In the Bradley in the Moors parish register for 1739, Elizabeth Byatt of Alton, is also recorded as Elizabeth Byard.

Lidgate/Lidgitt/Lidgett/Lydiate refers to a dweller by a swing gate; 1327:Geoffrey atte Lydegate of Waterfall; 1907:Frederick Lidgett (fitter), South Street, Fenton.

Moor, marsh and ford

Without a shadow of a doubt, the locality Podmore - "frog moor" - three miles west of Bowers, is at the root of a substantial number of the county's Podmores. Migrant families have brought the name from Podmoor near Kidderminster (of unknown meaning), with the Cheshire involvement boiling down to places such as " Letull Podmore (1457) in Chorley, "le Podemor" (1331) in Broxton Hundred (unidentified), Podmore Hollow in Mobberley, Podmore Meadow in Wheelock and Podmore Field in Wybunbury. Some of these, however, must take their names from previous landowners called Podmore; 1887:Joseph Podmore (painter and plumber), New Road, Talke; 1887:Frederick Podmore (hosier), Market Place, Burslem. Agnes Podmore, buried at Wheaton Aston in 1580, is found as Agnes Pogmore in 1538, but this name occurs much earlier in the 1379 Poll Tax returns for Yorkshire, where William de Poggemore is noted as a resident of the township of Brampton Bierlow in the parish of Wath-upon-Dearne, south east of Barnsley. Clearly there has to be some lost spot called Pogmore in south Yorkshire. Padmore and Patmore

Stafford High House in the 19th century

Blithfield Hall in the 17th century

STONE, 1810.

LOCAL
BILLHEADS
WITH
EXAMPLES OF
NAMES FROM
THIS SECTION

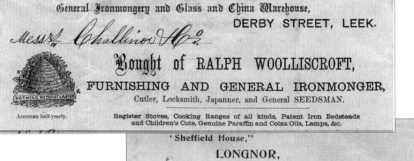

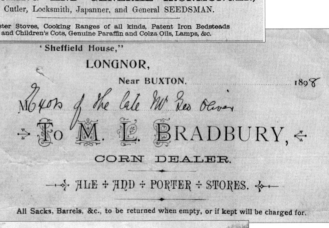

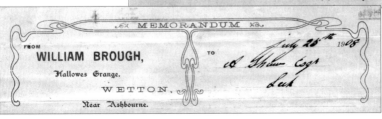

are two more modern variants of Podmore; 1687:Edward Padmore, buried at Seighford; 1907:George Patmore (potter), Furnival Street, Cobridge.

Whitmore, three miles north of Podmore - white moor" - is noted as "Wytemore under Lyme" in the Middle Ages, where "Lyme" echoes the old forest of Lyme, contained in Newcastle under Lyme and Burslem. This is one origin of the surname Whitmore, but contributions are also made by The Whitemoor (Farm) in Brewood and a toponymic for a dweller by a white moor. By a curious coincidence, these two surnames Whitmore and Podmore are joined together in marriage at Audley in 1583, when on May 12th of that year William Podmore wed Margaret Whitmore; 1887:Cyrus Whitmore and Son (dental surgeons and manufacturing dentists), Ivy Cottage, Broad Street, Hanley.

Ashmore is primarily derived from Ashmore Park near Wednesfield - "marshland where ash trees grew", but if Ashmore House near Biddulph is a medieval location, then this might also be considered as a source; 1851:William Ashmore (farmer) of Grindley, Drointon; 1887:John Ashmore (draper) of Parliament Row, Hanley.

Roughly halfway between Whitmore and Podmore lies the village of Maer reputedly named after a mere (a large pool) from which the River Tern rises before it flows through Shropshire to eventually join the Severn.

Meretown, which adjoins Aqualate Mere is from the same Saxon word "mere" - "pool, lake" and both localities are major bases for the surnames Mear(s)/Meares/ Meers/Meir, eg. Roger de Mere, assessed in the 1327 subsidy rolls at Radwood, Maer and Aston, and Yevan de Mere, fined six pence at Standon manor court in 1355 for allowing five cattle to trespass on to the Lord's corn. Alternatively, the names could denote residence near some lake or pool as exemplified by 1332:Richard atte mere of Leigh near Tean, but the situation is complicated by the fact that another Saxon word "(ge)maere" - "boundary", also exhibits medieval spellings such as "mere" as in Meerbrook, a stream that flows into the River Churnet - "Merebroke" (14th century) - "boundary brook". Meir and Meir Heath belong here as well, because they lay on the boundary which divided Normacot and Stone from Blurton and Trentham. Therefore, all these surnames could equally apply to someone who dwelt by some boundary or other. What is more important, however, is that the place Maer is pronounced as "Mare" and spelt as "Mare" by Plot in 1686, and in local parish registers we find Sarah Maer signing her own name as Sarah Mare at Stafford in 1760, whilst at Wolstanton, Elijah Mare (1746) is also quoted as Elijah Mayer in 1749. Again, the Saxon "(ge)maere", not to be outdone, is also converted into "Mare", as in Hand Mare in Blymhill and Brineton, and into "Mayre", as in Mayre Lane Leasow in Cannock. And so, the prolific local surname Mayer/Mayor is either from Maer or a toponymic for a dweller by a lake or boundary, and not derived from the imported Norman word "maire" - mayor of a borough", that is, an official title or an ironic appellation for someone who liked to put on the airs and graces of a mayor; 1841:John Mayer, aged 9, mould runner for Adolphus Hancock at Barker, Sutton and Till's Earthenware Factory, Burslem; 1907:Samuel Jennings Mayer (police constable), Park Road, Fenton; 1907:Frederick Meir (potter) of May Place, Fenton.

Far and away the most widespread surname for a dweller by a boundary, in north Staffordshire, is Vise/Vyse/Vize; 1421:William del vyse of Standon. This is a contracted form of Old French "devise' - "boundary", as preserved in Devizes, Wiltshire; 1762:Sarah Vise of Norton in the Moors; 1777:Andrew Vise (Vyse), overseer of the poor at Betley.

Another boundary dweller is indicated by March, from Old French "marche" - "boundary", but this is easily absorbed by Marsh, which is either a toponymic for a person who resided near some marsh; 1332:Thomas del mershe of Maer and Aston, or from Marsh near Castlechurch. At Stoke-on-Trent Robert Marsh (1651), occurs as Robert March in 1652.

Fenn - "dweller by a fen or marsh" - is very spasmodic in its distribution; 1332:Thomas in le fen of Madeley, near Uttoxeter; 1636:James Ffenne of Standon. Wagg is obscure, but it may be connected with an unrecorded Saxon wagge - "quaking bog, marsh", found in the dialectal "wagmire" - "quagmire" for Gloucestershire and Devon. Hence it is another toponymic for residence by a bog or marsh. Amongst those enrolled in the 1539 muster are Bartholomew Wagge at Penkhull, Alexander Wagge at Stone and Reynold Wagge at Betley and Balterley, whilst John Wagge and Phillip Wagg are exempt from hearth tax at Adbaston in 1666.

Doxey on the outskirts of Stafford - "land between two streams once occupied by a Saxon called Docc" - exists in three separate forms - the basic Doxey; 1758:Helen Doxey of Seighford; Doxsey; 1514:Richard Doxsey of Tunstall (Stoke-on-Trent) and the most persistent variant Docksey; 1599:Thomas Docksey of Chell; 1851:John Docksey (flint grinder) of Stanley, Endon; 1875:Anna Docksey (hay and straw dealer), Old Hall Street, Hanley. Several miles north west of Doxey is the little hamlet of Slindon, not far from Drake Hall open prison. Apparently it is compounded of the Saxon "slinu" - "slope" or "gently sloping ground", and "dun" - "hill", giving the tautological "sloping hill". The element also occurs in Slyne near Lancaster, pronounced "Sline" to rhyme with "shine". However, during the 1600s, Slindon appears as "Slin otherwise Slindon" in 1616 and as "Slyndon alias Slyne" in 1606, thus providing us with the origin of the North Staffordshire surname Slinn/Slynn; 1779:George Slin of Ranton, noted as George Slindon in 1784; 1851:David Slinn (salt dealer), Nursery Lane, Stafford; 1851:John Slinn (blacksmith), Cookshill, Caverswall; 1907:George Slinn (engine man), Stanier Street, Fenton. But what is more significant, is that, wherever the surname Slinn/Slynn crops up, it is invariably accompanied by spellings such as Slane, Slayne, Slaney, Slyne, etc; 1662:William Slyn of Chebsey, who is in all likelihood identical with William Slany (1667). The Seighford specimens include 1647:Robert Slaney, as opposed to Catheren Slynne of 1622, and so on. Throughout the sixteenth and seventeenth centuries the Slayne/Slane/Slaney/Slanye spellings besiege Slindon on all sides, especially around Cold Norton, Tittensor, Meaford, Darlaston (Stone), Kibblestone, Chebsey, Ranton, Ingestre and Stafford, and are far too early to be derived from the Irish name Slaney. Another crucial piece in the jigsaw is the location known as Sleen Field in Sandbach, from the allied word "slinn" - "slope". It follows, then, that we are dealing with the triplet Slaney-Sleen-Slyne, based on the sequence Sleigh-Slay-Slee-Sligh-Sly. Of course, some modern Staffordshire families called Slaney must have come from Ireland, traceable to the River Slaney - "health giving waters"; 1851:Thomas Slaney (saddler), Market Street, Cheadle.

Two miles south east of Slindon is Heamies, which is situated on a hill, at the foot of which runs the River Meece, so the place probably refers to a high spot by the said river, that is "High Meece", in contrast to the nearby Millmeece and Coldmeece. A form such as "Haymes" (1620) certainly validates this supposition. This locality is the major origin of the Staffordshire surnames Heames/Hemes/Heams, and Eames, minus the initial aspirate; 1666:Jane Hemes widow of Betley; 1851:James Heames (printer, bookseller), High Street, Tunstall; 1907:William H. Eames (licensee), Stag Inn, Waterloo Road, Burslem; 1907:Harvey Heames (potter), Oxford Street, Stoke.   Spellings such as 1581:Margery Haymyse (Hemyes) of Eccleshall could be confused with Haymes/Hames, which are from the Germanic personal name "Haimo", brought to England by the Normans as "Haim, Aymes"; 1175 Pipe Rolls:Hamo de Weston. Furthermore, the name Eames is occasionally from Middle English "eme" - "uncle", a surname of relationship; 1327:Roger le eme of Great Wyrley near Cannock.

Pyebirch Manor, south of Eccleshall, is an object lesson in the art of deception - no pies, no birches, just the medieval spelling "Pipebriche", as quoted in the 1298 surveys of the Bishop of Lichfield's demesne lands. This probably denotes some newly cultivated land with a pipe for drainage and evidently it also remains with us disguised as the surname Pybus; 1622:Thomas Pybus of Stafford and 1655:Alice Pibush (sic) of Seighford, married as Alice Bret in 1645 to Robert Bibus (sic).

Approximately two and a half miles north east of Pyebirch Manor across the River Sow and beyond Chebsey, we arrive at Izaak Walton's Cottage and Museum at Shallowford, adjacent to which is Halfhead Farm. This was once a homestead consisting of half a hide of land (about 60 acres). Included in the 1539 muster for Coton near Seighford was Leonard Halfehed, whilst Thomas Heyford was resident at Seighford in 1689. Clearly the latter is a variant of the former, passing through stages such as "Heyfhead" with dialectal "heyf" for "half" and then the "head" ending corrupted to "-erd" and "-ord". Families bearing the surname Hayford/Heyford could also be derived from Nether and Upper Heyford near Northampton or Lower and Upper Heyford south of Banbury, both alluding to a ford used at the time of the hay harvest. Another possible development is from Halfhead to Halford/Holford and even Alford, but here we are also looking at Halford near Stokesay Castle, Shropshire - "hawkers' ford" and Halford south of Stratford on Avon - "ford in a narrow valley"; 1698:Constance Halford of Ellastone; 1907:Walter Holford (potter), Bucknall New Road, Hanley; 1912:Frederick Alford (miner), Wise Street, Longton.

The full hide of 120 acres is preserved in Hyde near Chillington, The Hyde in Kinver and Hyde near Stalybridge, all of which are probably involved in the surname Hide(s)/ Hyde(s), but these may also designate a person who held and worked a hide of land; 1491:Nicholas Hyde, rector of Standon; 1851:Walter Hide (maltster) of Abbot's Bromley; 1907:James Hyde (fitter) of Garibaldi Street, Etruria.

The surname Walford has several origins - Walford near Standon - "ford of the Welsh or Britons", synonymous with Walford south of Ross on Wye, plus Walford near Baschurch, Shropshire or Walford south west of Ludlow, both referring to a ford over a river; July 8th 1680:William Wallford and Margarett Bacchouse, married at Seighford; 1851:John Austin Walford (watch and clock maker), Derby Street, Leek.

Fulford in the wooded hills north east of Stone - "muddy ford" - was presumably the birthplace of Adam de Fulford, who, in 1343, along with Stephen de Ireton (constable of Newcastle under Lyme), Ralph Lycoris and William Loveton..... *"entered upon the Priory of Trentham......against the will of the Canons there.....but they did not take or carry away any of the goods belonging to the same Priory, except only some victuals."* Subsidiary sources of the surname include the fieldname "ffulford" (1439) in Castlechurch, Fulford near York and Fulford north of Taunton, Somerset; 1851:Captain William Fulford, governor of Stafford County Gaol.

The county town Stafford - "ford by a landing place" - is not all that common as a surname. In the Middle Ages, of course, the Stafford family was amongst the most notable of the baronial lords, descended from Ralph de Toeni, a Norman knight who assumed the name of Stafford since his lands were concentrated near the town of that name. When Hervey Bagot married the sister and heiress of his feudal lord, Robert de Stafford, in 1194, he came into possession of the Stafford lands, and, following the usual practice of the Norman hierarchy, changed his name to Stafford. However, this connection between the Bagot and the Stafford families did not seem to meet with the approval of his sixteenth century descendant, Edward, Lord Stafford. This contempt for the name Bagot is revealed in a letter which Edward wrote to Richard Bagot in 1590, in which he concludes: *"No, surely, I will not exchange my name of Stafford for the name of a bag of oats, for that is your name - Bag Ote."* The etymology may be a trifle shaky, but the message is loud and clear! At the other end of the social scale, we find Thomas Stafford, his wife Ellen and their nine children, living at Gayton near Salt in 1532, a mere five miles distant from where their ancestors were born.

The simplest way of fording a river was by a footbridge, as in the dialectal "plat", which is probably contained in Platt Bridge west of Eccleshall, and hence one source of the local surname Platt(s). But external origins also come into the reckoning, e.g. Platt Bridge near Hindley in Wigan parish, Platt in Rusholme near Manchester and Helley Platt in Burnley chapelry. Besides, this same word "plat" often signifies a small plot of land or patch of flat land, and this would provide a further source; 1603:Elizabeth Shocobotham alias Plat of Slyndon. The Hotel Rudyard, which incorporated a house originally built for the reservoir keeper, was taken over about 1870 by Henry Platt, who enlarged it, notably with a ballroom in 1873; 1875:James Platt (brick and tile manufacturer), Stoke Road, Stoke; 1875:George Platt, licensee of the American Hotel, Waterloo Road, Burslem.

Ridges, headland and nooks

In this zone surnames derived from topographical features such as these are minor characters in the drama, but no less crucial to the development of the plot. About one and a half miles due north of Bury Bank (Darlaston) is Tittensor, whose high situation dates back to a former settlement on the ridge or slope here, attributable to a Saxon called Titten. In 1610, Thomas Tittensor was church warden for the parish of Stoke-on-Trent; 1851:Samuel H. Tittensor (chairmaker and wood turner), High Street, Tunstall; 1887:Eli Tittensor (cooper), King Street, Newcastle under Lyme.

Four miles south west of Tittensor lies Swinchurch Farm, Chapel Chorlton, which, at first sight, looks distinctly unpromising as the originator of a local surname. Yet, from this tiny locality has sprung one of the most complex of all Staffordshire locative surnames - Swing(e)wood/Swinswood. It is here, where Robert de Swynesheved of Chapel Chorlton is paying tax in 1327 and the original spelling of the place indicates a headland shaped like a pig's snout. Comparable placenames include Swineyard Hall in Rostherne, Cheshire, Swineshead north of Bedford and Swineshead near Boston, Lincolnshire, all formerly recorded as "Swinesheved' in the Middle Ages. At one time, all these places were thought to have been sites of pagan worship with animal heads as a prominent part of sacrificial feasts or a spot where the local hundred assembled for deliberation, with the head of an animal, say a pig, ram or goat, fixed to the nearest pole to mark the exact assembly point. But these ideas have now been abandoned. The actual progression from the original "Swynesheved" to Swinchurch on the one hand, and to Swing(e)wood/Swinswood on the other is not easy to detect, since there are several intermediary forms which are missing. However, a pairing such as Swindgett-Swindgewood/Swingewood is reminiscent of Bridgett-Bridgewood. Recordings for Seighford over the years comprise; 1623:Alice Swinshed spinster; 1631:Roger Swinshed (1666.Roger Swineshutt); 1797:Thomas Swingwood; 1804:Jane Swingewood; 1907:Daniel Swingwood of Ranscliffe Road, Kidsgrove; 1907:Joseph Swingewood (miner), Duke Street, Fenton; 1907:George Swinswood (labourer), Pitt Street, Fenton.

Several miles south west of Swinchurch Farm, beyond Podmore and Gerrard's Bromley is The Rudge, from whence came Stephen de Rugge, assessed in the 1327 subsidies for the village of Podmore. This is the Staffordshire dialect form of Standard English "ridge" - "ridge, a long narrow hill", preserved also in Rudge near Pattingham, a further source of the surname Rudge/Ridge. The modern Rudge can also be a nickname for a person with red hair, from Anglo French "rugge"; 1773:Margaret Ridge of Caverswall, married to Thomas Miller of Cheddleton; 1851:Joseph Ridge (maltster) of George Street, Longton; 1907:Thomas Rudge (potter), Albany Road, Stoke. In the Danelaw, Ridge was hardened to Rigg(s) owing to Scandinavian influence; Charles Riggs, one of the most noted clay pipemakers in Newcastle under Lyme, was apprentice to Francis Catherall from 1641 until 1648. The compound Smalldridge is perhaps for Smallridge - "dweller by a narrow ridge" - with intrusive "d", modelled on Allridge-Aldridge; 1907:William James Smalldridge (potter's fireman), Hulse Street, Fenton.

The constituents of the placename Eccleshall are the British word for a church - "ecles", from Latin "ecclesia", found in Eccles near Salford, Greater Manchester, and the Mercian "halh" - "land by a river". The locality means therefore "land of the church by the river" and the river in question is the Sow, which also retains its British name. The implication here is that there must have been a Romano-British church with a settlement growing around it already in existence when the Anglo Saxons invaded this area in the late sixth or early seventh century. At High Offley in 1779, Elizabeth Eccleshall married William Creswell widower; 1912:Mrs Eccleshall of Tunley Street, Stone.

Pershall north west of Eccleshall is another compound containing "halh", but the first component is obscure. Old English "peosu" - "pea" - has been proposed, referring to a wild pea plant such as the marsh trefoil, otherwise known as the buck-bean. William de Pessal of Pershall (1284 Feudal Aids) obviously has descendants whose family names are spelt Pessall or Pessoll; 1774:Sarah Pessal of Eccleshall; 1907:Thomas Pessoll of High Street, Silverdale. Other instances fluctuate between Pershall and Pearsall; 1597:Robert Pearsall of Charnes, four miles north west of Eccleshall, noted as Robert Pershall in 1598. Of course, there is inevitable overlap with Pursell/Purcell, which are either from Old French "pourcel" - "piglet, little pig", a nickname for a greedy individual; 1175 Pipe Rolls:William Purcel of Cotwalton near Stone, or from Purshull Green several miles west of Bromsgrove, Worcestershire, pronounced by the locals as "Persall". Schoolboy humour naturally associates the names with Persil, the well known washing powder and immediately burdens anyone named Pursell or Purcell "soapy" or "sudsy". In actual fact the brand name Persil is the French word for "parsley", an allusion to the sprig of parsley, trademark of Ronchetti who discovered a method of adding bleach to soap in 1907.

Moddershall near Stone - "Modred's nook" - occurs as "Mothershall" in 1609 and as "Mottershall" on a map of Stone coach roads (c.1800). Consequently this location is one possible origin of the surname Mottershaw/Mothershaw, following the pattern Ravenshall-Ravenshaw. Yet, a Cheshire source is also to be scrutinised - Murdishaw Wood in Sutton Weaver near Runcorn, recorded as "Mottershaw Wood" in 1831 - "the spokesman's wood"; 1761, December 28th:John Mothershawe, witness to the marriage of Benjamin Reynolds and Margaret Creswell at High Offley; 1851:Thomas Mottershaw (tailor) of Longton Road, Longton; 1912:William Moddershall (dipper), Wesley Sreet, Tunstall.

The village of Yoxall is situated near the meeting of the Swarbourn and the Trent, and was once the home of Izaak Walton's grandfather. It denotes a secluded piece of land small enough to be ploughed by a pair of oxen in one day; 1851:Edward Yoxall (grocer and coffee roaster) of Market Place, Burslem; 1851:Thomas Yoxall (joiner and builder) of Church Street, Stoke .

Woods, trees, clearings

In this zone surnames derived from "woods" are not very well represented at all. Wetwood/Watwood go back to Wetwood not far from Bishop's Wood, where glass was produced by Huguenot craftsmen from Lorraine in the sixteenth century, or from Wetwood north west of Tittesworth Reservoir - "Wethwode" circa 1230. Both refer simply to a wet wood; 1532:Humphrey Wettwode of Sandon (1539:Humfrey Whatwood); Castlechurch parish registers 1580:Elizabeth Watwood otherways called Wright, daughter of John Wright and Jone Watwood, unlawfully begotten; 1907:John Wetwood of Victoria Street, Cheadle.

William Hasshwode and his wife Alice, poll tax contributors in 1381 at Knightley, north west of Ranton, undoubtedly came from Ashwood close by Ranton Abbey - "ash wood, wood mainly consisting of ash trees", but the surname is also derived from Ashwood near Kingswinford, one of the Hays of Kinver Forest, Ashwood in Ravenscliffe (Tunstall) - 1836 Ordnance Survey map - or possibly Ashwood in Longton; 1875:James Ashwood (greengrocer), Sneyd Street, Tunstall; 1912:Walter Ashwood (collier), Park Road, Fenton. Dashwood retains the original "D" of "de Ashwood"; 1887:Alfred Dashwood of Newcastle Street, Burslem.

Haywood/Heywood are chiefly traceable to Great and Little Haywood near Shugborough - "enclosed wood", a meaning shared by "Heywood" (1584) in Brocton by Baswich, another likely source of the surnames, plus "le heyewode" (1364) in Brewood - "the high wood". If the name was brought into Staffordshire from neighbouring counties, then the principal origins are Heywood in Bury parish, Lancashire - "high wood" and several places in Derbyshire, Haywood in Bakewell, Haywood in Mapleton (just across the county boundary from Okeover) and "le heyewode" (1345) in Atlow near Ashbourne, all probably for "enclosed wood" or "high wood". Cheshire may have lent a hand with Heawood Hall in Alderley and the lost Heywood Barnes in Checkley cum Wrinehill, both denoting an enclosed wood; 1841:David Heywood, aged 8 years, mould runner for Joseph Smith at George Phillip's Earthenware Factory, Longport; 1851:Stephen Haywood (corn miller), Woodseaves (High Offley); 1875:Teresa Heywood (hatter), Newcastle Street, Burslem. Sometimes things get somewhat blurred, since Haywood tends to alternate with Hayward; 1767:Robert Hayward of Seighford, quoted as Robert Haywood in 1768. Hayward on its own designates a medieval manorial officer who was in charge of the Lammas lands (enclosed for corn). His main duty was to prevent cattle from straying into the fields and trampling down the crops; 1327:William le hayward of Hilderstone.

Callingwood north of Tatenhill - "wood of disputed ownership" - survives in the surnames Collingwood and Collingswood; 1907:Charles Edward Collingwood (potter's designer), Foley Place, Fenton.

One Scandinavian term of great relevance in North Staffordshire is "lundr" - "grove, copse", which is preserved in Lount Farm east of Colwich, cited as "Lund, le Lounde" in medieval deeds from the Chartulary of St. Thomas Priory, Stafford, The Lunts Farm in

Aston near Maer (The Lounts - 1833 Ordnance Survey map), "le lunde juxta Colemanesaker" (14th Century) in Field near Leigh and Lount Farm near Rolleston. Hence the surnames Lund, Lunt, Lount and Lowndes, but these could also be migrants from Danelaw places such as Lund in Kirkham parish, Lunt Heath in Prescot (St. Helens) and Lunt near Maghull on Merseyside (all in Lancashire), whilst the Yorkshire possibilities centre around Lund north west of Beverley and Lund near Selby. Also involved are Lound north of Retford, Nottinghamshire, Lount north east of Ashby-de-la-Zouch, Leicestershire, Lound near Witham on the Hill in Lincolnshire and Lound north west of Lowestoft, Suffolk; 1824:William Lowndes (silk throwster) of Upper Hulme; 1851:Mary Lowndes (milliner and dressmaker), Navigation Road, Burslem; 1851:Joseph Lunt (tailor) of Goldenhill, Tunstall; 1907:Edwin Lund (musician), Leek Road, Hanley; 1907:Thomas Lunt (flint miller), Chester Street, Burslem.

Lunn seems to be a variant of Lund or Lunt minus the final consonant, the nearest parallel being Chetwynd (Chetwynt) which is shortened to Chetwyn/Chetwin/Chatwin. This goes back to Chetwynd north west of Newport, Shropshire - "Ceatta's winding ascent"; 1666:Ellen Chatwin, exempt from hearth tax at Alstonefield; 1675:Catherine Chetwin, buried at Audley on September 4th; 1912:Henry Lunn (wagoner), Bryan Street, Hanley; 1912:James Lunn (carter), Lord's Square, Burslem. Regarding the surname Lowndes, there might be some confusion with the word "launde" - "glade, pasture", since the two names Launde and Lowndes occur at Hilderstone; 1532:George Launde, 1666:Thomas Lownes.

The triplet Aldershaw-Eldershaw-Oldershaw is exceedingly difficult to unravel. Aldershaw and Oldershaw are clearly derived from Aldershawe near Lichfield - "alder wood, alder copse", synonymous with "Alreschawe" (1283 Court Rolls) in Essington north of Wolverhampton, and possibly Oldershaws south west of High Offley; 1606:Thomas Ouldershaw of Burslem; 1725:Jane Aldershaw of Wolstanton. However, in the Baswich parish registers, John Owldershaw (1693) is recorded as John Oleranshaw in 1689 and John Eldershaw is buried at Baswich in 1701. The surname Eldershaw usually specifies anyone who dwelt by an elder wood, whilst the spelling "Oleranshaw" points to a derivation from Ollerenshaw (Hall) in Chapel-en-le-Frith in the Derbyshire Peak district - "alder wood"; 1673:Old Goodwife Eldershaw of Barlaston; 1875:William Ollerenshaw (greengrocer), Well Street, Hanley. Moreover, at Norton in the Moors, in 1798, Samuel Aldershaw signs his own name in the parish register as Samuel Alldersea. Now if the latter is the correct name, then the locative in question is Aldersey Green, north east of Farndon, Cheshire - "the river land of a Saxon called Aldhere or Aethelric"; 1800:Mary Aldersay of Norton in the Moors; 1907:Richard Aldersea (engineman), Brocksford Street, Fenton.

Alders produce a useful hard timber formerly much employed for submerged piles and supports because the wood was extremely durable under water. It is said that most of Venice is built on alder-wood piles. Adam in the olres of Milwich (1346 Assizes) built his home in the midst of some alder trees, and his progeny are now with us bearing names such as Alder(s)/Allder/Older/Nolder; 1666:Thomas Older, paying tax on one hearth at Fenton Culvert. The compound Greatolder signifies residence by some thick, stout alder(s); 1532:Thomas Grettholder of Millmeece; 1582:Jone Greatoulder widow of Standon.

The widespread Perry/Pirie/Pirrie denotes either a dweller by some pear tree; 1347:Hugh atte pirie of Stafford, or comes from Perry Barr north of Birmingham - "homestead by a pear tree"; 1887:Aaron Perry (glass and china dealer), Uttoxeter Road, Longton; 1907:Frank Perry (mouldmaker), South Street,Fenton.

Surnames in "-ley"

Practically every kind of tree native to the British Isles is incorporated in placenames ending in "-ley". Ashley west of Podmore - "ash wood" or "glade with an ash tree" has given us Ashley/Ashlee/Ashleigh, with minor contributions from Ashleigh in Great Wyrley," Ass(h)ele" (13th C) in Cannock and "Aschley"(1259) in Blymhill and Brineton. Cheshire Ashleys could trace their family tree back to Ashley north of Mobberley; 1851:John and Joseph Ashley (tailors), Hick Street, Newcastle under Lyme; 1887:William Ashley (tripe dealer), St. John's Market, Burslem.

This entire area of Staffordshire surrounding Ashley must have been heavily wooded long ago, judging by the "woods" and "-leys" scattered all about, e.g. Burnt Wood, Wetwood, Greatwood and Bishop's Wood to the south and Maer Hills Forest to the north. Several miles to the south east lies the village of Aspley - "aspen wood", synonymous with Aspley Heath near Tanworth in Arden, Warwickshire and Aspley Guise south west of Bedford. All these locatives are probably involved in our local families called Aspley; 1271:Nicholas de Aspley, prior at St. Thomas's Priory, Stafford; at High Offley in 1798, William and Fanny Aspley had a daughter, whom they christened Isabel. The variant Espley has arisen either by analogy with the couplet Asprey-Esprey or is derived from Espley near Hodnet in Shropshire or Espley in Caldwell, south of Church Gresley, Derbyshire, both perhaps for "aspen wood"; 1875:James Espley (grocer), Reid Street, Burslem; 1875:George Espley (tinman), Lord Street, Etruria.

On the whole, the Staffordshire Oakleys are traceable to Oakley near Mucklestone - "oak wood", Oakley (Farm) near Croxall, Oakley in Brewood or possibly Oak Leigh near Gayton. East Anglian migrants could have brought the name from Oakley near Denham, Suffolk, whilst other families might have roots in Oakley north west of Bedford, Oakley near Poole, Dorset, Oakley north east of Oxford, Oakley near Basingstoke, Hampshire, Oakley south west of Aylesbury or Oakley Green near Windsor, Berkshire; 1851:John Oakley (joiner) of Little Fenton; 1875:Joseph Oakley (forge manager), Chesterton.

Berk(e)ley/Barclay is not an indigenous Staffordshire surname, but an invader from Berkeley in Gloucestershire, a few miles south west of Slimbridge Wildlife Trust Centre, or Berkley near Frome, Somerset - "birch wood" - both pronounced "Barkley", or Barklye in Heathfield, Sussex; 1875:George Barclay (draper), Elliott Street, Newcastle under Lyme; 1907:John Barkley (potter), Beresford Street, Shelton. There is occasional interchange between Barkley and Bartley; 1686:Hennery Bartley of Penkridge, who is buried as Henery Barcley, pauper in 1727; 1907:William Bartley (forgeman), Austin Street, Hanley.

Homegrown origins of the surname Brierley/Brearley/Brealey comprise Brierley Hill, Dudley or Big and Little Brierley Leasow in Bradley south west of Stafford - "clearing overgrown with briars", and hence identical in meaning with Brierley north east of Barnsley, Brierley near Cinderford in the Forest of Dean, Brierley south of Leominster, Herefordshlre and probably Brearley near Halifax; 1875:Alfred Brierley (wine and spirit merchant), High Street, Hanley; 1907:James Brearley (carter), Avery Street, Hanley; 1907:Reginald Brealey(sic), Daisy Bank, Leek.

The group of localities Hadley, Hadleigh, Hedley and Heatley were all sited amongst heather.   Staffordshire representatives are Hadley End in Yoxall, "Hedlee" (1364) in Brewood and Heatley near Bagot's Bromley, with Hateley Heath in West Bromwich resulting in the surname Hateley; 1580:Hughe Hateley of Ellastone; 1851:John Hadley (farmer) of Hatton, Swynnerton; 1875:Samuel Hadley (plumber, glazier, painter), Edensor Road, Longton; 1907:Edward Hedley (ironfounder), Gilman Street, Hanley; 1907:Thomas Heatley (potter's placer), Rose Street, Northwood.

Wheatley, Whateley and Whatley signify clearings or fields where wheat was cultivated, as testified by Big Wheatley ln Brewood, Whateley Leasow in Cannock, Whatley in Dunston and "Whateley pitte" (1502) in Bradley south west of Stafford. Wetley Moor two miles south of Bagnall appears as "Whatley More" circa 1540 - "wet glade" - and this might provide a further source of the surnames; 1674:Joseph Whateley of Audley; 1851:Samuel Wheatley (agent), Butterton Hall, Trentham; 1875:John Wheatley (secondhand clothes dealer), Sutherland Road, Longton.

We have already seen how unpredictable the ending "-ley" can be - viz Critchlow-Critchley, etc, but nowhere is this more evident than in the doublet Barlow-Barley. At first sight Barlow seems to be connected with Barlow (old manor) in Manchester parish or Barlow in Norton (Runcorn), both of which refer to a hill where barley was grown. However, Barlow near Chesterfield, Derbyshire is mentioned as "Barleie" in the Domesday survey and means either "clearing where barley grew" or "boar clearing". It shares this etymology with Barley south east of Clitheroe and possibly Barley Hole north of Sheffield. On the other hand, Barlow south of Selby, Yorkshire is noted as "Berlay" in the Middle Ages and denotes either "clearing with a barn" or "barley clearing". In Staffordshire the fluctuation between Barlow and Barley is confirmed by Thomas Barlow of Longdon, alternatively known as Thomas Barley in a lawsuit of 1586. It is in this region of the county where the surname Barlow ramifies from the 1500s onwards, that is roughly from Cannock Chase in the west to Needwood Forest in the east and Blithfield Reservoir to the north, and it is almost certain that it is derived from the locality called "Hay de Berley" in Callowhlll between Newton and Bagot's Bromley, quoted thus in a 1257 deed from the Chartulary of St. Thomas's Priory, Stafford. The place alludes to " clearing where barley grew". Robert de Berleye, taxed at Newton and Blithfield in 1327, obviously came from this locality. The vacillation between Barlow and Barley continues well into the 17th century, e.g. 1617:Thomas Barlow of Upper Tean, who is ineligible for any hearth tax at Tean in 1666 (appears as Thomas Barleigh). By now the overwhelming majority of forms are spelt Barlow(e) or Barloe; 1666 Hearth tax returns:William Barlowe of Knypersley, John Barlowe of Chesterton, Ann Barloe of Weston Coyney, Joane Barlow of Whiston near Kingsley Holt; 1835:Benjamin Barlow, appointed choirmaster and organist at St. Edward's Church, Leek; 1851:William Barlow, licensee of the Eagle and Child, Bridge Street, Newcastle under Lyme; 1887:Samuel Barlow, sexton of Hartshill Church, Hartshill, 1907:Edwin Barley (potter), Hassell Street, Hanley.

Barley can also be an occupational term for a person who made and sold barley bread or cakes, or a merchant who dealt with this commodity, equivalent to Barleyman. This sense is inherent in Ailric Berley, witness to a twelfth century deed in the Staffordshire Chartulary. Yet around Knightley near Ranton the name Barley flits back and forth with Burley, imitating Barkley-Berkley; 1532:John Barley of Knightley; 1666:Thomas Burley of Knightley. Relevant here are Great Burley Field in Castlechurch, the Derbyshire trio of Burley in Duffield, Burleigh Plantation in Longford and Burley in Twyford and Stenson, the West Riding duo of Burley near Leeds and Burley in Wharfedale, a lost Burley in Cholmondeley, Cheshire and Burleigh near Great Bolas, Shropshire. All these refer to a clearing belonging to a fort or manor; 1887:Richard Burley (engine driver), Campbell Road, Stoke; 1887:John Burley (shoeing and general smith), Old Hall Street, Hanley. In the 1539 muster roll, two of those enrolled at Blithfield are Richard a Berley and Thomas a Byrley, which retain the vestigial remains of the old preposition "atte", thereby bequeathing us with one origin of the surname Abberley, but a secondary source is Abberley near Stockton on Teme, Worcestershire - "Eadbeald's clearing"; 1851:James Abberley (boot and shoe maker), Market Street, Longton; 1875:George Abberley, Vine Inn, London Road, Stoke. Habberley could be a variant of Abberley with initial aspirate, or from Habberley near Pontesbury Hill, Shropshire or Habberley near Kidderminster, both possibly for "glade of Heathuburg"; 1907:Thomas Habberley (watchman), Acton Street, Birches Head.

The Staffordshire Stockleys boast several separate branches. The chief line is from Stockley Park south of Tutbury, but others stem from Stockley in Scarcliffe near Bolsover, Derbyshire, Stockley Farm in Aston by Budworth, Cheshire, Stockley Hill near Tyberton, Herefordshire, Stockley several miles west of Avebury, Wiltshire, Stockleigh English north of Crediton or Stockleigh Pomeroy near Exeter (both in Devon). The meanings of the localities vary from "wood belonging to a monastery" to "wood where logs were obtained" or "clearing with tree stumps"; 1907:Richard Stockley (miner), Leek New Road, Cobridge; 1907:Edwin Stockley (potter's gilder), Spode Street, Stoke.

Langley and Longley - "long wood or clearing" - occur in so many counties, that it is best to narrow down our search to the most accessible locatives, e.g. Langley Lawn Farm in Brewood, a place recorded as 'Longeleye" near Bishop's Offley in the 1298 Surveys of the Bishop of Lichfield's estates for Eccleshall. Yet not to be sneezed at are places such as Langley south of Macclesfield, three locations in Derbyshire, namely Kirk Langley and Meynell Langley on the Ashbourne road west of Derby, plus Langley near Heanor, Langley in Middleton parish, Greater Manchester and Langley south west of Warwick; 1851:William Langley, (horse, gig, letters) Red Lion Square, Newcastle under Lyme; 1875:George Langley (mattress maker and wool flock dealer), John Street, Hanley.

Some woods or clearings were situated on a slope or ledge, as in Shelley farm in Solihull, Shelley south east of Huddersfield, Shelley a few miles south west of Ipswich, or Shelley near Chipping Ongar, Essex. During the sixteenth century the surname is most common in mid-Staffordshire; 1532:Robert Shelley of Milwich; Thomas Shelley of Berryhill and Knenhall; 1539:John Shelly of Ingestre; 1539:William Shelly of Sandon. In the March 7th edition of the Staffordshire Advertiser (1795), one item revolves around the discovery of a hoard of Saxon coins in the orchard of one Sampson Shelley of Oulton near Kibblestone. Most of the coins were retained by the Shelley family and cannot now be traced; 1851:Clement Shelley (farmer), Beacon Hill, Hopton and Coton; 1851:Robert Shelley (coal dealer), Newcastle Road, Stone.

Animals also feature prominently in compounds of "-ley". The suffix Harley in Shelton under Harley by Swynnerton Old Park is to be discussed along with Harley in Hartington Upper Quarter, Derbyshire, Harley north west of Much Wenlock, Shropshire and Harley north of Sheffield, Yorkshire. All these localities designate a wood frequented by hares or grey wood; 1907:Augustus Harley (horse dealer), Waterloo Road, Cobridge; 1907:Jane Harley (widow) of Carlisle Street, Longton.

In all probability, John Harteley, his wife Elizabeth and family, who settled at Tillington near Stafford in 1532, had ancestors who came from Hartley Green east of Sandon - "stag glade", synonymous with "Harteley meadow" (1567) in Forton, Hartley in Rochdale parish, Lancashire and Hartley in Derby, all additional sources of the surname. Northern migrants could also have introduced the surname from Hartley near Kirkby Stephen, Cumbria or Hartley on the north east coast, just north of Whitley Bay, whilst southern visitors brought it from Hartley near Gravesend or Hartley near Cranbrook (both in Kent) or from either of two localities north east of Basingstoke, Hampshire - Hartley Wespall or Hartley Wintney; 1875:Benjamin Hartley (modeller), West Parade, Fenton; 1875:Charles Hartley (parian manufacturer), High Street, Longton. Hartless is a curious late corruption; 1797:Dorothy Hartley of Weeford (1784:Dorothy Hartless); 1907:John Hartless (potter) of Newlands Street, Shelton.

Oxley near Wolverhampton - "pasture for oxen" - is the parent of many Staffordshire Oxleys, but some lines must be traced to Oxley in Chinley, Buxworth and Brownside near Chapel en le Frith or Ox Lee in Hepworth, West Riding of Yorkshire; 1875:Miss Clara Oxley of the Ladies' School in Belgrave Road, Dresden; 1875:Edwin Oxley (seedsman), Spring Garden Road, Longton. Shipley and Shepley - "pasture for sheep" - have a multitude of sources, chief amongst which are Shipley south west of Trescott, just over the Shropshire border, Shipley north of Ilkeston, where the American Adventure Theme Park is situated, Shipley near Bradford (West Riding of Yorkshire), a lost Shipley in Gawsworth, Cheshire, Shipley east of Billingshurst (West Sussex), Shepley in Ashton under Lyne, Lancashire, Shepley Farms near Bromsgrove or Shepley north east of Holmfirth (West Riding of Yorkshire). In the Rocester parish registers for 1800, one tragic entry reads: *"Thomas Shipley, aged 39 years, who was killed by accident at Uttoxeter (June 18th), by falling from a ladder as he was loading a waggon of cotton, by which he fractured his skull, and died almost instantly, leaving a wife and several children."* 1851:Charles Shipley (whetstone manufacturer) of Weston upon Trent; 1875:Thomas Shipley (beerseller), Newcastle Street, Silverdale.

Caution is the watchword in the treatment of the group Cowley/Coley/Colley. Cowley near Gnosall is certainly the principal source of the Staffordshire surname Cowley, it means "Cufa's glade" or "glade near a hill" or "glade where logs were obtained", and is identical in meaning with Cowley near Exeter, Cowley in Oxford and Cowley south of Buckingham. Cowley south of Cheltenham, Gloucestershire is the only Cowley that lives up to its name - "cows' pasture", but yet another Cowley, near Uxbridge, denotes "Cofa's glade" or "glade in a valley"; 1569: Ellon Cowley of Mucklestone, daughter of Elnor Cooley; 1907:Thomas Cowley (carter) of Dale Street, Burslem. What really clouds the issue, are two Derbyshire locatives - Cowley in Wensley and Snitterton, and Cowley in Dronfield, Woodhouse, plus Cowley in Gawsworth, Cheshire. All these exhibit medieval spellings such as Colley(e), Collei, Collegh and refer to a wood or clearing where charcoal was burnt or obtained. Hence they are synonymous with our local Coley near Great Haywood and Coley in Gnosall, and Colley (1547) in Pentrich near Ripley, Derbyshire. Moreover, they are the major origins of the Staffordshire surname Colley/Coley, although also to be roped in are two other Cheshire locatives - Colleye (1392) in Congleton and Collhey (15th century) in Rostherne - "charcoal enclosure". Besides these locatives Colley can be a nickname from the Saxon "colig" - "coaly, coal black" applied to the colour of a person's hair; Nicholas Coly, customary tenant on the Audley estates at Tunstall, Stoke-on-Trent in 1298. Colly was once a popular name for a blackbird, as in the traditional song *The Twelve Days of Christmas*: "The fourth day of Christmas my true love sent to me, four colly birds, three French hens, two turtle doves, and a partridge in a pear tree." 1841:John Colly, aged 11, maker of leaves for flowers in the Ornamental Flower Room at Minton and Boyle's, Trentham Road, Stoke; 1851:James Colley (beerhouse), Sneyd Street, Tunstall.

Often embedded in the locality is the name of the Saxon who hacked out the clearing in the forest or wood in the first place many centuries ago, as exemplified by Wolseley in Colwich parish, which contains the personal name "Wulfsige" - "wolf victory", and Bishop's Offley and High Offley, west of Eccleshall, both of which preserve the Saxon name "Offa". This name was made famous by the great King of Mercia who built Offa's Dyke in the 8th century to mark the boundary between England and Wales. Richard

Wolseley was in tenure of land at Bowers (Standon) in 1422 and Margaret Offley and Edward Dod were wed at High Offley on December 13th, 1729. Sedgley near Wombourne is "glade of Secg"; 1810:Joseph Sedgley bachelor of Chebsey; 1912:Wilmot Sedgeley (packer), Slater Street, Middleport. Fradley near Alrewas has been taken as "glade of Frod", but this is not compatible at all with the early spellings of the place, e.g. "Foderesleye" - 1262. It must remain an enigma for the time being; 1907:Frank Fradley, licensee of the Golden Cup, High Street, Hanley.

Surnames in "-ton"

Walton, located just south of Eccleshall on the River Sow and Walton near Stone, four miles away on the River Trent, provide conclusive evidence of the survival of a Romano-British population in this region, since both localities denote a homestead inhabited by Britons in a predominantly Saxon district. Walton on the Hill near Stafford (also on the River Sow), could well represent a third such settlement, although Walton Grange near High Onn apparently signifies a farmstead with ramparts or by a wall. At any rate, as a result of this plethora of locatives, the surname Walton multiplies rapidly across the county after the Middle Ages; 1413:John Walton of Huntebache (Humpage Green); 1532:Henry Walton of Drointon; 1640:John Walton of Marston and Whitgreave; 1875:Richard Walton (cratemaker), Back Sytch, Burslem; 1907:George Walton (shingler) of John Street, Hanley.

Many settlements were built by a tree or group of trees and this accounts for Acton north of Hanchurch Hills and Acton Trussell west of Cannock Chase Country Park - "farmstead by the oak(s)". The Trussell family owned land at the latter locality from at least 1342 and their name comes from Old French "trussel" - "packet", later a puncheon or mould used in the process of stamping coins. Acton Hill south east of Eccleshall, a third origin of the surname Acton, has an altogether different scenario, being recorded as "Hakedene" in 1254 - "hook-shaped valley". However, Shropshire is the "Acton" county, boasting no less than five of them - Acton north of Clun, Acton Burnell south of Shrewsbury, Acton Pigott right next door, Acton Round north west of Bridgnorth and Acton Scott south of Church Stretton. Migrant families from any one of these places could have augmented the Staffordshire Actons, reinforced by Cheshire migrants from Acton near Nantwich and Acton Bridge north west of Northwich; 1851:John Acton (wine and spirit merchant), Market Place, Burslem; 1875:Walter Acton (surgeon), Brunswick Street, Newcastle under Lyme.

Ashton is a little more vague. Principal local bases include Ashton in the parish of Gnosall, Ashtons Farm in Pershall and Ashton Hays near Longdon - "settlement by the ash tree(s)". But Ashton is a common locality and so the surname may have arrived in Staffordshire via Ashton by Delamere Forest Park, Cheshire, Ashton in Makerfield near Haydock, Ashton upon Mersey near Sale or Ashton under Lyne, Greater Manchester; 1851:John Ashton (clockmaker), Leek, Sheepmarket; 1887:William Ashton (herbalist) of Waterloo Road, Burslem. There is frequent confusion with Aston; 1797:Susannah Ashton of Seighford (1800:Susannah Aston).

Seighford Parish Register

Aug.	29	Margaret d. of Robt. Till	bapt.
Nov.	1	John s. of John Vnton	bapt.

1563-4

Jan.	6	Francis s. of James Knyght	bapt.
Jan.	23	Robert Beyly and Agnes Ansell	mar.
Feb.	2	Margaret d. of John Dampord	bapt.

1564

May	1	Alice d. of Richd. Bratt	bapt.
May	1	Ellen d. of Robt. Tyll	bapt.
Sept.	21	Ellen d. of Willm. Walter	bapt.
Oct.	22	Joan d. of Robert Baylie	bapt.

1564-5

Feb.	2	Thomas s. of Thomas Greatrax	bapt.

1565

Apr.	1	Eliz. d. of George Bratt	bapt.
Apr.	1	Humphrey s. of Thomas Whitgreave, gen.	bapt.
July	1	Thomas Chamberlin and Ellen Middleton	mar.
Aug.	5	Robert s. of Henry Hart	bapt.
Nov.	25	Humphrey s. of Ralph Walter	bapt.

1565-6

Jan.	20	Richd. s. of Robert Cockes	bapt.
Feb.	3	Richd. s. of John Vnton	bapt.

1566

Apr.	19	Willm. s. of John Dampord	bapt.
Oct.	6	Joan d. of Thomas Greatrix	bapt.
Nov.	1	Willm. s. of Willm. Walter	bapt.

1566-7

Jan.	19	John s. of James Harvie	bapt.

Seighford Parish Register 1563

Perton near Wolverhampton - "village where pear trees grew - is recorded as "Parton" by Kip in 1607/1610 and as "Purton" by Plot in 1686, and these variants are adopted as surnames; Parish registers for the Church of St. Mary, Stafford 1657:Richard Perton, cited as Richard Parton in 1654, and at Eccleshall in 1586, Elizabeth Purton is also known as Elizabeth Parton. On rare occasions the Purton spellings could conceivably go back to Purton near Berkeley or Purton in Lydney (on either side of the Severn estuary), Pirton near Hitchin, Hertfordshire or Pirton in Pershore, Worcestershire, all of which share the same meaning as Perton. Scottish families called Parton acquire their name from Parton near Loch Ken in Kirkcudbrightshire, whilst two locations in Cumbria (of unknown derivation) are unaccounted for, namely, Parton near Whitehaven and Parton several miles south west of Carlisle. 1851:Henry Parton (maltster and victualler) of The Brown Jug, Bishop's Offley; 1907:James Parton (tram inspector), Victoria Street, Hartshill; 1907:William Purton (warehouseman), Grove Place, Shelton.

It seems to be a case of take your pick regarding the surname Thornton - "place in the thorns" - since it is characteristic of northern counties such as Northumberland, Durham, Yorkshire and Lancashire. In fact Yorkshire is swamped with localities called Thornton of varying prefixes and suffixes (16 in all), with all other counties trailing miserably in its wake. Locations of the greatest interest for Staffordshire families bearing the surname Thornton are perhaps Childer Thornton and Thornton le Moors (both near Ellesmere Port, Cheshire), Thornton Hough south of Birkenhead, Thornton north of Blackpool and Thornton in Sefton on Merseyside; 1851:Thomas Thornton (last maker), Friar Street, Stafford; 1851:William Thornton (farmer) of Gilbert's Lea, Adbaston.

Now and again the allied name Brereton/Brearton/Breerton is from Brereton Green near Sandbach, Brearton in the parish of Knaresborough (West Riding of Yorkshire) or Brierton in Hartlepool - "farm in the briars", but these play second fiddle to our own Brereton near Rugeley - "hill where briars grew", from whence came Adam de Breredon, living at Kinvaston in 1352; 1851:Edmund Brereton (bricklayer and builder), Old Hall Street, Hanley. In 1675 the place is spelt as "Brewerton", and this modification persists as a rare variant; 1851:Edward Brewerton (watchmaker) of Longnor near Sheen.

Superficially, Hazleton/Hazelton is connected with Hazleton south east of Cheltenham, Gloucestershire, originally "Heseldene" (circa 1130) - "hazel valley", but during the sixteenth century the surname fluctuates between Hasulton and Haslynton, e.g. 1532:John Haslynton of Bishton near Colwich, noted as John Hasulton in 1545. The former spelling harks back to Haslington near Crewe or Heslington south of York, near Yorkshire Air Museum, both denoting a farmstead amongst hazels, or even Haslingden south of Oswaldtwistle - "hazel valley". At Newcastle under Lyme, Henry Hasselton (1811), is alternatively known as Henry Hasseldine in 1809, thus foreshadowing modern surnames such as Hazledine/Hazeldene. Other localities may have participated in these later forms, including "Hasuldene" (1369) in Long Eaton, Derbyshire, and two places in Cheshire - Hazledines in Tabley Superior and Haselden(e), 13th/14th century in Sandbach, all relating to a hazel valley. Hazelton Clump. near Ilam is probably named after some previous landowner of that name; 1851:William Hazledine (millwright) of Coldmeece; 1875:Richard Hesletine (china and earthenware dealer), Market Street, Kidsgrove; 1907:William Hazeldine (iron worker) of John Street, Tunstall.

From the close of the Middle Ages up to the advent of the Industrial Revolution the distribution of the surname Ellerton is quite precise. It is concentrated around Maer, Trentham, Wetwood near Eccleshall and Ranton, all in striking distance of Ellerton in Shropshire, just beyond the county boundary from Knighton. The place itself means "Aethelheard's farm" and is the ancestral home of Richard Elerton, resident at Wetwood in 1532, and Michael Ellerton, settled at Trentham in 1629. Outside help also comes from Ellerton north east of Selby in the East Riding of Yorkshire or Ellerton near Catterick in the North Riding - "farmstead amid alders"; 1875:Elizabeth Ellerton (stationer), High Street, Goldenhill, Tunstall; 1907:Henry Ellerton (placer), Hitchen Street, Burslem.

Withington near Church Leigh - "farmstead among willows" - is on a par with Withington Green and Lower Withington near Jodrell Bank, Cheshire, Withington east of Shrewsbury, Withington near Hereford and Withington near Levenshulme, Greater Manchester. All these are earmarked as possible sources for the surname Withington; 1636:Mary Withington of Stowe by Chartley; 1779:Timothy Withington of Shebdown Heath (High Offley); 1851:Charles Withington (farmer and road surveyor) of Consall.

Naturally, many villages grew their own crops, one of the main ones being barley. This has given us the ubiquitous locative Barton - "barley farm", which is native to over two dozen English counties. From the original meaning developed later senses such as "demesne farm" or "outlying grange", since several Bartons were actually granges attached to nearby monasteries. Barton under Needwood is certainly a former barley farm, but Barton near Bradley, south west of Stafford contains an obscure Saxon personal name beginning with the theme "Beorht - "bright". Be that as it may, both locations have produced countless divergent branches of the Barton family tree in many parts of north Staffordshire; 1851:William Barton (engraver), Edmund Street, Hanley; 1851:Mary Barton (schoolmistress) of Hanging Bridge, Mayfield; 1887:James Barton (glass and china dealer), George Street, Newcastle under Lyme.

The evolution of the surname Leighton is strewn with wrong turnings and dead ends. For example, in the Milwich parish registers, John Layton (1701) is mentioned as John Leyton in 1705, and we also find Elizabeth Leighton in 1708 in the same registers. From these recordings it is only logical to assume that they are derived from some place called Layton, Leyton or Leighton. One candidate which instantly springs to mind is a locality written down as "Layton in Pyrell Hundred" in the 1539 Muster Roll lists for the county, but this has not yet been positively identified. Outside sources include Leighton near Crewe, Leighton near Neston (Cheshire), Leighton south west of the Wrekin in Shropshire, Leighton north of Carnforth, Lancashire, Leighton Buzzard in Bedfordshire or Leighton Bromswold west of Huntingdon. All signify a village where leeks were grown, a meaning shared by East and West Layton north west of Scotch Corner in the North Riding of Yorkshire. However Leyton in Greater London is "farmstead on the River Lea". In the Ellastone parish registers, the parish clerk narrates that on August 1st 1634 Margrett Leighton was buried, having been *"killed in Wootton Parke by one William Copestake, a maddeman"*; 1851:Ann Leighton, licensee of the Three Anchors, Betley; 1875:George Leighton (postmaster and grocer), Apedale Road, Chesterton.

Some villages were tucked away in valleys, as illustrated by Hopton near Stafford in the Trent valley and Compton near Kinver, Long Compton west of Tittensor Chase and Long Compton south of Ranton. Here the initial elements are "hop" and "cumb", both meaning "valley". John Hopton was vicar of Eccleshall parish in 1532, and Elizabeth Compton married Richard Dermott at Audley on July 18th 1672. Migrant families brought the name Hopton from Hopton, south west of Wirksworth, Derbyshire, Hopton near Thetford or Hopton near Lowestoft (both in Suffolk), or from any one of seven locations in Shropshire - Hopton near Baschurch, Hopton east of Wem, Monkhopton west of Bridgnorth or four places within range of Ludlow, namely, Hopton Wafers and Hopton Cangeford to the east and north east, and Hopton Castle and Hopton Heath to the west. In the case of Compton, four more likely bases for the Staffordshire families bearing this name is a quartet from Warwickshire - Long Compton and Little Compton south of Shipston on Stour and Compton Verney or Fenny Compton east of Stratford on Avon. The great expanses of heathland and moorland across our county have provided us with the equally widely dispersed surnames Hatton and Morton/Moreton. Hatton is chiefly derived from Upper and Lower Hatton near Swynnerton, or The Hattons near Gunstone - "hamlet on a heath", but also on the agenda are external sources such as Hatton north east of Tutbury just across the border with Derbyshire, Hatton east of Runcorn, Hatton Heath south east of Chester, Hatton south of Church Stretton, Shropshire, Hatton near Warwick, and Hatton south east of Market Rasen, Lincolnshire; at a session of the Standon manor court in 1361, John de Hatton was granted possession of the lord's mill for four years, providing he rendered nine quarters of multure (ground corn) for the first year, and then ten quarters of multure annually for the following three years; 1875:Thomas Hatton (hosier), Newcastle Street, Burslem; 1875:William Hatton (hairdresser, photographer), Hope Street, Hanley.

The surname Morton/Moreton is traceable in the main to Moreton near Colwich, Moreton south of Aqualate Park or Moreton north of Draycott in the Clay - "hamlet by a fen or moorland". But Morton and Moreton are common placenames in umpteen counties and could easily have spawned other branches of the surname in our county. In the parish registers of St. Mary's, Stafford, one Puritan family, Robert and Mercy Morton, christened their twins Rebecca and Hopestill in 1633, and in 1841, Richard Moreton, aged 9, worked as a figure maker for his father William Moreton, at Hilditch and Hopwood's China Factory, Longton; 1851:Ann Moreton (milliner and dressmaker), Waterloo Road, Burslem.

Marston north west of Hopton in the Trent Valley and Marston near Wheaton Aston denote a hamlet by a marsh and both have given name to many Staffordshire families. The letter "t" is often omitted, giving Marson; 1717:Jonas Marston or Marson of Rugeley. In the eastern half of the County, from the Staffordshire Moorlands down through Tutbury and beyond, the strongest contenders as origins of the surname are Marston Montgomery, two miles east of Rocester, and Marston on Dove, north east of Tutbury; 1698:Thomas Marston of Audley; 1851:William Marson (farmer) of Cookshill, Caverswall.

Mitton near Penkridge sprang up at the junction of two streams - Church Eaton Brook and Whiston Brook and is the primary source of the surname Mitton/Mytton/Mutton, supplemented by Great and Little Mitton south west of Clitheroe and Mitton near Bredon, Worcestershire. Mutton, however, can also be a nickname from Old French "mouton" - "sheep", or an occupational term for a herder of sheep, a shepherd; September 28th 1719:Maria Mitton, buried at High Offley.

John de Warton, assessed for tax purposes at Sutton near Aqualate Mere in 1327, acquired his name from Warton (Grange) just north of Sutton. In the Middle Ages the place is recorded as "Wavertune, Waverton", and is thus identical in etymology with Wharton (Green) near Winsford, Cheshire, Wharton in Waverton parish south east of Chester, Wharton near Leominster, Herefordshire, and Warton near Polesworth, Warwickshire. All these refer to a farmstead near swampy ground or at a wavering tree. The surname is indecisive as to its spelling, swinging back and forth between Wharton and Warton; 1720:Mary Warton of Standon (1738:Mary Wharton). In certain instances the surname may go back to Warton near Carnforth, Warton by Freckleton (both in Lancashire) or Warton north west of Rothbury Forest, Northumberland - "lookout place"; 1851:John Wharton (potato dealer), Slack Lane, Hanley; 1887:Thomas Warton (stoker), Station Street, Longport.

The surname Hampton, borne by John Hampton of Mucklestone (1532), can be assigned to a whole host of locatives. At the forefront are places such as a lost Hampton in Newton (Draycott in the Moors), perhaps "home farm", a lost Hampton near Blithfield - "high village", two locations in Shropshire - Welsh Hampton near Ellesmere and Hampton Loade on the River Severn, Hampton not far from Malpas, Cheshire, Hampton east of Solihull and Hampton near Warwick, all for a farmstead in a high situation. Some Hamptons like Hampton in Newton above were originally "home farm", and this applies too to Hampton Lovett near Droitwich, Meysey Hampton east of Cirencester and Hampton Poyle north of Oxford. A third group specified a farmstead in a meadow, as characterised by Hampton Lucy near Stratford on Avon and a trio from Herefordshire - Hampton near Bodenham, Hampton Bishop and Hampton Wafer. In early sources, Wolverhampton is regularly shortened to "Hampton" - "high village", thus furnishing an additional origin in our county; 1851:Enoch Hampton, owner of a beerhouse in Joiner's Square, Hanley; 1851:Peter Hampton, carrier's service on Fridays from W. Sale's in High Street, Eccleshall to Stone and Longton. In 1861, James Hampton, the village police officer at Bagnall, was a boarder at Bagnall Hall.

Swynnerton - "village by the pig ford" - midway between Tittensor and Millmeece, exists as the surname Swynnerton and Swinnerton, with the latter having the slight edge in numbers; 1539:Robert Swynnerton constable at Eccleshall; 1739:John Swinnerton, overseer of the poor at Betley; 1851:Joseph Swinnerton, landlord of the Vine Inn, London Road, Stoke. Colton, south of Blithfield Reservoir - "farmstead where colts were reared" or "Cola's farmstead" - appears as "Coulton" on Kip's map of 1607/1610, and is thus responsible for both variants of the surname. But several other locatives enter the fray, including Colton south east of Coniston Water - "village on the river Cole", Colton west of Norwich or two locations in the West Riding of Yorkshire - Colton near Tadcaster and Colton near Whitkirk - "village of Cola or Koli", whilst Coulton north west of Castle Howard is probably "farmstead where charcoal was burnt"; 1907:William Colton (miner), Victoria Road, Longton; 1907:Thomas Coulton, brewer's agent, London Road, Oakhill.

A high percentage of places called Burton or Broughton were once farms near or belonging to a fort, fortified farms or manor house enclosures, as in Burton (Manor) near Stafford, Burton upon Trent and Broughton near Ashley. Other settlements known as Burton have numerous meanings, too varied to detail here, whilst some of the Broughtons were originally sited near a brook, and hence synonymous with Brocton and Brockton, as in Brocton by Baswich and Brocton near Eccleshall; 1851:Elijah Burton (plasterer), Chapel Street, Longton; 1875:Joseph Burton, (perambulator and general dealer), Broad Street, Hanley; 1875:Edward Broughton (tinplate worker), High Street, Longton; 1875:William Broughton, licensee of the Sir Robert Peel Inn, Peel Street, Dresden.

The Colton-Coulton interchange is seen in Olton-Oulton. Primarily these go back to Oulton north of Stone or Oulton near Norbury - "farmstead of the followers of Ealda", but credit must also go to Oulton south west of Rushton Spencer (of unknown meaning), Oulton in Over (Winsford) - "old farmstead" (identical with Olton near Acock's Green, Birmingham), Oulton south east of Leeds, Oulton in Lowestoft, Oulton west of Blickling Hall (Norfolk) and Oulton north west of Wigton, Cumbria (of varying etymologies); 1672:Maria Olton of Audley; 1875:William Oulton (wholesale druggist and dry salter), Market Square, Tunstall; 1907:Wignall A. Oulton (artificial teeth maker), Tunstall.

Personal names are concealed in countless placenames ending in "-ton". Lurking in Billington, one and a half miles south west of Stafford Castle, is the Saxon "Billa", but Billington north of Blackburn refers to the hill of the Billingas, with a rare third source, Billington near Leighton Buzzard designating "Billa's hill"; 1875:George Billington (bricklayer and stonemason), Lord Street, Etruria; 1887:Richard F. Billington (professor of music and teacher of brass, string and reed instruments), Bedford Street, Basford .

During the Middle Ages Amerton, west of Stowe by Chartley - "farm of Eanbeorht" - displays very similar spellings to Emberton north east of Newport Pagnell, Buckinghamshire, and indeed, the two places are identical in every respect except their modern form. Amerton, recorded as "Amberton" in a lawsuit of 1614, alternates with Emberton: Esdras Emberton, who is exempt from hearth tax at Audley in 1666, comes to light as Esdras Amberton in 1682. The "b" often goes missing too, becoming Emerton; 1872:Thomas Emerton, head teacher at Oulton School, Kibblestone; 1887:Daniel Emberton (greengrocer and fruiterer) of Cooper Street, Tunstall.

Loynton, south of High Offley - "Leofa's farm" - survives as Loynton/Lointon and probably Laynton and Lainton; 1875:Emma Lainton (milliner) of Stone Street, Stoke; 1907:John Loynton (warehouseman) of Well Street, Hanley.

The personal name inherent in Croxton north west of Eccleshall is the Old Norse "Krokr", a byname from "krokr" - "hook", "something crooked", a nickname for a person who was crookbacked, cunning or sly. The same name is contained in Croxton Green by Cholmondeley Castle and Croxton Hall near Middlewich (both in Cheshire), Croxton east of St. Neots in Cambridgeshire, Croxton south west of Immingham, Lincolnshire, two places in Norfolk - Croxton near Fakenham and Croxton near Thetford, South Croxton near Leicester and Croxton Kerrial north east of Melton Mowbray. The two latter localities are both pronounced something like "Crowson", thus yielding a plausible origin of the surname Crowson, whilst Cruxton is also a possible later variant; 1616:Symon Crowson of Codsall; 1851:Richard Croxton, owner of a beerhouse in Kingstone, near Uttoxeter; 1907:Henry Cruxton of Victoria Street, Chell.

The threefold combination of Whittington near Charnes, Whittington south east of Lichfield and Whittington not far from Kinver lies at the heart of the Staffordshire surname Whittington, but outside influence must be shouldered by such locatives as New and Old Whittington near Chesterfield, Derbyshire, Whittington near Oswesty, Whittington north of Docker (Lancashire), Whittington south east of Worcester and Great and Little Whittington north of Corbridge, beyond Hadrian's Wall, Whittington near Cheltenham and Whittington north of Atherstone, Warwickshire. The places denote the village of Hwita or the people of Hwita or simply white village. In the 1539 Muster roll for the county Roger Whittyngton enrols at Coldmeece, John Wyttyngton at Chatcull and William Whittington at Tunstall near Adbaston; 1912:Enoch Whittington (miner), Edward Street, Longton.

Winnington and Willington are best dealt with simultaneously, since they frequently interchange with one another; 1705:Robert Willington of Little Onn, quoted as Robert Winnington in 1712. If the original name is Winnington, then this is derived from Winnington north of Mucklestone - "farmstead of Wynna's people", Winnington in Northwich, Cheshire - "farmstead of Wine's or Wina's people" or possibly Winnington Green north east of Welshpool - no forms. On the other hand, if Willington has seniority, then the odds are in favour of Willington two miles north east of Stretton, Horninglow, south of the old Roman road running from here to Derby - "village amongst willows", Willington near Kelsall, Cheshire - "village of Winflaed or Wynflaed", or Willington south of Shipston on Stour in Warwickshire - "village of the people of Wulflaf or Wiglaf". Less attractive are Willington near Bedford - "village amongst the willows", Willington north west of Spennymoor, Durham and Willington near North Shields on Tyne and Wear, both referring to "village of Wifel's people"; 1907:James Willington (colliery fireman), Park

Street, Stoke; 1907:Mrs Mary Willington, Greyhound Inn, London Road, Stoke.

In the Danelaw shires the locatives Carlton and Carleton are widespread and refer to the village of the free men or peasants or Karli's village. Their Saxon counterparts are the equally prolific Charlton and Chorlton, as embodied in the two Staffordshire locations Chapel Chorlton and Hill Chorlton east of Maer. Both are recorded as "Charlton" in the eighteenth century parish registers for Swynnerton, hence the prevalence of the surnames: 1875:Christopher Charlton (tailor), Church Street, Hanley; 1907:George Chorlton (potter's fireman), Waterloo Road, Cobridge.

Knighton near Adbaston on the Staffordshire-Shropshire border and Knighton south of Woore -"village of the knights" - are behind most of our local families called Knighton, although the synonymous Knighton on Teme in Worcestershire and Knighton in Leicester are also to be taken into consideration. Of minimal importance are Knighton south east of Plymouth, two places in Dorset - Knighton south of Sherborne and Knighton north of Bournemouth, Knighton near Marlborough, Wiltshire and Knighton north west of Bridgwater in Somerset; 1666:William Knighton, not chargeable for hearth tax at Chesterton; 1912:Mrs Knighton of Queen's Road, Stoke.

Preston occurs in two dozen counties and designates a village established by priests. The principal native source is Preston near Penkridge, as in Richard de Prestone, paying poll tax at Penkridge in 1381. Preston is also a late variation of Presson, which stands for Priestson - "son of the priest"; John Priestson, resident at Balterley in 1482. George Preston of Church Eaton (1786) is alternatively known as George Presson in the same year. But, of course, in our county, where Weston is pronounced as "Wesson", this transition is run of the mill; 1701, November 10th:John Preston, married to Mary Badylie at Audley; 1875:John Preston (shoemaker), Northwood, Hanley.

STAFFORD, 1810.

The End

INDEX